PENGUIN BOOKS

DEATH IN ANCIENT EGYPT

Alan Jeffrey Spencer was born in Manchester in 1949 and studied Egyptology at the University of Liverpool, gaining the degree of Doctor in Philosophy in 1975. In April the same year he was appointed to the staff of the Department of Egyptian Antiquities in the British Museum, where he is now Assistant Keeper. He has travelled extensively in Egypt and has directed annual archaeological excavations for the British Museum since 1980. In addition to numerous reports on this fieldwork, his publications include *Brick Architecture in Ancient Egypt*, *Early Egypt* and the *Catalogue of Egyptian Antiquities in the British Museum, Volume V: Early Dynastic Objects*.

A.J. SPENCER

DEATH
IN
ANCIENT
EGYPT

PENGUIN BOOKS

PENGUIN BOOKS

Published by the Penguin Group
Penguin Books Ltd, 27 Wrights Lane, London W8 5TZ, England
Penguin Books USA Inc., 375 Hudson Street, New York, New York 10014, USA
Penguin Books Australia Ltd, Ringwood, Victoria, Australia
Penguin Books Canada Ltd, 10 Alcorn Avenue, Toronto, Ontario, Canada M4V 3B2
Penguin Books (NZ) Ltd, 182–190 Wairau Road, Auckland 10, New Zealand

Penguin Books Ltd, Registered Offices: Harmondsworth, Middlesex, England

First published in Pelican Books 1982
Reprinted in Penguin Books 1991
3 5 7 9 10 8 6 4

Printed in England by Clays Ltd, St Ives plc
Set in Linotron 202 Bembo

CONTENTS

◨

LIST OF PLATES

LIST OF TEXT FIGURES

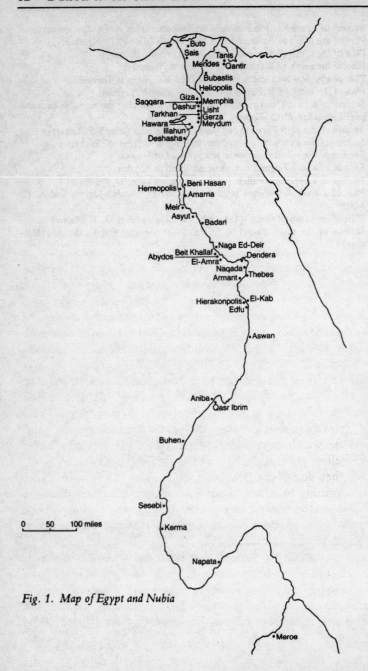

Fig. 1. Map of Egypt and Nubia

PREFACE

For some considerable time there has been a lack of a general synthesis of ancient Egyptian funerary practices in a form which would be suitable both for the general reader and for students of Egyptology. This deficiency was only too apparent when dealing with inquiries at the British Museum, since there was no easily obtainable book to which those interested in Egyptian funerary matters could be referred. In an attempt to fill this gap in the bibliography, a number of reprints have been made in recent years of the works of Wallis Budge, but these are now so out of date that they are best ignored except by those who already possess sufficient knowledge to distinguish the portions which are still valid from those which have been superseded. There are, of course, some excellent general works on parts of Egyptian funerary practice, but they do not draw together all the interrelated facets of the subject. Turning to scholarly publications we find much that is in need of revision, while many good pieces of work on aspects of mortuary belief are now out of print and available only to those with access to a specialized library.

It was with these problems in mind that this book was initiated, in an attempt to provide a starting-point for the study of the whole range of Egyptian funerary beliefs and practices, placing different aspects of the subject, such as mummies, coffins and pyramids, in their true context. The reading matter listed at the end of the book includes a number of works which deal with individual topics in greater detail.

One recurrent problem in Egyptological publications is the rendering of Egyptian names, in which scholars exhibit a justifiable inconsistency. This being the case, I have chosen to avoid all the diacritical marks frequently employed in the writing of names and other Egyptian words, as there is little to be gained by their inclusion in a book of this kind. The writing 'Khafrē'' is no more intelligible to the general reader than 'Khafre', and the student or scholar, who is aware of the significance of the diacritical marks, will not be inconvenienced by their absence.

For permission to use the quotations on pages 35 and 104, the writer is grateful to Purnell Books Limited and to the Loeb Classical Library (Harvard University Press: William Heinemann).

My thanks are also due to the following institutions and individuals for the use of photographs: The Egypt Exploration Society for plates 4, 5, 6, 14, 15, 18, 32, 36; The Trustees of the British Museum for plates 2, 3, 7, 8–13, 17, 19–31, 33, 34, 35; and T. G. H. James for plate 39.

1

THE CHARACTER OF ANCIENT EGYPT

The culture of ancient Egypt, more than any other early civilization, is symbolized for many people by funerary remains, particularly by bandaged mummies and their painted coffins. Indeed, it is precisely these items which constitute the main point of interest in Egyptian archaeology for the general public, although an understanding of the reasons why matters of death and burial seem so intimately linked with ancient Egypt is, unfortunately, often lacking. As will be explained later in this book, the Egyptians devoted a great deal of their resources to the preparation of tombs simply in order to provide a suitable home for their spiritual life after death, which was to continue indefinitely. Once the concept of an afterlife had developed, all other Egyptian mortuary practices were merely logical extensions of this belief, to guard and provision the dead. Tombs and funerary equipment were constructed during life and mortuary priests were appointed, so that when death came one was fully prepared for it and was guaranteed a safe passage to the next world. Failure to make the necessary preparations would result in total annihilation from memory, which was the Egyptians' greatest fear.

Archaeology has benefited greatly from the results of ancient Egyptian funerary beliefs, particularly from the custom of preserving the body for use in the afterlife and the provision of tomb-furniture. The objects in Egyptian tombs provide a valuable source of information on ancient material culture, as do the paintings and reliefs of decorated tomb chapels. The excavation of tombs is not in any sense a sacrilege, but is simply a means of acquiring information, just as archaeology also requires the investigation of ancient temples and settlements. By studying each kind of site it is possible to build a more complete picture of the culture involved, since details which may be lacking in the archaeological record of the settlements may be found in the cemeteries, and vice versa.

In the early days, before any scientific principles had been established, tombs were opened for the sole purpose of acquiring rare or valuable objects, which were generally dispersed among collectors without record. At this stage, possession of the objects was everything, and no regard was given to the gathering of historical information. Groups of objects from burials would be split up, the valuable items being taken away and the commoner objects left in the tomb. The actual embalmed bodies of the ancient Egyptians had attracted attention very early on, and came to be used by the apothecaries of the sixteenth and seventeenth centuries in the preparation of drugs. A remarkable trade developed, with mummies being shipped to Europe from Alexandria in order to satisfy the demand for this strange medicine. Powdered mummy was employed for the treatment of wounds, and the substance could be taken internally in cases of illness. Occasionally, the supply of genuine Egyptian mummies would run short and would have to be supplemented by the corpses of executed criminals, treated with pitch to resemble the real thing. Other strange uses for mummies survived to much more recent times, a notable example being their importation for use in the manufacture of bituminous paint. This practice was still going on in the early part of the twentieth century!

From the more enlightened viewpoint of archaeology, a tomb may be regarded as a sealed unit, within which information of different kinds is locked. The amount of this information which can be recovered depends upon the methods of excavation and recording. All kinds of points are worthy of note because they may be paralleled in other graves and provide evidence of a regular custom. For example, we now know that the attitude of the body in Egyptian burials varied at different periods and we can detail these changes, but this knowledge would never have been possible had excavators not taken the trouble to mention the position of the body in their reports. The same is true of a whole series of other features which, recorded individually from a large number of excavated cemeteries, now provide a body of evidence from which we can distinguish the characteristic trends and fashions of different ages. Our ability to write generally about such matters as the development of tombs or coffins, the provision of offerings, tomb-robbing, mummification, or the history of everyday objects placed in graves, depends on the small and apparently trivial details gleaned from the excavation of hundreds or even thousands of tombs.

Certain tombs in Egypt can be dated very precisely by their inscriptions, but the majority of funerary monuments are fixed by comparative means to a range of dates rather than to a fixed date expressed in years B.C. Egyptologists make use of a convenient system of dynasties and periods in reference to the subdivisions of Egyptian history, which, although imperfect, has yet to be bettered for providing general dates. The system originates in the works of the Egyptian historian, Manetho, a native of Sebennytos in about 280 B.C., who divided the history of the country into thirty-one dynasties extending down to 332 B.C. His source material was incomplete, and we know that the breaks between individual dynasties do not always represent a real change in the ruling family. Other sources, particularly the lists of kings compiled by the Egyptians at certain periods, have supplied the names of many more rulers to fill out the dynastic framework, and the whole system has been correlated with a scale of years by fixed astronomical dates, by synchronisms with events in the Near East and by scientific methods such as carbon-14 dating. Groups of dynasties are linked together into kingdoms or periods covering broad spans of time, as shown by the summary chart on page 18. For the sake of readers not familiar with the main phases of Egyptian history, the salient features of each stage are summarized overleaf, as constant reference will be made to dynasties and periods

in the account of Egyptian burial practices in the later chapters.
Those who would like to read about the history of ancient Egypt
in detail will find a number of suitable titles in the list of recommended reading at the end of this book.

CHRONOLOGICAL TABLE

Dynasties	Years B.C.	Period
	before 3100	Predynastic
I	3100–2890	
II	2890–2686	Early Dynastic
III	2686–2613	
IV	2613–2494	
V	2494–2345	Old Kingdom
VI	2345–2181	
VII–VIII	2181–2160	First
IX–X	2160–2040	Intermediate
XI	2134–1991	Middle Kingdom
XII	1991–1785	
XIII	1785–1633	
XIV	1785–1603	
XV	1674–1567	Second
XVI	1684–1567	Intermediate
XVII	1650–1567	
XVIII	1567–1320	
XIX	1320–1200	New Kingdom
XX	1200–1085	
XXI	1085–945	
XXII	945–715	
XXIII	818–715	Third
XXIV	727–715	Intermediate
XXV	747–656	
XXVI	664–525	
XXVII	525–404	
XXVIII	404–399	
XXIX	399–380	Late
XXX	380–343	
XXXI	343–332	
	332–305	Macedonian
	305–30 B.C.	Ptolemaic
	after 30 B.C.	Roman

Prior to 3100 B.C. Egypt was not a unified state; the Nile Valley was populated by individual groups now known as the Predynastic cultures. The first evidence for the existence of these people appeared in 1895 as a result of the excavations carried out by Petrie at Naqada in Upper Egypt. The graves were of a new type and were confirmed by later work to belong to a period earlier than anything yet known in Egypt. It soon became apparent that the Predynastic Period itself was divisible into different stages, but, since no fixed dates were available, the remains could only be arranged in order by relative dating. There was a tendency for the new discoveries to be labelled with terms derived from the names of the sites at which they were first encountered, and, as a consequence, a range of names grew up which were later found to duplicate one another in some cases. At Naqada, evidence of two cultures was found, the one preceding the other, and so the names Naqada I and Naqada II were coined. Later discoveries at El-Amra, El-Gerza and Semaina produced the terms Amratian, Gerzean and Semainean, each of which in fact overlaps with Naqada I and II. However, these old names are still found in Egyptological literature, even in some quite recent works, and it is worth knowing their significance. All the objects of the Semainean culture were later shown to be of early First Dynasty date, while Amratian and Gerzean duplicate the terms Naqada I and Naqada II respectively. Even earlier than the Naqada I period are the Badarian and Fayum cultures, which are the earliest settled communities of which we have knowledge.

Towards the close of the Predynastic Period we see in Egypt clear evidence of influence from Mesopotamia, which seems to have assisted the move towards unification of the country, generally thought to have occurred in about 3100 B.C. under King Narmer. The first three dynasties were the formative period of Egyptian history, during which rapid advances were made in art, architecture and technology. The evidence for this progress is best illustrated from the excavation of Early Dynastic sites at Abydos, Saqqara, Helwan, Tarkhan and elsewhere. Many of the characteristic emblems and symbols of Egyptian culture, which were to last for thousands of years, first appear in the Early Dynastic Period. Particularly strong among these are references to the fact that the land had formerly been divided into two parts, north and south, just prior to the conquest of the Delta by the southerners. Upper and Lower Egypt had their own distinctive royal crowns, local deities, symbolic plants and individual shrines, and all these features regularly appeared on monuments throughout historic times whenever reference was made to the unified state of the country. The king wore the combined crowns of Upper and Lower Egypt (fig. 2), and, when shown with his full complement of regalia,

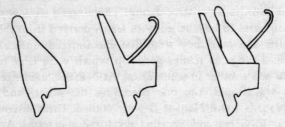

Fig. 2 The crowns of Upper and Lower Egypt, and the double crown

had the emblems of the vulture and the cobra – that is the goddesses Nekhebet and Wadjet of south and north respectively – attached to the front of his headdress. Allusions to the dual nature of the Egyptian kingdom are regularly found in mortuary contexts, examples being the buildings in the Step Pyramid complex of Djoser, representing the national shrines of the two lands, and the occurrence of the goddesses of north and south on coffins. The design in figure 3 is taken from a coffin of the Twenty-First Dynasty, and shows the vulture of Nekhebet and the cobra of Wadjet above the lotus and papyrus, symbolic plants of Upper and Lower Egypt. The concept of Egypt as two lands was all-pervasive, and indeed, the ancient Egyptians themselves used the term 'The Two Lands' as a common name for the country.

The period from the Fourth to the Sixth Dynasties, known as the Old Kingdom, was one of the most stable in the history of the land, characterized by strong central government with power concentrated in the hands of the king. The Old Kingdom is sometimes referred to as the Pyramid Age owing to the adoption of the true pyramid as the standard form of royal tomb. Under the Fourth Dynasty, the pyramid-builders attained their highest degree of achievement, showing how a mastery in the art of working in hewn stone had grown quickly from the more tentative beginnings seen in the construction of the Third Dynasty pyramid of Djoser. The pyramids of the Old Kingdom were built on the desert fringes to the west of the Nile Valley, in the region close to the capital at Memphis. From tomb inscriptions of certain nobles we learn of trading and military expeditions beyond the frontiers of Egypt into Asia and Nubia, particularly in the Sixth Dynasty.

The stability of the Old Kingdom was not to last, and at the close of the Sixth Dynasty the land fell into anarchy, which continued throughout the First Intermediate Period. During this span of some 130 years, different areas of Egypt came under the control of local rulers, until two distinct power centres emerged, one based at Heracleopolis in the north and the other at Thebes in Upper Egypt. After a struggle of considerable duration, the Theban rulers extended their control over their rivals, until King Mentuhotpe II of the Eleventh Dynasty brought the whole country

Fig. 3. Nekhebet and Wadjet

under his authority in about 2050 B.C. This event marks the beginning of the Middle Kingdom, an age which saw the restoration of strong government, leading to major achievements in art, architecture, literature and foreign conquest. Egyptian power was once again extended into Nubia and the construction of a series of fortresses in that region was initiated. At the start of the Twelfth Dynasty, the seat of government was moved from Thebes to a new location close to the village of El-Lisht at the entrance to the Fayum oasis, so as to be better placed to control both Upper and Lower Egypt. In an attempt to strengthen further the hand of central government, the power of the local princes was severely curbed by the later kings of the dynasty, particularly by Sesostris III. The authority of the king appears to have faltered, however, at the very end of the Twelfth Dynasty, and declined still further in the Thirteenth, as a new era of instability arose in the land.

As will be seen from the dates in the chronological table (p. 18), the Thirteenth to Seventeenth Dynasties, which make up the Second Intermediate Period, were to some extent contemporaneous, ruling over different parts of Egypt. During this period Asiatics moved into the Nile Delta and established their own dynasty, gradually extending their influence southwards. These foreigners are known as the Hyksos, from a corruption of an Egyptian term meaning 'rulers of foreign lands', and later Egyptian records describe them as oppressive invaders. They were not expelled from the country until a vigorous line of rulers from Thebes, known as the Seventeenth Dynasty, attempted to regain control of the north and drive the Asiatics beyond the frontiers. War between the two sides continued during the late Seventeenth Dynasty, with the Egyptian side steadily achieving greater success. The last ruler of the dynasty led his forces against the Hyksos capital, a city called Avaris in the eastern Delta region, and under Amosis I, founder of the Eighteenth Dynasty, the foreigners were completely driven from Egyptian soil.

With the commencement of the Eighteenth Dynasty in about 1567 B.C. we reach the New Kingdom, which extends to the end of the Twentieth Dynasty. Following up the expulsion of the Hyksos from the country, the kings of the New Kingdom, particularly those of the early Eighteenth Dynasty, embarked on a programme of foreign wars which extended Egyptian military conquests to the Euphrates in the north and to the fourth cataract of the Nile in the south. Great wealth flowed into Egypt as a result, and much of it was used for the construction and furnishing of new temples. By the reign of Amenophis III Egypt's authority over its new empire had been firmly established and little was required in the way of military action. In this reign we see the beginnings of the movement to alter the state religion to a new system, in which great emphasis was placed on the deity embodied in the disk of the sun, called the Aten. This development was carried to its conclusion under Akhenaten, successor of Amenophis III, by the building of a new capital city at El-Amarna, well away from the old centre at Thebes, and the banning of the old religion in favour of the worship of the Aten. This phase of Egyptian history is known as the Amarna period, after the site of the new capital, although the ancient name of the city was Akhetaten, which means 'the horizon of the Aten'. Nothing was done to maintain control of the empire during the reign of Akhenaten and the Asiatic vassal states began to rebel. An unconventional art style was introduced at this time, at first in a very exaggerated form, but the naturalistic innovations were later restrained to some extent. The Amarna experiment, which may well have been entirely political, aimed at limiting the power of the priests of Amun at Thebes, ended with a return to the old capital and the restoration of the previous religious system under Tutankhamun. In the records compiled at later periods the whole Amarna interlude was deliberately omitted.

In the Nineteenth Dynasty the royal residence was transferred to the eastern Nile Delta, although royal burials continued to be made at Thebes. Egypt remained prosperous; military exploits were again carried out against the Nubians, Libyans and Hittites; many new temples were founded or older ones enlarged. By the Twentieth Dynasty, Egypt had to defend itself against foreign invasion by the so-called Peoples of the Sea, but the campaigns of Ramesses III were successful in holding the enemy at bay. It was during this dynasty that the royal tombs at Thebes suffered so severely from plundering that a special investigation was made, the records of which are preserved for us in a number of hieratic papyri.

The Third Intermediate Period, from the Twenty-First to the Twenty-Fifth Dynasties, began with the kingdom divided between a line of kings at Tanis in Lower Egypt and a family of High-Priests of Amun who controlled the area of Thebes. This situation was altered by Shoshenk I, founder of the Twenty-Second Dynasty, who installed his own son as High-Priest of Amun in Thebes and thereby ended the old hereditary system. Towards the close of this dynasty, in about 730 B.C., the kingdom again broke up into separate units under local rulers. All these parallel minor dynasties were ended by the invasion led by King Piye (the name was formerly written Piankhy) from Nubia, where a separate kingdom had existed for some considerable time. The invasion came in about 727 B.C. and marked the beginning of the Twenty-Fifth Dynasty. Piye did not remain in Egypt, returning promptly to his homeland, but his brother Shabako consolidated the Nubian hold on the land and ruled from Thebes as king. The Nubian rulers were thoroughly saturated with Egyptian culture, so the change of dynasty did not alter the basic nature of life in the Nile Valley. They ruled as pharaohs, with all the regalia of Egyptian royalty, and carried out building works on the temples of the Egyptian gods. Their burials, however, were made near their home town of Napata, far to the south. At the end of the dynasty the Nubian kings were involved in conflict with the Assyrians, who eventually invaded Egypt and sacked Thebes, after which the Nubians withdrew to their own home territory.

The Assyrians appointed a certain Psammetichus as vassal ruler in Sais, but he gradually extended his authority over the whole country and became the first king of the Twenty-Sixth Dynasty. The phase of Egyptian history from this point down to 332 B.C., including dynasties XXVI–XXX, is known as the Late Period. During the Twenty-Sixth Dynasty the prosperity of the country revived greatly, coupled with a resurgence of high-quality art and architecture. Greek traders were present in the land and Greek mercenaries were employed in the army. At the end of the dynasty, Egypt was invaded by the Persians and became a province of the Persian Empire. The Twenty-Seventh Dynasty consisted entirely of Persian kings, ruling Egypt indirectly, and it was not until 404 B.C. that native rule was re-established by Amyrtaeus, the sole king of the Twenty-Eighth Dynasty. The final stage of the Late Period was a time of repeated struggle to maintain this independence, although some degree of stability was achieved under the Thirtieth Dynasty, when some notable temple-building projects were completed. The last native ruler, Nectanebo II of the Thirtieth Dynasty, fled southwards in about 343 B.C., as Egypt once more succumbed to Persian conquest. Only a few years later, in 332 B.C., the Persian domination was ended by their defeat at the hands of Alexander the Great. Although Alexander and two of his successors were recognized as legitimate kings of Egypt, real power devolved upon a certain Ptolemy Lagus, sent to govern the country by Philip Arrhidaeus. By 305 B.C. Ptolemy had become the independent ruler of Egypt and founded the Ptolemaic Dynasty, containing twelve kings of the same name and Cleopatra VII. Egypt during the Ptolemaic Period was rather different from its earlier state: the administration was essentially Greek, wealthy Egyptians attempted to gain Greek education, and Greek influence appears in art and architecture. The Ptolemies continued the old Pharaonic traditions in the building of temples to local divinities, and they are shown in the temple reliefs in the regalia of Egyptian kings. After the deaths of Antony and Cleopatra in 30 B.C. brought Egypt under the rule of Rome, the practice of temple-building continued, with the Roman emperors appearing in the guise of pharaohs in the reliefs, although Egypt was in fact governed by a prefect as a province of the empire. Many other aspects of ancient Egyptian civilization survived in some form well into the Roman Period, including characteristic Egyptian burial customs, which were adopted by Roman settlers in the country as well as being retained by the local population. It was not until the coming of Christianity that the lingering remnants of the old culture were finally submerged during the fourth century A.D.

The above outline of Egyptian history will give some idea of the extraordinary longevity of the civilization, the characteristic features of which appear over some 3,400 years. The span of time separating King Djoser of the Third Dynasty from King Nectanebo II of the Thirtieth Dynasty is about the same as the time from Nectanebo II to the present day! The ability of Egyptian culture to survive over such a period of time, despite repeated interludes of foreign domination, owed much to the nature of the country and its effect on the character of the inhabitants. There was a tendency for customs and traditions to persist relatively unchanged for centuries, or even millennia, giving rise to the often-repeated statement that the Egyptians were an extremely conservative people. This conservatism must have been linked to the fact that life in the Nile Valley proceeded at a measured pace, dramatic events affecting the lives of the ordinary people being conspicuous by their absence. Each day was filled with similar activities, usually of an agricultural nature for the mass of the population, and the near-constant sunshine itself induces a feeling of timelessness. The flat land of the valley, being intensively cultivated, varies little from one place to another, as any traveller who has taken the day train from Cairo to Luxor will confirm. For several hundred miles the monotonous scene of green cultivated fields, palm trees, irrigation channels and mud-brick villages is repeated, with the desert cliffs visible as a background. The Nile Valley is a green strip around the river, boxed in between the eastern and western deserts, the barrenness of which tended to discourage travel (plate 1). In this environment there was little stimulus to think about the world beyond the Nile Valley and hardly any thirst for knowledge for its own sake. The inventions made by the inhabitants were mostly of a practical kind, to deal with particularly local problems, such as irrigation and other agricultural matters. However, once a working device had been invented it was rarely superseded by an improved version, because the immediate problem had been solved. There was a corresponding slowness to take up the technical innovations brought to Egypt by other peoples, such as the use of the wheel, or of iron instead of bronze.

Interesting sidelights on the Egyptians' view of their own land are found in their religious and mythological writings, the ideas expressed in them being distinctly conditioned by the environment. The story in the creation myths of a primeval ocean from which the first land appeared is derived from observation of the annual Nile flood, which covered all the flat land of the valley before receding to leave a deposit of fertile silt. In the creation legend of Hermopolis, the first inhabitants of the island which emerged from the waters were eight divinities, known collectively as the Ogdoad. The group was composed of four frog-headed gods and four snake-headed goddesses, and it is apparent that the choice of these animal forms was linked with the kind of fauna which appeared upon the Nile mud as the waters of the inundation receded.

Just as creation myths reflected the physical environment of the Nile Valley, so the local view of the universe was conditioned by geography. The world was considered to be a flat plain, as the valley floor is flat, and the sky was like a flat plate supported above it. According to different legends, the sky was upheld on four supports at the limits of the world, or it rested upon two mountains. The latter concept is influenced by the presence of the desert cliffs, running like walls down the edges of the valley and acting as an inducement to a strong introspective attitude. The idea that the deserts marked the limits of the world persisted long after the Egyptians had become aware of lands beyond the confines of the valley, and is frequently encountered in ancient texts. In tomb-scenes showing offerings being brought to the deceased, we can find the inscription: 'Everything which is brought to him from the estates and towns of Upper and Lower Egypt, together with what is between the two desert margins.' Other texts state that the sun was considered to rise from the eastern horizon and set behind the cliffs of the west, encircling all that existed in the process. With ideas so heavily conditioned by the environment, the Egyptians were surprised by anything which was not paralleled in their own land, as shown by their description of the river Euphrates as 'reversed water which goes north in going south', because the river did not flow northwards like the Nile. According to Egyptian religious beliefs, the ideal condition of the land was preordained by the gods from the outset, so that rather than striving for progress and change, one should only endeavour to maintain this divinely appointed state of affairs. This belief was probably a major factor in the ability of the local culture to reassert itself essentially unchanged after interludes of anarchy or foreign domination. Statements in certain literary texts make it quite clear that the Egyptians regarded their own land and culture as far preferable to anything devised in the neighbouring states of the Near East, and consequently they did not wish to imitate foreign customs. Not until the Ptolemaic Period was the native culture seriously affected by foreign ideas, and even at this late date many of the Greeks who settled in Egypt tended to be assimilated into the local way of life. The tolerant nature of Egyptian society, an offshoot of the polytheistic religious system, assisted the process by which foreigners could be absorbed into the culture of the Nile Valley without leading to radical change.

The Egyptian system was a recipe for a lasting and stable civilization, of which the Egyptians were justly proud. The records compiled in the temples listed the rulers of the country right back to the establishment of the kingship, and there is no doubt that the educated Egyptians of later periods were aware of the long continuity of their civilization. The love of stability and permanence is reflected in the monuments of the land; the temples and tombs were solidly built of enduring materials, and the inscriptions state plainly that these buildings were intended to stand forever. As the surviving monuments of Egypt are now generally between two and five thousand years old, it could be said that the aim of the builders to create monuments for eternity has, in terms of the human scale of time, been virtually achieved.

2

BEGINNINGS OF MUMMIFICATION

The earliest burials known in Egypt, dating to a period well before 3000 B.C., already display evidence of a belief in continued existence after death in the provision of various kinds of funerary gifts in the graves. This belief was to develop and gain in strength until it became one of the most powerful single influences upon the Egyptian civilization, which would not only condition the thoughts and hopes of the population but would also directly affect their art, architecture, technology and even their legal practices. Without the belief in the afterlife, many of the features which are considered to be typical of ancient Egypt, including pyramids, mummies and sarcophagi, would never have existed. We would also have known much less about the daily life of the Egyptians, since most of our information on this subject is derived from tombs, which contain examples of the objects used in life and paintings showing day-to-day events.

Belief in continued existence after death is common to many civilizations but it may have been a particularly logical development in Egypt, conditioned by the nature of the country. The earliest graves were very simple affairs consisting of shallow circular or oval pits in the ground, in which the body was placed in a contracted position, with the knees drawn up under the chin and the hands normally lying before the face. These graves were situated on the low desert spurs which fringed the fertile Nile Valley, and, although exceptions occur, the Egyptians preferred at all times to bury their dead in desert tombs rather than in the soil of the valley. One reason for this may have been a desire not to occupy the cultivated land with cemeteries, but a more important motive was probably the wish for permanence; a grave in the moist soil of the cultivation could not be expected to survive so well as one constructed in the dryness of the desert. Since the early graves contained little or no provision for keeping the sand away from the body, this dryness had a remarkable effect on the preservation of the burial, the corpse becoming desiccated very rapidly after interment. The decomposition fluids did not remain in contact with the body but were absorbed by the dry sand, thereby saving the corpse from complete decay. Many examples of these burials have been found with well-preserved skin and hair still adhering to the bones (plate 2). This natural preservation must have been observed by the Egyptians themselves, as, even before the appearance of tomb-robbers, burials would have been exposed by erosion or by animals, as well as by the accidental cutting of a new grave into an older one. It may be that seeing the still-lifelike bodies of the dead was the origin of the Egyptian belief in a continued existence in which survival depended upon the preservation of the body in a recognizable form. This belief was to become the driving force behind much of Egyptian funerary practice, the aim of everyone being to prepare for death by ensuring that all possible steps were taken to build tombs in which their bodies would survive forever, in order that the spirit of the deceased would always have a body in which to reside. Without the body the spirit had no place to rest and consequently could not exist.

As mentioned already, the graves of the earliest period of which we have evidence are very simple, but they nevertheless contain a number of objects apart from the burial itself. These items are early examples of the practice of supplying goods for the dead, to be used in the next life; they consist of pottery vessels, beads, flint tools and other objects, some of which may have been of amuletic value, showing the early introduction of magic into funerary belief. Simple burials of this kind belong to the Predynastic Period, that is, the period before the unification of Egypt into a state, an event which probably took place around 3100 B.C. The Predynastic Period is itself subdivided into a number of different cultures, as explained in the previous chapter. Although the characteristic products of each Predynastic culture are easily distinguishable, the style of the graves themselves changed little until the late Naqada II period, when they became more elaborate. Throughout the bulk of the Predynastic age most graves were mere pits, and it is ironic that the best-preserved burials are frequently found in the poorer graves, since these contained nothing to separate the body from the filling and thereby retard the process of dehydration. Already in the Badarian period burials were commonly covered by goatskins or by woven matting, but the pit of the grave itself was not normally roofed over until considerably later. The introduction of methods to protect the body from the filling of the pit was motivated by a desire to improve the conditions for the dead, as clearly demonstrated by three graves of children at Mostagedda in Upper Egypt, in which a basket had been placed over the head of the corpse to insulate the face from the surrounding sand. Similar concern for the well-being of the departed is seen in the provision of a pillow of leather, found beneath the head of the corpse in certain Badarian graves. During the middle and late Predynastic Period the practice of wrapping the burial in animal skins gradually gave way to other forms of protection, particularly the use of basketwork trays upon which the body was laid out, with covers of similar material placed on top. Wooden coffins, made of rough planks jointed by dowels, became increasingly common towards the end of the Predynastic Period. These coffins were short, being designed to hold a body in a contracted position. But the main advance in Predynastic tomb design was the gradual introduction of wood-roofed graves, of which many late Predynastic examples are known. The development of a wooden roof to the pit effectively separated the burial from the sand by creating an underground chamber, admittedly of small dimensions, within which the burial could be placed in a small coffin surrounded by items of funerary equipment (fig. 4). The roofing of the graves consisted of beams of wood laid across the width of the pit, covered by thinner branches and consolidated with mud. Probably the introduction of roofing was responsible for the change in shape of the grave from oval to rectangular, the latter form being easier to cover effectively with wooden rafters. The pits of roofed graves were frequently lined

Fig. 4. *A late Predynastic burial with coffin and grave-goods*

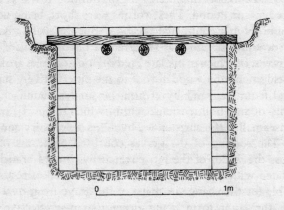

Fig. 5. *A wood-roofed grave with brick lining.*

with mud-plaster or wood, as an additional barrier between the body and the ground. Near the close of the Predynastic Period this lining could be more substantial, consisting of a wall of mud-brick with plaster on its interior face (fig. 5).

The development of the Egyptian grave during the Predynastic Period, as we have seen, was a process of steady improvement in the degree of protection given to the actual burial, isolating it from the ground by means of a coffin and the lining of the chamber. Continued refinements in this direction were achieved as a result of major advances in tomb architecture following the unification of the country under a single ruler in about 3100 B.C., at which time there was a corresponding outburst of technological progress in all spheres of ancient Egyptian life. An important consequence of the added separation between the body and the filling of the grave was the loss of the natural preservative effects of direct contact with the dry sand, formerly the essential component in preserving some of the soft tissues by rapid drying. By doing their best to provide the dead with additional protection and comfort, the Egyptians had unwittingly created the conditions for the total decay of the body, an effect completely opposite to the one they desired. It is unlikely that they understood at this period why burials in sand were preserved but those in coffins were not, as they did not yet have any experience of embalming. Even had they done so, there could be no question of returning to the simple form of grave, because the desire to isolate the body from the ground had become firmly established and was supported by the belief that the tomb would function as the eternal dwelling of its owner. This concept was to lead to the further enlargement of the burial chamber and its later subdivision into separate rooms in order to provide space for the funerary gifts. Another consideration, which was to ensure the continued separation of the burial from the surface sand, was the increasing necessity to protect the tomb from plunderers. Tomb-robbing was a common practice as early as the Badarian period, and the greater numbers of valuable objects placed in graves of subsequent ages only encouraged the activity. The shallow grave in the desert surface offered little security; it could easily be rifled in a short time by a few men. Roofing over the pit hardly gave any better protection, indeed, it almost constituted a weakness, since it enabled the robbers to tunnel in under the roof and loot the burial without the trouble of first emptying the pit. Shortly after the unification of the country the more elaborate tombs of the rich began to make use of chambers at a deeper level than had previously been attempted, going below the surface sand and gravel into the rock itself. This development, which was to lead to much deeper chambers in later periods, took the burial further from the plunderers but also involved a complete departure from the earlier shallow graves in the desert sand.

Throughout the Predynastic Period no attempts were made to preserve the body by artificial means, and the burials which were insulated from the sand by coffins or similar enclosures are generally found to have been completely reduced to skeletons (plate 3). The more widespread use of coffins at the beginning of the Dynastic age only aggravated the problem of decomposition and the Egyptians became unpleasantly aware of the fact that their bodies were unlikely to survive intact for continued use after death. Early in the First Dynasty, so far as our present evidence goes, they made the first tentative attempts to achieve by artificial techniques the kind of preservation which had formerly been conferred by the effect of burial in sand. The early processes were not very extensive; they seem to have consisted largely of the simple business of wrapping the corpse in many layers of linen bandages. The earliest piece to show this kind of treatment was the arm found by Petrie in the tomb of King Djer at Abydos. Although the bones had been moved from their original location by plunderers they certainly belonged to the tomb, since they were still encircled by four bracelets of gold, turquoise and amethyst, of unquestionable First Dynasty date (plate 4). On seeing the jewellery, Petrie assumed that the arm must have been that of a woman, and suggested that it may have belonged to the wife of Djer, but it is far more likely to have been the arm of the king himself, because we know that jewellery was worn by both sexes in ancient Egypt. The arm had been wrapped in linen and was important in itself as an example of the beginnings of mummification, but unfortunately it was not regarded with enthusiasm in all quarters. Petrie describes its eventual fate:

When Quibell came over on behalf of the Museum, I sent up the brace-lets to Cairo by him. The arm – the oldest mummified piece known – and its marvellously fine tissue of linen were also delivered to the Museum. Brugsch only cared for display; so from one bracelet he cut away the half that was of plaited gold wire, and he also threw away the arm and linen.[1]

Other examples of the use of linen wrappings are known from the Second and Third Dynasties, but it was not until the end of this period that any attempt was made to tackle the problem of decomposition by removing the internal organs from the body. Recognizing that they could not preserve the flesh, the Egyptians adopted a technique involving the use of bandages soaked in resin to retain an apparent semblance of life in the features of the deceased. The wrappings were carefully moulded to the shape of the body in order to reproduce the features, particular attention being paid to the face and genital organs. As the resin dried it consolidated the linen wrappings in position, preserving the appearance of the body for as long as it remained undisturbed. The corpse itself decom-posed very rapidly within this linen shell, practically all the tissues disappearing in a process of slow combustion to leave the inner-most wrappings in close contact with the skeleton. Very often, the inner bandages have been charred by the decomposition process. A number of Second Dynasty burials of this type have been found at Saqqara, certain examples having eight layers of cloth around the limbs and fourteen over the chest. These wrapped bodies were found in the contracted position, which had continued in use since Predynastic times, usually lying on the left side in a short wooden coffin. Early in the Third Dynasty the same kind of wrappings were apparently used to prepare for burial the body of King Djoser, the builder of the Step Pyramid at Saqqara. In a granite chamber at the bottom of a deep pit under the pyramid the remains of a human foot were discovered, probably from the original burial, with the external features carefully modelled in the linen with which the bones were wrapped. This poor relic was the only frag-ment of the burial to have survived the attentions of successive visits by plunderers.

The wrapped bodies of the first three dynasties were not truly mummified, since no treatment other than the use of linen bandages and resin was employed, but at the commencement of the Fourth Dynasty we encounter the first evidence of deliberate attempts to inhibit decomposition by removal of the soft internal organs from the body. Extraction of the viscera, particularly the liver, intestines and stomach, improved the chances of securing good preservation because the emptied body-cavity could be dried more rapidly. The greatest amount of evidence for the introduction of these techniques comes not from actual mummies, very few having survived from this period, but from the design of the tombs. If the internal organs were to be removed from the body it was essential that they should be deposited in some safe place in the tomb, in order that the body of the deceased should be complete once more in the netherworld. The separation of the organs from the body was not regarded as an obstacle to continued exist-- ence, since it was considered that they would re-unite by magical means. A special recess was prepared in the wall of the burial chamber, usually on the south side, to receive the viscera, themselves wrapped in linen for protection. Numerous examples of tombs with such recesses are known from a cemetery at Meydum, dating to the beginning of the Fourth Dynasty, although in most cases the contents of the recesses had disappeared. They are clearly the prototypes of similar recesses regularly used to contain the viscera in tombs of the Fifth and Sixth Dynasties. One of the Meydum tombs, belonging to a noble called Ranefer, still had the remains of linen-wrapped organs in the recess. These packages were not protected by any kind of outer container; in the early part of the Fourth Dynasty such refinements seem to have been available only to persons of the highest rank. Queen Hetepheres, the mother of Khufu, had an alabaster box with four internal compartments for the viscera in her tomb at Giza. At the time of its discovery the box still guarded its original contents, wrapped in linen and immersed in a dilute solution of natron (fig. 6). The use of receptacles for the viscera was extended to people of lower status in the Fifth and Sixth Dynasties, the organs being placed in limestone jars in a chest of wood (fig. 7). Many of the tombs which were furnished with these do not have any recess in the wall of the burial chamber, the protection of the chest alone being considered sufficient, but in some Sixth Dynasty tombs the box itself was installed in a niche. Burial chambers of the Fourth Dynasty frequently have a small pit in the floor instead of the wall recess, four examples occurring in the early cemetery at Meydum and many more in the tombs surrounding the pyramid of Khufu at Giza. It is interesting to note that the space prepared for the viscera in the burial chamber, whether in a niche or a floor-pit, is nearly always situated in the south-east corner, although the exact significance of this is not clear.

From the beginning of the Fourth Dynasty a significant number of burials occur in which the body was placed in the coffin in a fully extended position, in contrast to the earlier contracted attitude. The new custom first appears in the tombs of the wealthy, while contracted burials continued to be made in poorer graves, but gradually the extended position gained popularity until it became the standard type. This diffusion of new ideas from the richer classes to the poor is a regular feature of the development of Egyptian funerary practices, and means that archaic customs were often preserved in poor cemeteries long after they had ceased to apply in the wealthier tombs. The change from contracted to extended burials may well have been directly connected with the

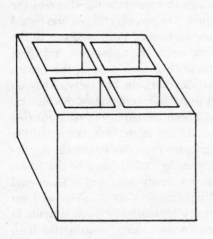

Fig.6. The alabaster Canopic box of Queen Hetepheres

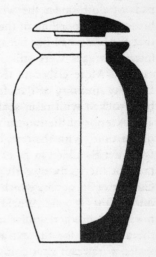

Fig. 7. Old Kingdom Canopic jar

introduction of more elaborate embalming techniques, it being far easier to remove the internal organs from an extended body. In support of this theory, it is worth pointing out that the rich tombs in which extended burials first appear belonged to individuals who would have been able to afford the latest embalming processes.

Apart from the removal of the viscera, which must have been accomplished as in later times by means of an incision in the side of the abdomen, the mummies of the Old Kingdom are not much better preserved than those of earlier periods. The technique of wrapping the body in resin-soaked linen, in which the features could be modelled, was still the standard form of treatment. In some cases the details of the face were added in green paint – green being the colour associated with resurrection – on the outside of the bandages, in order to heighten the lifelike appearance of the mummy. For the same purpose the outermost wrappings could be cut to imitate the form of clothing. A mummy of a woman of the Sixth Dynasty, discovered in a rock-cut burial chamber at Giza, was found wearing a long linen dress above the usual wrappings. The dress had the V-shaped neckline and broad shoulder straps typical of the period, as represented on female statues. Beneath this outer garment the body had been elaborately bandaged, with thick pads of cloth under the wrappings to reproduce the shape of the breasts and modelling of the figure. On investigation, it was found that the body had not been truly embalmed as the remains of the internal organs were still present inside the abdominal and chest cavities. More elaborate techniques had been used in the Fourth Dynasty mummy of Ranefer at Meydum, the body cavity having been packed with resin-soaked linen after removal of the viscera. The exterior of the mummy had been treated in the usual manner of the time, with the features modelled in the wrappings and the facial details added in paint. Unfortunately this specimen, important for the study of early embalming, was housed in the Royal College of Surgeons, which was practically destroyed in an air-raid during the Second World War. Reisner's excavations at Giza unearthed another similar mummy in which the incision made in the abdomen for the extraction of the internal organs had been sealed with resin after completion of the process.

A more widely publicized example of the achievements of the

Egyptian embalmers of the Old Kingdom is the Fifth Dynasty mummy discovered in a tomb at Saqqara in 1966. This burial, which has erroneously been described as the earliest mummified body, was found in a rock-tomb inscribed with the name of a certain Nefer, but the identification of the deceased is uncertain as the tomb had later been used as a family burial-place, associated with no less than eleven shafts. The excellently preserved male mummy still lies in its wooden coffin in a recess at the base of the pit in which it was discovered. As usual, it had been enveloped in many layers of linen, but instead of using resin to mould the cloth into shape, the embalmers had coated the exterior of the wrappings with plaster. This had been carefully worked so as to follow the contours of the body, particularly over the head, where the plaster not only reproduces exactly the appearance of the face, but also copies the form of the typical curled wig of the Old Kingdom. A moustache was painted on the upper lip and a false beard of linen was attached to the chin. The occasional use of plaster as a substitute for resin is known also from Giza, where a few bodies had been coated in their entirety, and others had received this treatment only over the head. The latter practice is an indication of the importance attached to re-creating the features in a lifelike fashion; even in mummies which were completely modelled in plaster or resin the greatest attention was always reserved for the head. Although they were not able to preserve a body, the embalmers of the Old Kingdom effectively transformed it into a kind of portrait statue, which would provide an acceptable home for the spirit of the deceased for as long as it survived intact.

The excavation of burials of Predynastic to Old Kingdom date has occasionally revealed some rather surprising results, which seem to contradict the Egyptian wish for the body to be preserved in its complete state. In 1895, digging at Naqada, Petrie cleared a number of Predynastic graves in which the bodies appeared to have been treated in a peculiar fashion, the bones having been separated into scattered groups. In some cases the skull stood apart from the rest of the skeleton, or was missing entirely; in other burials the lower arm bones had been placed separately. But there was evidence of even more drastic mutilation: bodies with all the ribs detached and lying in a heap, or miscellaneous leg bones laid parallel but not joined to the pelvis. Sometimes the bones seemed to have been sorted into types before burial, as described by Petrie: 'We find in grave T.42 all the bones of the body laid out, lotted according to their nature; the leg bones in the north corners crossing just as grasped in a handful; the ribs laid in a handful by them; the vertebrae ranged round in a circle; and the arms in the middle of the tomb.'[2] A good deal of evidence is given by Petrie to show that these peculiar arrangements were not the result of plunderers scattering the contents of the tomb in search of valuables. Many of the examples of dismembered skeletons were found in intact graves, with the burial still enclosed in a walled recess. The undisturbed nature of other graves was revealed by the funerary gifts being still in place, despite the disorder of the bones; in some the bodies lay at the base of the pit with pottery jars in their original order above them.

What was the reason for the strange distribution of the bones? Petrie examined the facts carefully and came to the conclusion that the bodies must have been cut up prior to burial, and that the extent of the mutilation could vary from the simple removal of the head to the complete dismemberment of the corpse. He considered that parts of the body, especially the head, might have been kept for a while by relatives as a reminder of the deceased; the head would then have been interred some time later than the rest of the body, which would explain its separate location in the grave. Those cases in which the skull was completely absent would be the result of the head never having been returned, perhaps because the exact location of the grave had been forgotten. To explain the more elaborate instances of dismemberment, Petrie suggested that some bodies had been completely cut up in order that parts of the flesh could be eaten, because of a primitive belief that this was a way of acquiring the virtues of the individual so consumed. The bones from one grave at Naqada are said to have shown marks of gnawing, and to have had the marrow scooped out.

More evidence of dismembered burials was collected from a late Predynastic site at Gerza, also excavated by Petrie with the assistance of Gerald Wainwright. Once again, apparently intact burials were discovered in which various parts of the bodies were missing or out of their true position, particularly the feet, head and pelvis.

The advocates of the dismemberment theory proposed that the custom of defleshing the corpse had been widespread in Predynastic times, and then had continued sporadically down to the Sixth Dynasty. The Old Kingdom examples are of particular interest, since evidence of the displacement of bones was found within wrapped mummies which appeared externally intact, showing that the various parts of the body must have been already separate at the time of wrapping. It is worth quoting a couple of the most marked cases recorded by Petrie in a Sixth Dynasty cemetery at Deshasha:

No. 28, when his hands were cut off and laid on the chest, and his knee-caps laid lower down the body, and his feet laid on the stomach. All inside complete wrappings...

No. 78, when an ankle bone was put on the breast; when the thighs were wrapped up in one roll with the shins and right forearm, without any hand; and when the splint bones were removed and one lost; and when the feet were gone all but the toe bones. All inside wrappings.[3]

A similar state of affairs was found in a tomb of the late Third or early Fourth Dynasty at Meydum, in which the atlas vertebra of the skeleton was in its correct position, but upside down. Wainwright recorded a number of points about this burial to demonstrate that the bones had been clean of flesh when wrapped, as the linen appeared to have entered even into the joints and beneath the kneecap. In support of the dismemberment theory, a selection of passages from the Pyramid Texts were quoted which seemed to allude to such a custom. A typical example of this type of spell reads, 'Awake, O King, raise yourself, receive your head, gather your bones together, shake off your dust and sit upon your iron throne...'[4] However, an examination of more detailed passages which contain similar references to dismemberment shows that the text is really connected with the legend of Osiris, who was cut up by his brother Seth and subsequently reconstituted by Isis and avenged by Horus:

Stand up for me O my father; stand up for me O Osiris the King, for I am indeed your son, I am Horus. I have come for you in order that I may cleanse you and purify you, that I may cause you to live and gather together for you your bones, that I may gather your soft parts for you and collect your dismembered parts for you, for I am Horus who protected his father.[5]

Now, since the dead king was regarded as identical with the god Osiris, the events of the Osiris legend, including the dismemberment by Seth, were applied to the king, but this did not mean that the king's own body had to undergo a similar dismemberment. Such a process would have been contrary to the real purpose of the texts, which was to prevent any kind of decay or damage from affecting the body:

O flesh of the king, do not decay, do not rot, do not smell unpleasant.[6]

Osiris was slain by his brother Seth, but he who is in Nedit moves, his head is raised by Re; he detests sleep and hates inertness, so the king will not decay, he will not rot, this king will not be cursed by your anger, O gods.[7]

The evidence for a ritual dismemberment based upon individual burials has been called into question by some scholars, who claimed that the disturbance in the graves was the result of plundered burials being restored by relatives. This supposition could explain the absence of a number of bones from the grave, or their peculiar arrangement, if the body had been broken up by thieves and some of the bones lost in the process; subsequently the relatives of the deceased might have gathered the remaining bones and replaced them in the grave. To the excavator, the grave would have all the appearance of an intact burial, although it would in fact be a re-burial. The same theory can be used to explain the wrapped bodies of Deshasha and Meydum with their misplaced bones; in these cases there would have been an attempt to rebuild the mummy and re-wrap it from the scattered remains left by plunderers. This explanation seems ideal, but unfortunately there is a serious fault in it. The body in mastaba 17 at Meydum, presented as an example of dismemberment by Wainwright, was certainly not a reburial, as the stone sarcophagus was found prised open at the time of the excavation of the tomb. Also, this type of tomb had no entrance passage, the burial chamber having been sealed before the construction of the superstructure above it. The chamber was robbed by someone with a good knowledge of the internal layout of the tomb, who entered through a narrow forced tunnel, and it is unlikely that the theft would have been discovered until long after the event. In any case, the relatives or mortuary priests would certainly not have entered the tomb through the robbers' tunnel, the location of which would soon have been obscured. The failure of the reburial idea in this one case throws doubt on the whole proposition, although it is possible that some of the apparent examples of dismemberment may be explained this way.

The question of defleshing of bodies has been coloured by the nature of the original arguments, which tended to lack objectivity. On the one hand, Petrie and his supporters were doing their best to prove the case for a ritual dismemberment, by presenting evidence from individual graves; the opposing faction, led by Elliot Smith, strove to defeat the idea by the use of anatomical investigations of mummies and the theory of reburial. Part of the problem stems from the fact that the controversy deals with an early period, because there is a tendency to equate 'early' with 'primitive' and to explain all problems in terms of ceremonial rites. Many wrapped mummies of the Late Period, or of Graeco-Roman age, exhibit considerable disarray within the bandages, with the bones in the wrong places or missing entirely, and yet no one has suggested that these individuals were ritually dismembered. They are normally explained as examples of carelessness in the embalming workshop, or as bodies which had already reached an advanced state of decay before they could be wrapped. If this explanation is sufficient for Late Period mummies, there is no reason why it should not apply to disarranged burials of any period.

Egyptian embalmers were not always entirely conscientious in their duties, especially as the relatives of the deceased had no means of checking that the remains of their dear departed were in as good order as the neat appearance of the external wrappings implied. In the case of the Predynastic graves we cannot blame the embalmers, because the burials belong to an age before the development of mummification, but it is possible that the separation of the bones may have been due to the activities of tomb-robbers who left so little evidence of their means of entry into the tomb that it was overlooked by the excavators. Investigations of early cemeteries at a number of sites have shown that tombs were often plundered through holes cut into them through the roof or the side, large enough only for the insertion of an arm to rummage for valuables.

Although the improvement in the effectiveness of mummification during the Old Kingdom was limited, the removal of the viscera being the only major advance, progress in the preparation of the burial-place was rapid. Deep vertical tomb shafts, rock-cut burial chambers and heavy stone sarcophagi characterize the richer funerary monuments of the Old Kingdom. Examples of brilliant technical achievements of the period are not lacking, particularly in the field of pyramid construction, but the preservation of the body which was to rest in these splendid tombs was beyond the ingenuity of the age.

3

PROVIDING
FOR THE DEAD

An important factor in the development of the Egyptian tomb was the necessity to provide storage space for the items of funerary equipment which were considered so essential for continued use by the deceased in the hereafter. In the small graves of the Pre-dynastic cultures this had not been a great problem, as the burial gifts were limited in number and consisted primarily of pottery vessels, together with a few small objects such as flint tools or slate cosmetic palettes. These goods could easily be accommodated within a grave-pit of modest dimensions, grouped around the body in a single chamber (fig. 4). But the great increase in the wealth of some sections of the population following the unification of the country led to a corresponding increase in the quantity of material which they wished to include in their burial equipment, leading to the development of much larger tombs with special store-chambers in the superstructure. These monuments were built of sun-dried mud-brick and were rectangular in plan; they stood approximately five metres high and were decorated with a system of intricate recesses in the brickwork, originally covered with brightly painted designs (plate 5). The patterns were derived from a copy of the reed-matting which had been the earliest building material of the Nile Valley. This type of tomb, together with any other similar rectangular superstructures of later periods, is usually described as a mastaba, because of its resemblance to the shape of the low bench-seat (Arabic *mastaba*) commonly seen outside Arab houses in the modern villages of Egypt. The First Dynasty mastabas of the rich were equipped with large numbers of magazines for the storage of funerary gifts. Throughout the earlier half of the dynasty, the capacity of these magazines gradually increased, as ever larger quantities of material were deposited in the tombs. The earliest known tomb of this kind is that usually ascribed to Queen Neithotpe, situated at Naqada in Upper Egypt; this contained twenty rooms in the superstructure, excluding the burial chamber itself. In tomb 3357 at Saqqara, dated to the reign of Hor-Aha and therefore only slightly later than the Naqada mastaba, there are twenty-seven magazines above ground-level and a further four in the substructure. By sinking the burial chamber and the rooms immediately around it into the rock – a procedure not used at Naqada – a considerable amount of extra space could be gained, the underground chambers being roofed with wood and the magazines of the superstructure carried right over them (fig. 8). This practice remained standard in later mastabas at Saqqara down to the middle of the First Dynasty, each tomb having a small number of storerooms in the substructure in addition to the magazines above. The amount of storage space in the tomb depended simply on the wealth of the owner. Two of the tombs at Saqqara each had forty-five magazines above ground-level, providing space for vast quantities of burial equipment. Some idea of the richness of the burials is given by the numbers of fine objects which were recovered during the excavation of the cemetery, despite repeated plundering in antiquity. Vessels and tools of copper, stone and pottery vases, wooden and ivory furniture elements, weapons, cosmetic articles and board-games all accompanied the tomb-owner into the afterlife. Such great wealth was available only to a few; there were also great numbers of smaller tombs, ranging from medium-sized mastabas of lesser officials down to the small graves of the poor, the

Fig. 8. Section of a large mastaba of the early First Dynasty

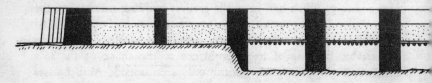

latter being little different from burials of the late Predynastic Period. The common feature which linked all social levels, however, was the desire to make the best provision they could afford for their tomb – a desire which continued right through the history of ancient Egypt.

Although the problem of storing masses of objects in wealthy mastabas had been solved by the development of magazines in the superstructure, this was not an ideal location in which to house such a quantity of valuable material. The magazines were too accessible to plunderers, and for this reason their number decreases dramatically after the middle of the First Dynasty, as they were replaced by underground storerooms cut in the bedrock. This trend continued in the Second Dynasty, when very extensive substructures were made, consisting of long passages with many side-galleries at intervals (fig. 9). The mastaba superstructure was now made completely solid, usually by filling the brick-built shell with rubble. There is some evidence to suggest that the idea of taking all one's possessions into the afterlife was more literally followed in the early dynasties than in later times, particularly in the case of private individuals as distinct from those of royal status. The tombs

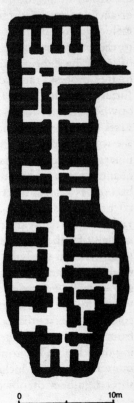

0   10m

Fig. 9. Plan of the substructure of a Second Dynasty tomb

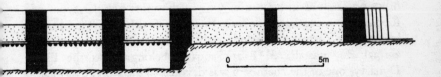

0   5m

of the wealthy nobles of the New Kingdom, for example, had far more restricted accommodation for grave-goods than did the large mastabas of the archaic period. One likely reason for the decrease in the quantities of equipment provided for the dead was the greater use of substitutes for the actual objects, in the form of small models or mere painted representations. In addition, many of the items included in the burial equipment of Early Dynastic tombs belonged to classes of objects which gradually became obsolete and fell out of use. The enormous numbers of stone vessels are an example of this process; they formed a large part of the standard tomb-furniture of the Early Dynastic Period, but with the introduction of wheel-made pottery at the end of the Second Dynasty the stone vases became redundant for everyday purposes, surviving only in the tombs because they had become a traditional element in the funerary equipment. As such they continued to be made in some quantity for royal burials down to the Sixth Dynasty, but the numbers of vessels manufactured and the range of types declined rapidly after the Third Dynasty. In private tombs, vases of hard stone were very rare by the reign of Khufu, being replaced by small jars and models of alabaster. The disappearance of the stone vases from the tomb reduced the bulk of the grave-goods by a large extent, particularly in the tombs of the kings. Some idea of the amount of space which was required simply for the accommodation of stone vessels in an Early Dynastic royal tomb can be gained when one considers the fact that some 40,000 stone vases have been extracted from the galleries of the Step Pyramid of Djoser without exhausting the supply. The tombs of later kings may well have contained more lavish items, including great amounts of goldwork, but for sheer numbers of objects the Early Dynastic tombs are unsurpassed.

A very important part of the material provided for the dead took the form of actual offerings of food and drink, which the deceased would require for his very survival, before he could enjoy all the other possessions in his tomb. One of the most popular types of food-offering consisted of choice cuts of beef, although it gradually became the custom to include only the head and foreleg of the animal. In mastaba 3111 at Saqqara, belonging to the First Dynasty, one of the chambers was devoted to the storage of meat, in this case consisting of large cuts from the ribs. Similar remains of the same age were found in tomb 385 H.4 at Helwan, but here two large flint knives had been placed in the magazine with the meat. Other mastabas at these two sites contained brick-built granaries; these were circular structures with an opening at the top for filling and another near the base where the grain could be removed (fig. 10). Liquid refreshment was not lacking in the tombs, for they contained masses of pottery jars full of wine, each vessel being closed by a clay stopper with a seal impression giving a royal or official name. It is ironic that much of our knowledge of the administration of Egypt in the Early Dynastic Period is derived from the seals of wine-jars. Sometimes, particularly in later mastabas, the jars contained only mud; the lack of the correct contents was due to a belief that the sealed jars would magically serve their purpose just as though they had been full. By the Second Dynasty, the supply of food and drink could take the form of a complete meal, carefully set out in the tomb on stone and pottery dishes. One such funerary meal (plate 6), found in a tomb at Saqqara, comprised the following menu:

Fig. 10. Section of a brick granary in Saqqara tomb 3038

loaf of bread	ribs and legs of beef
porridge made from ground barley	stewed fruit
a cooked fish	fresh *nabk* berries
pigeon stew	small cakes with honey
a cooked quail	cheese
two cooked kidneys	jar of wine

There were two further items in addition to the above, but their identity could not be established. Clearly, with a repast of this kind in the tomb, the deceased did not intend to go hungry. Such a meal could be enjoyed in perpetuity, as only the destruction of the offerings, or their removal from the tomb, could deny the deceased the benefits of the food. The fact that the provisions were never actually consumed meant that they would always be available in the burial chamber, so that the spirit of the owner could obtain sustenance as necessary by magical means. In later times the food-offerings were simplified, or replaced by magical substitutes, but the tombs of the Old Kingdom were frequently supplied with the basic head and foreleg of a bull, which might be left in the burial chamber itself, or in the pit just outside.

The offerings which did not take the form of foodstuffs could either be specially made items, destined only for funerary use, or they could be possessions of daily life which the owner desired to take with him into the next world. To have a complete set of funerary equipment made must have been an expensive matter, available only to wealthier individuals and to royalty. The great masses of goods in archaic tombs must have been specially made for the burials, although some items, particularly those of a more personal nature such as jewellery, may well have been used in life. Certain objects show clearly by their condition that they had been extensively used prior to inclusion in the tomb: an ivory gaming-piece in the form of a lion, found in a small grave at Abydos and now in the British Museum, had received so much use that the sides are worn smooth where it was held in the fingers. At the opposite extreme, items could be manufactured even at the site of the tomb and be placed with the burial just before it was sealed. This was particularly true of objects which were becoming tradi-tional rather than functional, such as the flint implements in tombs of the early Fourth Dynasty at Meydum. In a number of cases these flint blades can be fitted together to reconstitute the core from which they were struck – a circumstance which is most unlikely to occur unless they had been made at the graveside. Similarly, a flint scraper in mastaba 3505 at Saqqara had been broken in the course of manufacture and the fragments left in the tomb.

The preparation or transport of funerary equipment is illustrated upon the walls of New Kingdom tombs at Thebes, giving us some idea of the kind of material which was provided for private burials at that period. This is fortunate, as hardly any wealthy tombs of the New Kingdom have been found intact, although a variety of objects which can only have come from such tombs are scattered in museums. A large proportion of the objects consisted of items of furniture – boxes, chairs, beds and similar goods – but cosmetic equipment, toys, musical instruments, tools and weapons are also known to have come from tombs. More elaborate provision, including a large amount of specially made material, occurs in New Kingdom royal tombs, as demonstrated by the great assemblage of objects in the tomb of Tutankhamun. Here again, items made only for funerary purposes were found together with some of the personal possessions of the king. But Tutankhamun's tomb-furniture, despite its magnificence, would have been far inferior to that which must have belonged to the greater kings of the New Kingdom. In later times there was a reduction in the quantity of goods included in the royal tombs, with more emphasis on smaller objects. The royal tombs of the Twenty-First and Twenty-Second Dynasties at Tanis contained many very fine pieces of jewellery and similar items, but the bulky gilded furniture and chariots like those in Tutankhamun's tomb were not included.

The actual installation of the burial and its equipment was at all periods accompanied by certain rituals, which took place just outside the tomb. Our knowledge of these rites is best for the New Kingdom, since the tomb scenes of that age show exactly what occurred, but similar practices were already in use during the Old Kingdom and earlier. The transport of the body to the tomb took the form of a ritual procession, normally beginning on the east bank of the Nile and crossing over on ferries to the cemeteries on the west. On landing, the corpse would be placed upon a sledge covered by a shrine and drawn by oxen to the tomb itself, with a second sledge following to transport the chest containing the viscera (plate 7). Close to the mummy stood two women, impersonating the divine mourners Isis and Nephthys. The precise order of the members of the procession varies in different tomb-scenes, but the same elements usually occur. These include groups of mourning women, most of whom were probably hired professionals rather than relatives, a detachment of nine officials, referred to in the texts as the 'Nine Friends', and a number of servants carrying items of tomb-furniture. The sledge was preceded by several men, some of whom appear to have been mourners while others acted as priests. One of the latter burnt incense and sprinkled a libation of milk as the procession wound its way onwards. A vivid description of the scene is given to us by a contemporary inscription:

A goodly burial arrives in peace, your seventy days having been completed in your place of embalming, being placed upon the bier...and being dragged by young bulls, the road being opened with milk until you reach the door of your tomb. The children of your children, united with one accord, weep with loving hearts. Your mouth is opened by the lector-priest and your purification is performed by the Sem-priest. Horus adjusts for you your mouth and opens for you your eyes and ears, your flesh and your bones being complete in all that appertains to you. Spells and glorifications are recited for you. There is made for you an Offering-which-the-King-gives, your own heart being truly with you, your heart of your earthly existence, you having arrived in your former state, as on the day on which you were born. There is brought to you the Son-whom-you-love, the courtiers making obeisance. [You] enter into a land given by the king, into the sepulchre of the west...[1]

Part of the above text refers to ceremonies which occurred on arrival at the tomb. Here, the bier was greeted by ritual dancers, known as the Muu, and by a lector-priest who read from a papyrus sections of funerary spells in honour of the deceased. There now took place the most important ceremony of the entire burial proceedings, called the Ritual of Opening the Mouth. The purpose of this rite was to restore to the mummy the powers of speech, sight and hearing – in short, to bring the body magically back to life for its posthumous existence. This ceremony was an extremely ancient one, usually performed on a statue of the deceased, but from the end of the Eighteenth Dynasty it became customary to substitute the actual mummy for the statue. The body, in its anthropoid case, was held upright before the entrance to the tomb by a priest who wore a jackal-headed mask in impersonation of the god Anubis. Two other priests, known as the Sem-priest and the 'Son-whom-he-loves', touched the mouth of the mummy with various ritual implements, including an adze, a chisel-like implement and other amuletic objects, thereby restoring the senses (plate 8). The full ritual was quite complex, but it is frequently shown in only an abbreviated form in ancient representations, in which the presentation of the adze by the 'Son-whom-he-loves' is singled out for individual depiction. The next stage consisted of an offering of clothing, ointment and incense, followed by small offerings of food. Finally, there was a full-scale funerary banquet, presented by the priests as one of their number recited the offering formula. The different foodstuffs included in this meal were listed in the inscriptions on the walls of the tomb. Once the mummy had been installed in the burial chamber the rites were concluded and all the footprints were swept from the floor before the tomb was sealed.

Such were the ceremonies which accompanied the burial of a wealthy Egyptian, but there can be no doubt that the standard ritual must have been greatly simplified in very many cases. As mentioned above, most of our knowledge is based on the tomb-scenes, but these show the ritual as it was intended to be and not necessarily as it was in fact. Not all the rites depicted were always carried out, especially as the tomb-scenes themselves could magically act as a substitute for the actual ceremonies. This is demonstrated by the inclusion of scenes showing mysterious rites which linked the funerary ceremonies with the legend of Osiris, depicting a boat journey to Abydos and other important religious centres; this journey, however, can hardly ever have actually taken place. In funerary beliefs traditions tended to linger long after their original purpose had been forgotten, and a considerable part of the rituals of the New Kingdom shows the preservation of earlier customs. The burial rites of private individuals had been taken over from the royal ceremonies of the Old Kingdom and many influences remained. For example, several of the objects shown amongst the funeral furniture of the New Kingdom tombs are items of royal regalia, which had no place in a private monument. Similarly, the titles borne by the officials who took part in the burial procession are archaic terms originally applied to the members of the royal burial service, and do not accurately describe the state of affairs at a private funeral, where the participants were relatives of the deceased or hired mourners. In the Old Kingdom, only the dead king was identified with Osiris and the burial rites were designed to suit this identification, the Opening of the Mouth ceremony itself being said to have been first performed by Horus for his father Osiris. This is connected with the priestly title, 'Son-whom-he-loves', the 'Son' being Horus, whom the priest represented. Now Horus was not only the son of Osiris, but his heir in the classic sense, avenging the murder of his father and assuming the kingship which Osiris had previously held. Consequently, the Egyptians believed that the person responsible for carrying out the burial rites of an individual would thereby establish his right as heir, since he fulfilled the role of Horus. An illustration of this belief is found in an interesting ancient text, recording a dialogue between a man and his soul: 'Be patient, my soul, my brother, until my heir appears, who shall make offering and who shall stand at the tomb on the day of burial...'[2] This had its effect on the principles of inheritance, and it became accepted that a man's son, by performing the burial rites of his father, confirmed his right to inherit his property. Of course, if a son chose to delegate the responsibility to a paid priest this could not have affected his rights, since the son was still providing the means for the proper burial ceremonies. With royal burials the custom had most important effects, as in theory the person who attended to the burial of the king thereby obtained a claim to the throne. Consequently, each new king would be careful to provide for the burial of his predecessor, to fulfil his role of Horus burying Osiris and receiving his inheritance. A tenuous claim to the throne could be strengthened in this way; for this reason the Pharaoh Ay had himself depicted in a painting in the tomb of Tutankhamun performing the Opening of the Mouth ritual for the dead king.

The relatives of the dead, particularly the eldest son, were also expected to make provision for the continued well-being of the deceased. It was not sufficient simply to leave offerings in the tomb at the time of burial; a regular supply of food and drink had to be brought to replenish the provisions in the tomb. In fact this onerous task could be delegated to a staff of mortuary priests, although it is still the son of the deceased who appears in the tomb-reliefs and paintings as the bringer of offerings. From the Middle Kingdom it was possible to combine the funerary cult with that of a nearby temple, the food offerings being presented to a statue of the deceased in the temple itself. This contrivance helped the cult to be rather more permanent, because the priests were not obliged to make the long journey to the tomb in order to present the offerings. Some legal contracts on this subject, made between a certain Hapdjefa of Asyut and the priesthood of the local temple, record the gifts which the priests would offer to the deceased and the payment they had received for their services. An extract from one of these contracts reads as follows:

> The contract made by the count, overseer of priests, Hapdjefa, justified, with the temple staff of Wepwawet, lord of Asyut, namely: the giving to him of white bread by each one of them, to his statue, in the charge of his mortuary priest, in the first month of Inundation, day 1, New Year's Day, when the house is given to its lord after the lamp is lit in the temple; together with their going forth until they reach the northern corner of the temple, as they do when they glorify their own nobles [on] the day of the lighting of the lamp. What he gave to them for it: a *hekat* of northern barley from each field of the estate, from the first of the harvest of the count's estate, as every commoner of Asyut does with the first of his harvest.[3]

The presentation of the daily food-offerings took the form of a set ritual, again descended from the royal mortuary cult of the Old Kingdom. In its original form the ritual included many stages, all of which were probably carried out in the Old Kingdom royal mortuary temples, in which the rites would have been enacted before a statue of the king. The figure would have been ceremonially washed and purified with incense, then it would have received the ritual of Opening the Mouth to confer life on it. Following this, a small meal was presented, after which the statue was anointed with cosmetic and clothed in its royal regalia. Then came the offering of the full banquet, the individual parts of which are recorded in lists in the Pyramid Texts. This list of offerings was copied in private tombs, although the ritual was greatly simplified. In the Old and Middle Kingdoms, when many tombs had their own priestly staffs, the offering ritual may well have been recited in the tomb chapels at regular intervals, although the actual gifts of food may have been limited in number or entirely lacking. By the New Kingdom the procedure had probably been further simplified, amounting to only the occasional recitation of the offering formula and the presentation of small gifts of food. The necessity to provide for the daily requirements of the dead was an enormous burden on the living, and it was inevitable that the supply of offerings to any tomb would gradually be neglected and eventually be discontinued.

The need to provide offerings of food at the tomb had a profound effect on the evolution of the tomb itself, since it had to combine the function of a burial-place with that of a mortuary chapel in which the priests could officiate. In the earliest times, the first consideration would have been to have marked the site of the grave in order that the offerings could be brought to the correct spot. Small burials of the Predynastic Period were probably covered by low tumuli of rubble, beside which some simple offerings could have been made. Somewhat later, at the beginning of the First Dynasty, several small mastabas at Tarkhan illustrate how a special area adjacent to the tomb came to be enclosed by a low wall to encircle the offering-place, and stacks of pottery jars were indeed found in and around these primitive chapels. Once we reach the First Dynasty proper more elaborate provision is found, the royal tombs at Abydos having enclosed but unroofed chapels marked by stelae, and the large mastabas of the nobility possessing a special

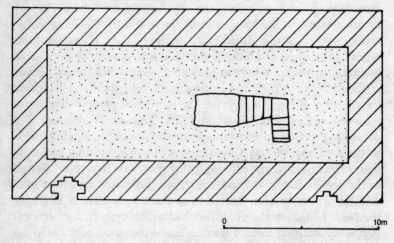

0   10m

Fig. 11. Plan of a typical mastaba of the Second Dynasty

offering-niche. This niche was simply one of the recesses which adorned the facades of such tombs, situated near the south end of the east side and singled out to serve as an offering-place. Two mastabas at Tarkhan had a wooden floor in this recess, showing its greater importance over the remaining niches. In the Second Dynasty the mastaba was simplified and built with plain walls, except for one recess at each end of the east face (fig. 11). The southern niche was the actual offering-place; the north recess was provided for the sake of symmetry and was normally of simpler design. With the continued development of the tomb, discussed in more detail in a later chapter, we find that the offering-niche grad-ually extends deeper into the superstructure until the original niche becomes no more than a doorway into a complex series of rooms (fig. 12). This trend continued in the stone-built mastabas of the Old Kingdom, culminating in the Sixth Dynasty, when practically the entire superstructure was filled with internal chambers, all forming part of the offering-chapel. In fact, the superstructure becomes nothing else but the chapel, and the burial apartments have their own location in the rock beneath it. This division between a chapel on the ground surface and a burial chamber

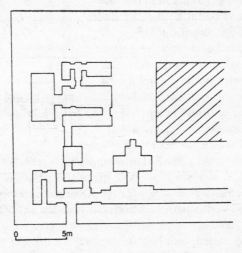

Fig. 12. Plan of the offering-chapel in Saqqara tomb 3518

underground exists all through the history of ancient Egyptian tomb development. Even in rock-cut tombs the burial chamber is always reached by descending a pit or sloping corridor further into the rock.

The focal point of the chapel was the stela, before which the offering ritual was enacted. This stela usually took the form of an imitation door carved in stone, and consequently it is normally known by the term 'false door' to Egyptologists (plate 9). Although it was completely solid the Egyptians believed that it would function as a real door for the spirit of the deceased, allowing him to leave the burial chamber at will in order to receive the offerings in the chapel. The false door itself bears the standard offering formula, and, in many cases, a scene showing the tomb-owner seated before a table piled with foodstuffs. The position of the offering-room and the false door were related to the location of the burial chamber below, so that in many cases the body in its coffin lay directly under the floor of the chapel (fig. 13).

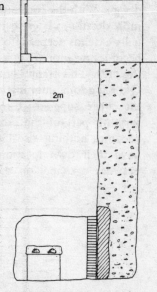

Fig.13.Relative positions of offering-chapel and burial chamber in the Old Kingdom

In Egyptian belief there were two main spiritual forms of the deceased, called respectively the Ka and the Ba. The former was supposed to dwell in the tomb, or, more precisely, in the mummified body, and it was the form in which the dead received their funerary offerings. The usual offering formula reflects this, in statements like, 'A thousand loaves of bread and jars of beer, together with all good and pure things for the Ka of the deceased', followed by the name of the person concerned. It seems that the Ka represented the life-force of an individual; it was created at the time of his birth, remained with him throughout his life and subsequently lived in the tomb. The dead were sometimes referred to as 'those who have gone to their *Kas*', and the tomb chapel could be called 'the house of the *Ka*'. Ordinary people had only a single *Ka* but gods and kings had several. The other spiritual manifestation, the *Ba*, is usually represented as a human-headed bird. It left the body at the time of death and was free to travel from the tomb during the daytime, but it returned to dwell in the mummy at night (fig. 14).

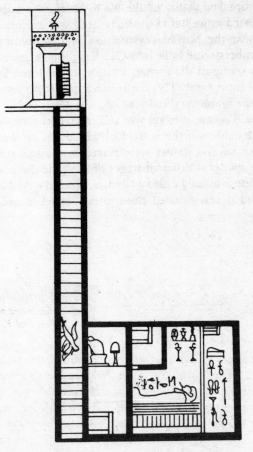

Fig. 14. The Ba descending the shaft of the tomb

A vivid representation of the emergence of the deceased from the underground chamber to receive his offerings is to be found in the mastaba of Idu at Giza, in which a portrait bust of the tomb-owner is shown as if rising from the ground at the base of the false door. In other tombs, both of the Old Kingdom and later date, the conventional false door is replaced by a type containing a statue of the deceased within the central recess. In this way the statue served as a link between the burial chamber and the chapel, since the *Ka* could reside in the mummy underground or in the statue in the superstructure. The ability of the *Ka* to dwell in a portrait figure of the deceased as well as in the body itself was exploited as a safeguard against the possible destruction of the mummy. Special sealed chambers were built into Old Kingdom mastabas in order to house a statue of the owner, completely enclosed by masonry and hidden from sight. This statue was intended to serve as a substitute for the mummy; should the latter be destroyed by any event, the *Ka* would continue to survive and receive its food-offerings so that the eternal life of the individual would not be threatened. In certain cases several statues were placed in a single tomb, representing the owner at different stages of life. The chamber containing the statue is usually called a 'serdab', from the Arabic word for a cellar, and it was situated close to the chapel in order that the

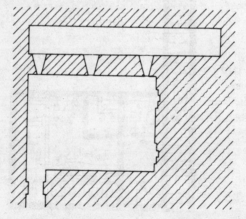

Fig.15. Plan of the apertures linking the chapel and serdab

figure would be near to the provisions supplied by the relatives or priests. In many cases, the wall between the chapel and the serdab was pierced by a number of holes or slots, to allow the statue to see out and the benefits of the offerings to pass inwards (fig. 15). In making a statue to act as a substitute body, the essential requirement was that it should be as lifelike as possible, so the figures, whether of wood or stone, were painted in colours. Particular attention was paid to the face, the animation of which was sometimes improved by the insertion of inlaid eyes of quartz crystal and obsidian. As an additional precaution the identity of the figure was confirmed beyond doubt by inscribing upon it the name of the owner. Most of the fine Old Kingdom statues now in museums were originally made as serdab statues, to be sealed forever into tombs; their purpose was strictly functional and it is only the modern world which has labelled them as works of 'art'. Before a figure was walled up in the serdab there would have been performed upon it the ceremony of Opening the Mouth, to endow it with life as a true duplicate of the deceased.

The tomb chapel, as mentioned above, normally formed part of the superstructure of the tomb, but for royal burials the chapel was enlarged to such an extent that it became a complete temple for the cult of the dead king. In the Old and Middle Kingdoms the mortuary temple was situated adjacent to the king's pyramid, forming an integral part of the monumental complex. The earliest pyramid temple, that belonging to the Step Pyramid of Djoser, was located on the north side of the pyramid, but the increasing importance of solar worship during the Old Kingdom led to the east side becoming the standard position for the temple in the later true pyramids. This is first seen at Meydum, where the pyramid must belong to the end of the Third or the commencement of the Fourth Dynasty, depending on whether it was erected by Huni or Sneferu. The temple at Meydum, although simple, has all the necessary architectural features to serve as an offering-place, the most important portion being the inner courtyard containing the two stelae and the offering-table; only the inscriptions are lacking (fig. 16). It is at Meydum also that we see the prototype of the causeway extending from the mortuary temple to a valley temple on the edge of the cultivation; both the causeway and the lower temple were to remain

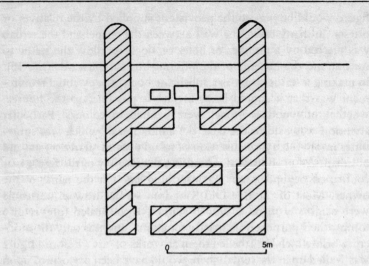

Fig.16.Plan of the mortuary temple of the Meydum pyramid

as permanent elements of later pyramid complexes. Their function was separate from that of the mortuary temple: the valley temple served as a reception-point for the body of the king, and the cause-way ensured that the mummy could be carried up to the pyramid without again leaving the ritually pure precincts of the complex, or being exposed to eyes other than those of the priests. The early causeway at Meydum was open to the sky but later examples were roofed over and their walls were decorated with reliefs. The pyramid temples of the Fourth to Sixth Dynasties, and those of the Middle Kingdom, were fairly complicated in plan but their essential purpose remained the same: to act as the chapel for the continuance of the cult of the dead king. Some of the wall-reliefs reflect directly the function of the temple as a mortuary chapel, showing rows of offering-bearers carrying all kinds of provisions towards the sanctuary; such scenes are common in private mastabas on a smaller scale. But as a divine being the king is also shown in the pyramid temples in the company of the gods with whom he was considered equal; the latter scenes depict an aspect of the royal mortuary cult which separated it from that of ordinary mortals, the purely religious subjects being unconnected with the prime function of the temple as an offering-place.

The pyramid temples, like the chapels of private tombs, were built as close as possible to the actual burial-place which they served, so that the presentation of the offerings and the intended recipient were not greatly separated. However, the abandonment of the pyramidal form of tomb for royal burials in the New Kingdom in favour of rock-cut tombs in the Valley of the Kings at Thebes made it impossible to continue building the tomb and its cult-centre close together. The mortuary temples of the kings of the New Kingdom were built instead along the edge of the cultivated land on the west bank of the Nile at Thebes, some considerable distance from the tombs themselves, but this was no longer regarded as a serious impediment to the receipt of the offerings by the dead. Gradually these mortuary temples came to combine the functions of an offering-chapel and of a temple for the cult of the god Amun, with whom the dead king was to some extent identified.

The efficient functioning of any kind of funerary chapel depended on the relatives of the deceased or on an employed priesthood to carry out the correct and regular rituals. But no mortuary cult could continue indefinitely, as was desirable for the well-being of the dead, and safeguards were needed to prepare for the possible cessation of actual food-offerings. We have already seen how a statue could substitute for the body and become the resting-place of the *Ka*, but this kind of belief went much further, extending to the reliefs and paintings on the chapel walls, so that the scenes could magically provide all the requirements of the deceased. This is the reason why so much of the tomb decoration consists of repetitive scenes showing the bringing of food, or the tomb-owner seated before a sumptuous meal. The very depiction of such images on the walls acted as a substitute for the events represented and ensured the continued existence of the person for whom the tomb had been prepared. The extraordinary logic of the ancient Egyptians carried this magical provision to great lengths by showing not only the food on the offering-table, but also all the stages in the production of the food, including the sowing and harvesting of the crops, the fattening of the fowl, the rearing of cattle and their subsequent slaughter in the butcher's shop (fig. 17). To refer to the tomb-scenes as 'decoration' is really to give a misleading impression, since they were intended to be strictly functional. Even the

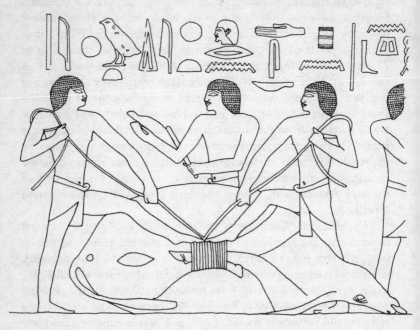

Fig.17.Scene of butchers at work from a Sixth Dynasty tomb

scenes which show the deceased in leisure activities, such as hunting, were included to enable him to continue to enjoy such pursuits in the afterlife. The power of the representations to provide for the needs of the dead would survive so long as the scenes themselves lasted, which was likely to be a good deal longer than the funerary cult. A clear illustration of the ability of carvings and paintings to replace actual objects is given by the large numbers of stone offering-tables which bear permanent reliefs on their upper surfaces showing the food and drink which may have been lacking in more edible form (fig. 18). During the Middle Kingdom it was customary to depict food-offerings amongst the paintings on the coffin,

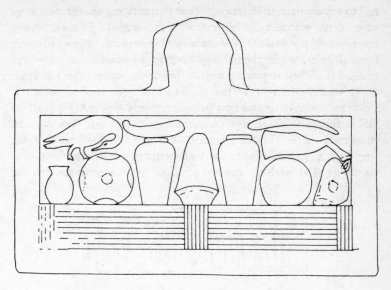

Fig.18.Offering-table with reliefs of food and drink

together with illustrations of other items of funerary equipment, all of which would have been available to the owner through the magical properties of pictorial representation. Normally the precise contents of the scenes were clarified by the addition of inscriptions labelling the various objects.

The functional nature of Egyptian paintings and reliefs had a profound effect on the conventions which governed the production of such images. The characteristic appearance of Egyptian art was not due to lack of expertise but simply to the fact that strict rules had to be followed if the scenes were to fulfil their intended purpose. Figures and objects were not drawn as they actually appeared but in the most recognizable and complete form possible, because an incomplete representation would be unable to function properly for the benefit of the deceased. Paintings of the human figure deliberately distort the true state of affairs in order to show both arms, by drawing the shoulders from a frontal view even though the rest of the body is in a mixture of three-quarter view and profile. Similarly, although the head is in profile, the eye is drawn in full to ensure its completeness. More illuminating are the paintings of gardens, common in New Kingdom tombs at Thebes, where the pond in the middle is shown in plan with the trees radiating from all sides, whilst the fish and birds in the pond are in side-view (plate 11). When depicting objects inside containers the Egyptian artist would often draw the object above the box in which it belonged, simply to make its presence clearly evident (fig. 19). So far as funerary belief was concerned an object not seen was an object not there. The rules were only relaxed with scenes of lesser importance, not so vital to the well-being of the deceased, such as paintings of animals or servants. In these areas we can see that the

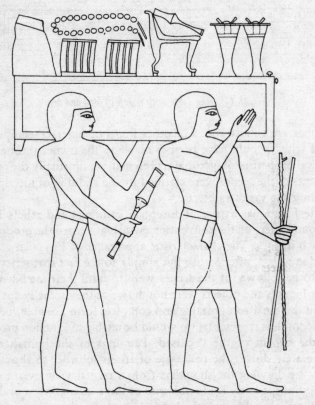

Fig.19.Funerary goods depicted above the containers in which they are carried

Egyptians were capable of excellent naturalistic artistry when free from the restrictions which controlled most tomb art.

As an alternative or a supplement to the provision of reliefs and paintings, the supply of offerings could be guaranteed by models, which were considered to serve the dead just as well as the full-size objects they replaced. The earliest kinds of models to be used were small copies of stone and pottery vases, already common in tombs of the First Dynasty. Their use was greatly extended in the Old Kingdom, when many large mastaba-tombs had complete sets of model offering-vessels in place of their larger equivalents, in addition to models of copper tools and vases (plate 10). But the Middle Kingdom was the period at which greatest use was made of funerary models, not only as copies of individual objects but also to depict activities of everyday life. The latter type functioned magically to sustain the deceased in the same way as the wall-paintings, and consequently we find that the majority of models illustrate episodes in the preparation of food or drink, such as baking, brewing, cultivating the fields and storing the grain. The models are made of wood, covered with a thin plaster coat and painted in colours (plate 12). One of the finest groups of such models was found in the tomb of a noble called Meketre, who lived during the Eleventh Dynasty. All kinds of day-to-day activities on the estate of a wealthy noble are illustrated: cattle-rearing, bread and beer making, weaving and carpentry are each represented in minute detail. In addition, there are models of Meketre's house and his sailing-boats, and, with more obvious funerary connection, figures of servants bringing food-offerings to the tomb. But more impressive than the range of subjects is the fine detail of the individual models. Servant-girls carry baskets of food on their heads and in the baskets are the separate cuts of meat, loaves of bread and jars of beer, carefully modelled in painted wood. In the butcher's shop the freshly cut joints are shown hanging from lines on a balcony. The carpenters hold model tools of copper with wooden handles, and, in order that the work should not be hindered by the tools becoming blunt, spares were provided in a wooden box at the back of the shop, together with spare adze blades of the correct size for the handles. The largest model in the tomb shows Meketre seated under a columned portico, inspecting his cattle as they are driven by. In life, a great nobleman would have possessed many servants to perform duties on his estate; in death their place was taken by their model counterparts, who would carry out the same tasks for eternity. During the First Dynasty the servants of royalty or of high officials had actually been slain to accompany their master in the next world, but this custom was soon abandoned. The purpose of these servant-burials was the same as that of the model attendants of the Middle Kingdom: to enable the wealthy noble to enjoy the same kind of life-style after death as he had during his lifetime.

In later times the responsibility for carrying out tasks on behalf of the deceased was transferred to a special kind of funerary statuette, known as a shabti-figure. Shabtis begin to appear in tombs of the Middle Kingdom, at which time they usually consisted of a rough mummiform figure of wood or wax, often enclosed in a model wooden coffin. In the New Kingdom the figures were more elaborate affairs of stone, wood, metal or glazed composition, and they frequently bore a magical text to ensure that they would be effective in carrying out their tasks, although poorer examples were marked only with the name of their owner. The duties which they were intended to perform were largely agricultural, reflecting the everyday life of the Nile Valley, and, as a consequence, the shabtis of the New Kingdom and later are shown carrying hoes, mattocks and baskets (plate 13). Shabtis continued to be a regular feature of burials down to the end of the Dynastic Period but the quality of the figures varied greatly over this span of time. After the fine examples of the Eighteenth and Nineteenth Dynasties there was a decline in the standard of production down to the Twenty-Second Dynasty, when very many shabtis of extremely rough form were made, often devoid of any text. A revival is found in the fine shabtis of the Twenty-Fifth and Twenty-Sixth Dynasties, to which period belong some of the best figures of this type. At the beginning of their development, in the Middle Kingdom, it was usual for only one shabti to be provided in a tomb, to act as a deputy for the deceased, but in later times much larger numbers were supplied, and they gradually took on the role of serfs. Large numbers of shabtis were considered to be organized in separate gangs, like the workmen on a large estate, and so special 'overseer' figures were added in the late New Kingdom to keep the ordinary servants in control. The overseers are distinguished by their being represented in the dress of daily life instead of as a mummiform figure, and they carry whips to indicate their rank. Also in tombs of the late New Kingdom, the shabtis could be accommodated in special inscribed boxes provided for the purpose, but in the Late Period the position of the figures in the tomb could be more varied, examples having been found walled up in recesses in the sides of the burial chamber.

The inscriptions on shabtis leave no doubt as to their function. The full version of the text mentions specific tasks which the deceased might be called upon to perform in the next world, including cultivating the fields, irrigating the canals and transporting sand. In the event of any such request to the deceased, the text states that the shabti was immediately to say, 'Here am I', indicating that the figure was ready to carry out the tasks on behalf of its owner. It is interesting to note that shabtis were purchased, their manufacture being apparently under the control of the temple workshops. A papyrus in the British Museum records the sale of a set of shabtis to a certain Espernub, the figures being destined for the tomb of his father, Inhafy. The text is more than a simple deed of sale; it also urges the shabtis to work efficiently because the correct payment had been received:

Pedikhons, son of Espenankh, son of Hor, the chief modeller of amulets of the temple of Amun, has declared to the beloved of the god, the priest Espernub, son of Inhafy, son of Iufenkhons: as Amun the great god endures, I have received from you the silver [i.e. the price] of these 365 shabtis and their thirty-six overseers, 401 in all, to my satisfaction. Male and female slaves are they, and I have received from you their value in refined silver [namely the price] of the 401 shabtis. [O shabtis] go quickly to work on behalf of Osiris, for the beloved of the god, the priest Inhafy. Say, 'we are ready' whenever he will summon you for service of the day.[4]

The shabti formula is a good illustration of a concept important in Egyptian funerary belief – namely, the power of the written word to cause events to occur by magic. To write something down was to give it substance; the shabti text, by simply stating that the figures would respond to any calls upon the deceased, actually ensured that they would function as desired. But the power of the written word to influence events also extended to the inscriptions in the tomb itself, enabling the texts, like the pictorial representations, to provide for the needs of the deceased long after the supply of daily offerings had lapsed. This ability of the written word to have a positive effect is best seen in magical texts designed to ensure the well-being of the dead, and particularly in the Pyramid Texts, which had the specific function of conferring protection on the dead king. Again and again, the texts deny the death of the king and state that no evil will have the power to harm him. The inscriptions themselves had the power to safeguard the king's eternal existence, which would only be threatened if the texts should be entirely destroyed. A typical passage runs as follows:

O King, you have not departed dead, you have departed alive; sit upon the throne of Osiris, your sceptre in your hand, that you may give orders to the living.[5]

Another text assures the king of protection:

O Osiris the King, behold you are protected and alive, so that you may go to and fro daily and none will interfere with you.[6]

The provision which the Egyptians made for death was wholly concerned with ensuring their safe existence in the afterlife, and we have seen how this provision took various forms, beginning with the basic essentials of preserving the body itself and supplying the necessities of food and drink, then gradually developing to include magical methods of providing the same requirements. Although the magical offerings, whether in the form of models or pictures or inscriptions, duplicated the actual funerary gifts, the latter were not abandoned as obsolete, since the Egyptians rarely discarded old ways in favour of new ideas. The guarantee of both material and magical security for the dead made it extremely difficult for an individual to lose his chance of a second life, because this would only happen if all the means for his survival were to be totally destroyed. If all else was lost the spirit could find ultimate refuge in the preservation of his name, either in written or spoken form, which really means that the survival of the Ka could depend on the lasting memory of the deceased among the living. This concept is clearly revealed in a text of New Kingdom date, parts of which are quoted below, extolling the advantages of the scribe's profession:

But if you do these things, you are knowledgeable in writings. Those learned scribes from the time of the successors of the gods, [those] who foretold the future, it has come about that their names endure forever, although they have gone, having completed their lives, and [although] all their relatives have been forgotten. They did not make for themselves pyramids of copper with tombstones of iron. They did not know how to leave heirs, namely children [who would] pronounce their names, but they have made heirs for themselves of the writings and the books of instruction which they made...

There were made for them doors and halls but these have fallen to pieces. Their mortuary priests are [gone], their tombstones are covered with dirt and their tomb-chambers are forgotten. [But] their names are pronounced because of the books which they made, because they were good, and the memory of him who made them is for ever more.[7]

This then was the final key to eternal life: to have one's memory perpetuated and one's name spoken by the living. An often-repeated sentiment in tomb inscriptions also shows the value of having one's name preserved in writing:

I made live the names of my fathers which I found obliterated on the doorways...Behold, he is a good son who perpetuates the names of his ancestors.[8]

On the other hand, if you destroyed a person's name you ended his existence in the next world. This is demonstrated by an inscription from Coptos, designed to terminate the memory of a certain Teti, son of Minhotpe:

Let him be cast out on the ground from this temple...let him be driven from his office of the temple from son to son and heir to heir...his name not being remembered in this temple, as is done to his like...[9]

For the same reason, the names of individuals are frequently found to have been hacked out from the walls of their tombs.

The pronouncing of the name of the deceased is only one example of the power of the spoken word to benefit the dead; in addition, recitations formed an integral part of the offering ritual.

It follows that if pictures and inscriptions had the magical ability to influence events, then the spoken word would naturally have similar powers. An important part of the offering ritual took the form of oral recitations, and many tomb chapels contain the following plea to visitors to recite a prayer for offerings on behalf of the owner:

O ye living who are upon earth, who shall pass by this tomb. So surely as you wish your gods to favour you, may you say: a thousand of bread and beer, a thousand of flesh and fowl, a thousand of alabaster and clothing for the Ka of the deceased...

Individuals who respected the tomb and who recited the formula were promised benefits by the deceased, but the inscriptions display a quite different attitude towards those who damaged the chapel:

Now as for all people...who shall make a disturbance in this tomb, who shall damage its inscriptions or who shall do damage to its statue, they will fall under the anger of Thoth.[10]

From the foregoing it will be apparent that the Egyptians regarded the dead as being very much alive, dwelling in their tombs as they had formerly lived in their houses. The link between the tomb and the house was very important, the tomb chapel often being called 'the house of eternity'. Various points in tomb architecture illustrate the identification of the tomb with a dwelling. Already in the Second Dynasty the substructures of large mastabas possessed chambers which duplicated the apartments of a house, even lavatories being provided. In later times, particularly in the New Kingdom, it was customary to have a garden with trees just outside the chapel, just as a wealthy person would have a garden outside his house. Cemeteries, too, tended to be town-planned like living cities. The best example of this is seen at Giza, where the original mastabas were laid out in regular streets to the east and west of the pyramid of Khufu, but, as in any town, the design was complicated by the construction of later tombs in the streets between the older monuments. A very late reflection of the concept of the tomb as a house is found in the Graeco-Roman cemetery at Tuna el-Gebel, in which many of the tombs were built in the form of houses of the period. The Egyptians themselves described the land of the dead as a dwelling-place. Although the dead depended on the living for their survival, they were considered to have the power to influence events, and letters were written to the dead asking for their help in disputes. The dead were not, however, thought to be particularly malevolent, as is often the case in other cultures. The Egyptians were not obsessed with death; the study of their funerary beliefs shows that it was the love of life which drove them to make such elaborate preparations for burial, since death accompanied by the correct rituals was only the beginning of eternal life. Their fear of losing this second existence is very apparent. Possibly the attitude of the living towards the dead in their cemeteries is best shown by an inscription on a Middle Kingdom stela from Abydos. The text is set in the form of a song above the figure of a musician playing the harp before his master:

The singer Tjeni-aa, he says, 'How well-established you are in your place of eternity, in your everlasting tomb. It is filled with offerings and with food. It encloses every good thing. Your *Ka* is with you and it does not depart from you. O seal-bearer of the King of Lower Egypt, chief steward, Nebankh, yours is the sweet breath of the north wind.' By the singer who causes his name to live, the revered singer Tjeni-aa, whom he wished to sing for his *Ka* every day.[11]

4

SECURITY
OF THE TOMB

It is a sad fact that the vast majority of ancient Egyptian tombs
have been plundered in antiquity, and archaeologists are generally
left with only the scattered and broken wreckage of once fine burial
equipment. A few seasons' work on the excavation of any cemetery
makes this point abundantly clear, as each tomb-chamber proves
to contain little or nothing of great significance. Intact burials are
frequently very poor ones, the ancient plunderers having known
well that they were not worth the trouble of investigation. The
intact rich burial is a rarity, preserved usually by some freak of
chance, such as its location having been obscured by later buildings.

It is of interest to give some account of the methods used in the
excavation of a tomb, for there are often quite clear indications in
the early stages of the work to reveal whether or not the burial has
been plundered. The majority of the larger burial chambers of all
periods lie at the foot of deep pits in the rock, and the clearing of
the filling from the pit is a protracted task. Shafts may vary in depth
from a matter of only a couple of metres to as much as thirty
metres, and the usual manner of clearance is to haul all the filling
up in baskets on ropes. For the average pit of about 2 m square and
8 m deep, a gang of six or seven workmen is required; two men
fill the baskets at the bottom of the pit as it descends, two more
haul on the ropes to bring the material to the surface and two or
three more carry the baskets to the dumping area, usually close at

hand. When excavating a series of shafts in a compact group of tombs, it is often most convenient to dump excavated material from one pit into another after the clearance of the first shaft, thereby keeping the surface of the site unencumbered by large spoil heaps and avoiding having to leave dangerous deep pits standing open. To remove the filling from an eight-metre shaft will take a week of hard work before the burial chamber is reached, and some more days to clear out the chamber itself.

It is not safe to assume that a shaft will contain only a single chamber; in many Old Kingdom mastabas the shaft will continue downwards past one burial chamber to a second one at a deeper level (fig. 20). Normally, the pits narrow as they descend, but this is not always true. One recently excavated shaft of the Sixth Dynasty at Saqqara was only about 1.30 m square at its mouth, but widened to over 2 m close to its base, making the clearance a much longer job than the excavators had first imagined.

It is usually possible to tell very soon after the beginning of the clearance of a tomb-shaft whether it has been cleared previously since the time of the original filling. Shafts were normally filled with the rubble which resulted from their own excavation, and this is the kind of material which should remain in them if they are untouched. Loose sand indicates a pit which has been completely cleared and allowed to fill again over the years with sand blown in by the wind; fragments of pottery, stone vessels, wood or other broken antiquities in the filling show that the burial has been robbed and the worthless items thrown back into the pit; a very hard-packed filling of mud and broken bricks reveals that the shaft

Fig.20. Section of an Old Kingdom tomb-shaft with chambers on two levels

stood open while the mud-brick superstructure of the tomb collapsed into it, to be compacted by the occasional rain storms. All these indications can aid the excavator, by providing advance warning of a robbed burial. Nevertheless, it is not unusual for there to be a quickening of interest in the excavation as the top of the burial chamber is reached. At first it is difficult to see what is inside, since the loose fill from the pit has spilled down into the entrance, covering its floor, but a little more clearance provides sufficient room to crawl a short way into the undercutting of the shaft and to examine the state of the chamber by torchlight. The all-too-familiar scene is one of complete devastation, with broken pottery, bones and fragments of wood scattered around among the dust. The stone sarcophagus, if one is present, may have had its lid displaced or broken, or the plunderers may have penetrated it by simply cutting a hole through one side. Despite the disappointing appearance of the chamber, it must nevertheless be carefully and completely excavated, measured, planned and published, together with a record of any remaining objects, so as to rescue as much information as possible from the wreckage left by the plunderers. With careful recording, even badly robbed tombs can tell us much about ancient customs and technology, particularly when the information gleaned from many such tombs can be combined to give an overall picture. Robbed tombs, quite obviously, also tell us a great deal about the practice of tomb-robbing itself, which, as a regular feature of ancient Egyptian life, is no less deserving of study than others.

In considering the activities of Egyptian tomb-robbers, it is first necessary to define the basic problem faced by the builders of the tombs. The essential weakness in the security of any Egyptian burial was the fact that the tomb had to contain objects of value, but, with the Egyptian view of the afterlife, there was no alternative. Consequently, the designers of tombs were forced to employ increasingly complex devices to prevent entry to the burial chamber, and particularly to protect the body itself, upon which the most valuable objects lay. The early effects of plundering upon tomb development, leading to the transference of the storage facilities from the superstructure to subterranean levels, has already been described in an earlier chapter, but the threat of robbery had far more extensive repercussions right through Egyptian history. Simple burials, like ordinary Predynastic graves or poor tombs of later ages, offered virtually no defence against robbery, but their very simplicity meant that they did not attract the tomb-robbers so much as the tombs of the wealthy, which, although more difficult to penetrate, offered the promise of greater rewards. In spite of this fact, all but the poorest of graves were commonly robbed to some extent, for the sake of even the smallest items of value. Ordinary cemeteries could be robbed at any time, and the evidence shows that the first plundering took place very soon after the time of interment; royal tombs were quite a different matter, and they may well have survived intact until a period of weak central authority created the conditions in which an attempt to penetrate the burial chamber could succeed. Such periods of turmoil are not lacking in Egyptian history, and the effect of a relaxation of control is clearly described for us in a well-known ancient text: 'Truly, the land turns round as does a potter's wheel. The robber is a possessor of riches. [The wealthy man?] has become a plunderer.'[1] The poor social conditions and famine which prevailed during these unstable phases of Egyptian civilization would in themselves have prompted a greater number of people to turn to tomb-robbing as a means of existence. In the late Twentieth Dynasty, a period for which we have a wealth of documentary evidence about tomb-robbing, the practice was clearly encouraged by economic factors, including the very familiar phenomenon of a high rate of inflation. A woman, questioned about some silver in her possession, replies, 'I obtained it in exchange for barley in the year of the hyenas, when there was a famine.'[2]

To return to architectural matters, the earliest defensive mechanisms for the protection of the burial chamber appear in mastaba-tombs of the First Dynasty, which were entered by means of a stairway descending initially from the east side, but, at a slightly later date, from the north. The stairway, cut in the rock, was closed by the use of portcullis blocks of limestone. These were tall and narrow slabs let down into grooves in the sides of the stairway, in exactly the same manner as the portcullis gate of a castle, hence their name. There might be only one such portcullis, or they could be duplicated at different points along the stair, although the use of more than two such blockings did not occur until the Second Dynasty. A good example of a tomb with multiple portcullis blockings is the Third Dynasty mastaba K.1 at Beit Khallaf, which had portcullises let down through the body of the superstructure (fig. 21). The stones were lowered on ropes, and often have holes in their upper ends through which these were passed. As an additional deterrent, the sloping stairway descent was filled up with gravel. In fact, this filling was probably a greater obstacle to the robbers than the portcullises, which, being of limestone, were speedily pierced (plate 14). This may have been the reason for the transition from the sloping stairway to a vertical shaft during the Third Dynasty, although the earlier type of entrance was retained in the royal stepped pyramids of the dynasty, and the unfinished pyramid of Sekhemkhet had a portcullis to close the ramp. Vertical tomb-shafts are standard in mastabas of the Old Kingdom, with only a few exceptions, and remain common in other types of tombs of later periods. A typical Fourth Dynasty mastaba possessed a single portcullis block immediately before the entrance to the burial chamber, and the only real obstacle to the plunderers was the quantity of filling in the shaft. Obviously, the deeper the shaft, the more difficult it would be to rob the tomb, since the business of emptying the pit would require a number of people and a considerable amount of time free from disturbance. Very shallow pits, on the other hand, could easily be cleared out in a single night by a few determined men. For some, the practice of robbing tombs could

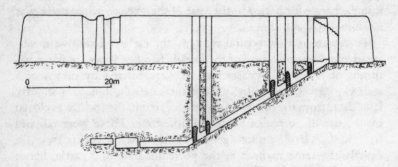

0   20m

Fig.21. Section showing the portcullises in
mastaba K.1 at Beit Khallaf

be conveniently combined with a legitimate job, grave-diggers being particularly suspect. New shafts not infrequently cut into pre-existing chambers, providing easy access to the valuables they contained for any of the diggers who were less than honest. Such collisions of underground passages were inevitable in very crowded cemeteries, but it is also quite likely that a large number were not accidental. The grave-diggers would be quite well aware of the locations of any recent burials, and no doubt took special note of those of any great wealth. A related practice, which likewise shows a good knowledge of the exact positions of tomb-chambers, was that of tunnelling from one chamber to another underground, robbing each in turn. In a recently excavated shaft at Saqqara a tunnel led off from each side of the pit at its base, and a further passage had been cut from the south-west corner of the chamber, each of these routes breaking into several nearby burial chambers in which the broken remains of mummies lay scattered about. The robbers were not troubled by any thoughts of respect for the dead; bodies were regularly smashed up to gain access to the jewellery and amulets beneath the wrappings. A body might be pulled out of the chamber into the pit, or even to the surface, for the sake of better visibility. Alternatively, only those parts of the corpse on which jewellery was to be found were removed, arms and fingers being wrenched away for the sake of bracelets and rings. The bones of the Prince Mereruka, found in his tomb at Saqqara, were scored by the knives used to hack up the mummy. Bodies were also set on fire after robberies, perhaps with the intention of avoiding any evil influence of a magical character which the dead might bring upon the despoilers of their tombs. In one case at Thebes, however, the reason was more prosaic, mummies of children having been ignited for the purpose of illuminating the chamber while the robbers carried out their work.

Once the thieves had succeeded in entering a burial chamber the only remaining obstacle in their way was the coffin. Wooden coffins offered very little protection and, from the Third Dynasty, coffins began to be made of stone. The majority of Old Kingdom sarcophagi were made of soft limestone, although some royal sarcophagi and those of very wealthy private individuals could be made of harder materials such as granite. Details of the style and decoration of coffins and sarcophagi are given in Chapter 7. Limestone coffins offered little protection for the mummy, since the lid could be broken, or the side of the sarcophagus could be pierced by chiselling. Sarcophagi of granite or quartzite were more of a challenge, but they were generally opened by displacing the lid to one side just sufficiently to reach the body. The robbers usually lifted the lid by using wooden levers and then propped it open with stones (plate 15). In the burial chamber of mastaba 17 at Meydum, the sarcophagus lid was found to have been rolled back on two wooden mallets. Another fairly simple method of opening a sarcophagus was to tip the whole coffin over on to its side, so that the lid immediately fell off. To counter this the coffins were sometimes set down into the floor up to the level of the lip, as in the pyramid of Khafre at Giza. Alternatively, to avoid the labour of making a socket for the coffin, a rubble floor could be built up artificially around it. Some details of the robbing of certain sarcophagi reveal once more that the robbers had accurate knowledge of the layout of the chamber; in

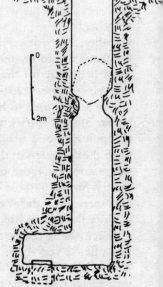

one tomb at Dendera the sarcophagus stood tightly up against one wall, and it had been rifled by someone tunnelling through that wall and the side of the sarcophagus in a single operation, without even entering the chamber. Other cases are known of sarcophagi being robbed through passages cut under the floor of the burial chamber and emerging precisely into the bottom of the coffin. Effective counter-measures to plunderers in the Old Kingdom are rare, the imagination of the designers of private tombs being limited to deeper shafts and heavier sarcophagi. The tomb of Ny-ankh-Pepy at Saqqara, however, had a most unusual device for closing the shaft, consisting of a large block of red granite placed above a constriction in the diameter of the pit (fig. 22).

Fig. 22. The granite plug in the shaft of Ny-ankh-Pepy

This circular plug sealed the tomb rather like a cork in a bottle, and was used in addition to the usual filling of the pit. The only other remotely similar arrangement, although of earlier date, is found in the pyramid of Djoser, where the burial chamber is sealed by means of a granite plug set into the entrance through the roof. In the case of Ny-ankh-Pepy the granite block was found still in its original position in the shaft, but the burial had been robbed by thieves who had tunnelled into the north-west corner of the shaft at its base, having begun their tunnel from a nearby tomb.

Royal tombs, naturally, were given the most elaborate protection, and the arrangements for closing the burial chambers of the pyramids belonging to both the Old and Middle Kingdoms are particularly interesting. The standard methods of sealing pyramids in the Fourth to Sixth Dynasties involved the use of portcullises and plug-blocks. The latter were rectangular blocks of stone let down into the entrance passages of the pyramids until they jammed tight at a pre-selected point. This was achieved by a slight reduction in the width of the corridor at one end, bringing the walls sufficiently close to hold the block. It will be clear from this mode of operation that the construction of the passages and the trimming of the plug-blocks had to be done with precision. Limestone plugs may have been used in the pyramid of Meydum and were certainly used in the two Fourth Dynasty pyramids at Dashur, but it was not until the construction of the pyramid of Khufu at Giza that granite plug-blocks were employed, on account of their greater resistance to tunnelling. Portcullises, being much thinner than plugs, could be easily broken or pierced if not made of hard stone, as a smashed limestone portcullis in the Bent Pyramid of Dashur clearly demonstrates. This particular barrier was of most unusual design, sliding downwards and sideways on a diagonal to close the corridor, instead of falling vertically in the more conventional manner (fig. 23). There were two portcullises of this type in the pyramid but only one had been moved into position. Later pyramids had granite portcullis blocks, either as single barriers or in groups of three (fig. 24). A common technique of the tomb-robbers was to ignore the portcullises or plug-blocks and to cut a fresh passage round them, through the softer limestone masonry of the pyramid.

To counter this process, the walls of pyramid passages were often lined with granite throughout the section in which the portcullises were located.

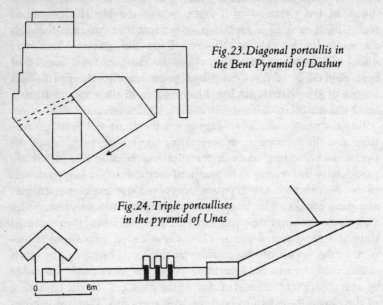

Fig.23.Diagonal portcullis in the Bent Pyramid of Dashur

Fig.24.Triple portcullises in the pyramid of Unas

One of the major weaknesses of the pyramids in the Old Kingdom was the lack of variation in the position of the entrance, which was always situated somewhere around the middle of the north face, although it might vary from pavement level to some fifteen metres above the base. The retention of the northern entrance in spite of the obvious security risk involved shows that the religious beliefs which required the entrance to be on the north side were given overriding importance. In the Old Kingdom, it was believed that the king would travel to the circumpolar stars, to continue to exist among them, and it was towards those stars that the pyramid entrance was aligned. Viewed from the latitude of Egypt, the circumpolar stars are never seen to set, with the result that the Egyptians regarded them as immortal, naming them the 'Imperishable Stars', or the 'Untiring Stars'. By the identification of the dead king with a star in this group he was to be assured of the same eternal existence: 'O you who are high exalted among the Imperishable

Stars, you shall never perish.'³ On the other hand, it was of little use to orientate the entrance of the royal pyramid towards the stars which symbolized perpetual survival if in so doing the burial itself was to be put at risk. But it was not until the Middle Kingdom that the rule of placing the entrance on the north of the pyramid was broken.

The earliest pyramids of the Twelfth Dynasty were generally similar to those of the Old Kingdom, although of inferior construction. Sesostris II was the first ruler to break away from the use of the northern entrance, in his mud-brick pyramid at Illahun.

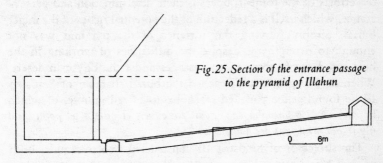

Fig.25. Section of the entrance passage
to the pyramid of Illahun

0   6m

Instead, the burial chamber was reached through a sloping passage from a vertical shaft on the south side (fig. 25). The innovation, however, was not sufficient; the magnificent granite sarcophagus found inside the pyramid by Petrie proved to be empty, and there was no trace of its lid. In a room adjoining the burial chamber a few relics of the tomb equipment were discovered, consisting of a variety of beads and a remarkable figure of the royal cobra, or uraeus, made of gold with inlays of coloured stones. In the subsequent pyramids of the dynasty the location of the entrance was shifted to various points around the monument, in a clear attempt at concealment. The arrangement in the brick pyramid of Sesostris III at Dashur was rather similar to that of the Illahun pyramid, except that the shaft entrance was located on the west side instead of the south. There can be no doubt that this moving of the entrance away from the north face made things considerably more difficult for the robbers, as well as for later archaeologists. Jacques de Morgan, who excavated the pyramid of Sesostris III in 1894–5, was forced to cut exploratory tunnels beneath the pyramid at three different levels before he met with any success. It is interesting to note that the first ancient passage he discovered was not one of the original corridors of the tomb, but a rough tunnel cut by robbers, who had searched beneath the structure in exactly the same manner. This shows that the whole process of robbing a royal tomb had now become a very protracted affair; it was necessary to burrow at random into the monument in the hope of striking an original passage, unless, of course, the plunderers had prior knowledge of the position of the chamber. Another factor which emerges from the efforts of the tomb-robbers is their determination and perseverance, which itself is a reflection of the potential riches of the intact burial. Simply moving the entrance of the pyramid was not enough to deter them, despite the difficulties of working in the heat and dust of subterranean passages under the Egyptian desert. When de Morgan finally reached the burial chamber of Sesostris III he found a fine panelled sarcophagus of red granite, of which he writes: 'Le sarcophage . . . avait été ouvert et pillé à tel point qu'il n'y restait même pas des poussières.'[4]

The successor of Sesostris III constructed two pyramids, both of mud-brick, one at Dashur and another at Hawara in the Fayum. It was de Morgan, once again, who excavated the Dashur pyramid, by the same laborious method of tunnelling. Since the burial chamber of Sesostris III had been in the north-west part of the superstructure, the excavator first searched in that region, but the builders had changed the design and had placed the burial apartments towards the south-east (fig. 26). The actual entrance lay on the east side, well to the south of the centre. The corridors and chambers were quite extensive and some may have been intended as blinds to distract plunderers from the burial chamber, in which case the interior layout of the tomb foreshadowed a far more complex development in the pyramid of Hawara.

The Hawara pyramid, because of its special internal arrangements and its huge mortuary temple, was probably the tomb actually used for the burial of King Amenemhat III. The entrance was situated on the south side, although Petrie, who excavated the monument, first reached the burial chamber by means of a tunnel he cut under the north face, and then found the remaining passages

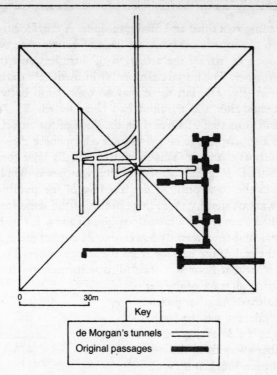

*Fig.26.Plan showing de Morgan's tunnels in
the pyramid of Amenemhat III at Dashur*

by exploring back from the interior to the entrance. This pyramid
was the earliest to make use of concealed passages closed by sliding
trap-doors of stone, and the whole design represents a magnificent
achievement in the provision of security for the burial chamber.
The descending stair from the entrance led to a small room and an
apparent dead-end, but a stone in the roof slid sideways to reveal
another chamber on a higher level. From this a false passage,
carefully blocked with stone, led straight on northwards, but the
correct path was a corridor leading to the east, closed only by a
wooden door. Some plunderers had been misled by the trick, and
had spent a long time and much effort cutting a path through the
stone blocking of the false passage. At the end of the correct tunnel
there was a second trap-door in the roof, giving access to a higher

passage leading to a third and final trap-door. A corridor from this point led to the antechamber, in the floor of which were two false pits, left open to attract the attention of intruders and to waste their time further. The burial chamber lay immediately to the south of this room (fig. 27), but there was no connection between the two chambers after the pyramid had been sealed. The original entrance had consisted of a trench in the floor of the antechamber, leading to a short passage below floor-level, opening directly into the sarcophagus chamber. This room had actually been formed by cutting it out of a single block of quartzite, which was then lowered into a pit in the rock prior to the building of the pyramid. The chamber was covered by three huge beams of the same stone, one of which had been left in a raised position to allow for installation of the burial, and subsequently lowered to its correct place, thereby blocking the end of the passage from the antechamber. The trench in the antechamber floor was then filled with masonry to conceal it, eliminating all trace of the path to the sepulchre. Another puzzle for the plunderers was the fact that the whole side of the antechamber away from the burial had been blocked up with stone, much of which was later broken and tunnelled in futile searches. Two more chambers lay above the burial chamber, to take the pressure off the roof of the latter, the uppermost having a pointed roof of limestone blocks. All these precautions would have been more effective if they had been correctly used; for some reason only the first trap-door had been closed, the others having been left in their recesses. It is quite clear that the traps laid for the thieves were effective in

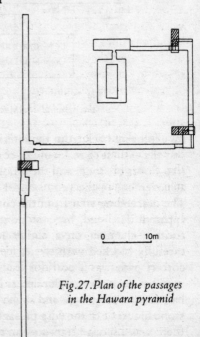

Fig.27.Plan of the passages in the Hawara pyramid

delaying their penetration of the sepulchre, demonstrated by the pointless cutting they made into the decoy blockings in the false passages and antechamber, but it was inevitable that the burial chamber would eventually be discovered. Once the trench in the antechamber floor had been located and emptied of masonry, the plunderers had only to get under the roofing beam which barred the end of the passage. This they achieved by chipping and scaling away the bottom edge of the block to make an opening just large enough to squeeze through. The burial chamber contained two sarcophagi, one for King Amenemhat III and one thought to have been intended for his daughter, the princess Neferuptah, but both had been robbed and only fragments of the burial equipment remained. Despite the presence of a second sarcophagus in the pyramid, and of an offering-table inscribed for Neferuptah, it has been more recently found that this princess was not, after all, buried in her father's pyramid. A separate pyramid, only thirty-five metres square, was discovered just over a mile away, and proved to be the true burial-place of Neferuptah. Practically all the mud-brick superstructure had been swept away, with the result that the burial chamber could be excavated from above, simply by raising the blocks of the roof. The layout of the passages in this pyramid is unknown, since they had not survived, but they are unlikely to have been more complex than those in the pyramid of Amenemhat III. In spite of this, the burial was found to be intact, preserved by some freak of chance to modern times, while all the elaborate security devices of the king's pyramid had failed. This is rather like the situation at Dashur, where the princesses' tombs around the pyramids of Sesostris III and Amenemhat III still contained marvellous jewellery, in contrast to the sad state of affairs in the pyramids themselves. The rich adornment of the mummy of Neferuptah shows why the plunderers habitually made the body their primary objective; the princess had been interred wearing a necklace and a collar with beads and terminals of gold, bracelets and anklets of gold and carnelian, and a gold falcon amulet.

The two pyramids of Mazghuna were ascribed by Mackay to Amenemhat IV and Queen Sebekneferu because of their similarity in design to the pyramid of Hawara. This assumption may well be correct, although it is also possible that the pyramids belong to the early Thirteenth Dynasty. They both contained security devices similar to those in the pyramid of Amenemhat III, including false passages, stone trap-doors and a concealed entrance to the burial chamber. Despite the care taken in the preparation of the blocking systems, in neither pyramid had all the trap-doors been moved to the closed position, a carelessness already seen in the pyramid of Hawara. Perhaps the difficulty of moving these enormous blocks – two of the stone traps in the Northern Pyramid of Mazghuna weighed twenty-four and forty-two tons respectively – led the builders to abandon the attempt to make them slide.

The pyramid of Khendjer at South Saqqara, together with the pyramid of unknown ownership nearby, both of the Thirteenth Dynasty, display an interesting technical advance in the method used to close the burial chamber, in the hope of achieving still greater security. The passage leading to the chamber opened under one of the roofing blocks, which had been left propped up until after the interment, as in the pyramid of Hawara. But the means of support for the slab was entirely new. At either end, where it overlapped the length of the chamber, it rested upon granite props, which in turn stood upon the sand filling of two special shafts in the masonry. To lower the beam, the sand was released from the shafts through apertures in the base, with the result that the supporting props gradually descended until the massive block rested in its correct position, barring the end of the entrance corridor at the same time. Narrow passages were provided to enable the workmen to reach the sand-filled shafts in order to operate the mechanism (fig. 28). In the pyramid of Khendjer the roof had

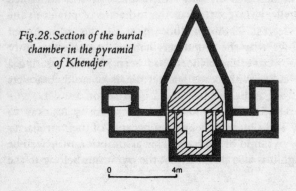

Fig.28. Section of the burial
    chamber in the pyramid
        of Khendjer

0   4m

been lowered, but the robbers had eventually reached the chamber, aided, once again, by the fact that two of the stone trap-doors in the outer corridors had never been closed. Their final entry into the burial chamber had been made through a small hole which they cut in the roof. In the similar pyramid nearby, the stone roofing-beam itself had never been lowered, and it may be that the tomb remained unused. Jéquier, who excavated these two monuments, believed that the same technique for lowering the roof on sand had been employed at Mazghuna, although this is not certain. It was in any case a superb technical achievement in tomb design, which was to reappear in an adapted form much later on.

Private tombs of the Middle Kingdom were, in general, not very different in the security aspect from their Old Kingdom counterparts, but at a few sites some of the defensive methods developed for royal pyramids were copied and adapted in rich private tombs. Mastabas continued to be built during the Middle Kingdom, but there was also an increase in the popularity of rock-cut tombs built in the limestone cliffs bordering the Nile Valley. The latter type of tomb was the very reverse of secure; set upon a hillside with an ostentatious facade, it advertised its presence and invited the attentions of plunderers. Nor did most rock-tombs contain any technical devices to hinder access to the burial chamber; the majority had simple rubble-filled shafts descending vertically or on a slope from below the floor of the chapel. Probably their owners, who were in many cases powerful district governors, thought that their tombs would be safeguarded by the regular visits of mortuary priests, but no offering cult lasted forever, and the priests themselves could not always be trusted. A few rock-tombs had false burial chambers to deceive intruders, with the true sepulchre concealed at a lower level, but these efforts were usually futile. Some of the mastaba-tombs of the period display considerably more ingenuity and make use of some systems not previously employed. One of the most remarkable tombs is that of Senwosretankh at Lisht, a large stone mastaba whose superstructure had been extensively destroyed. The substructure consisted of a sloping descent to a horizontal passage, which was barred by four portcullises, beyond which lay the burial chamber (fig. 29). The first deterrent to robbers was the existence of a vertical shaft from the surface to the beginning of the horizontal corridor, opening just before the first portcullis. This pit, which increased in diameter as it descended, was filled with loose gravel and sand, while the sloping ramp was closed with more tightly packed rubble. Anyone clearing out the sloping passage and beginning to remove the blocking in the corridor at its base would take away the support from beneath the filling of the vertical shaft, bringing down more rubble and

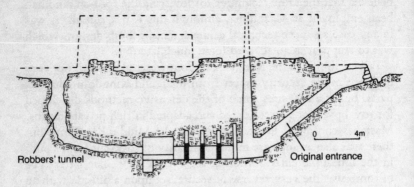

Fig.29.Section of the tomb of Senwosretankh at Lisht

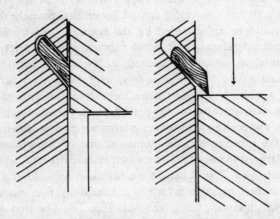

Fig.30.The lock on the portcullises in the tomb of Senwosretankh at Lisht

sand from above to fill up the space. This device effectively deterred the treasure-seekers from any attempt to enter the burial chamber from this direction, and it certainly surprised the modern excavators of the tomb, who were not in the least expecting a rain of loose rubble from above. Behind this obstacle lay the four portcullises, the first of which at least had a special feature of its own. In the sides of the grooves in which the block was to slide were cut holes sloping downwards to contain metal or wooden bolts. These were held back in their sockets by the block itself prior to it being lowered, but dropped downwards as the top of the portcullis descended past them, preventing it being raised again (fig. 30). These precautions, although ingenious and highly original, did not prevent the ultimate plundering of the burial. The seekers, despairing of effecting an entry through the correct entrance, simply dug a shaft into the bedrock, turned towards the chamber and broke through its southern wall. One of the most interesting points about this mastaba and its unusual defensive mechanisms is the identity of the owner, who included the distinction of 'Royal Sculptor and Builder' among his titles. Is it possible that the innovations in this tomb were the products of his own architectural genius, ideas which he carefully guarded for use only in his final resting-place. This is mere speculation, but it becomes more plausible when we find that another Twelfth Dynasty tomb with rather unusual security devices also belonged to an architect. The tomb in question is the mastaba of Inpy at Illahun, close to the pyramid of Sesostris II. In front of the tomb there was a deep open pit, to hinder access by unauthorized persons. Intruders entering the substructure of the tomb would pass through the two rooms A and B to reach an apparent burial chamber at C, complete with its recess on the east side for the mummified viscera (fig. 31). The true burial chamber, however, lay hidden behind the stone wall at the north end of this room. Nothing was found in this chamber; either the tomb had never been used or it had been very completely robbed.

Among the less elaborate tombs of provincial cemeteries, organized robbing by the necropolis guards seems to have been a standard procedure. At Riqqa there was evidence to show that the bodies were still pliable when robbed, indicating how soon after burial the

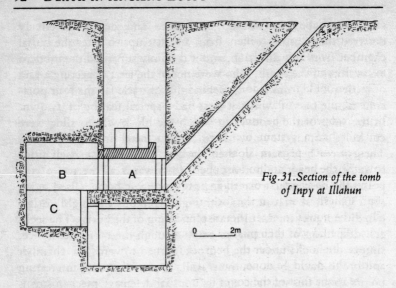

Fig.31.Section of the tomb
of Inpy at Illahun

0   2m

tombs were re-opened. Certain shafts at the same site contained a number of chambers, some of which had been entered, while others remained intact. In every case the intact chambers proved to be very poor, which is precisely why they had been left alone. Only the undertakers or the guards could have possessed such detailed information. A number of tomb-shafts had been marked on their sides, and the excavator of the site suggested that these marks had been made by the thieves to indicate which pits had already been looted. One plunderer, at least, came to grief in his activities: shaft 124 at Riqqa led down to a rock-cut chamber, the roof of which had fallen in, bringing down several tons of loose rock. This was removed by the archaeologist to reveal a crushed skeleton lying on the remains of a wooden coffin. On top of the skeleton were the arm bones of another body, the remainder of which lay in a group nearby and had also been flattened. The likely explanation of these conditions, suggested by Engelbach in his report, was that the arm bones belonged to a tomb-robber who had lifted the corpse from its coffin and was crouching beside it to tear off the wrappings when the roof collapsed and crushed him instantly. This theory is supported by the richness of the burial, for on the body was found a splendid set of jewellery in gold and semi-precious stones, which, but for the collapse of the roof at that moment, would never have survived to the present day. It is now in the Egyptian galleries of the Manchester Museum.

In the Middle Kingdom, certain coffins from wealthy burials were equipped with a special locking mechanism to prevent their being re-opened. The inner anthropoid coffin of the lady Senebtisi at Lisht had a system of copper hooks fixed to the lid, which engaged with pegs in slots in the base. The hooks all pointed towards the head, and to lock the coffin the lid was first placed in position with a slight overlap at the foot, to allow the hooks to enter their respective slots. The lid was then pushed up to engage the hooks under the pegs, but, before this could be done, a metal swivel in the foot of the cover had to be raised to clear the edge of the coffin, until it dropped into a slot cut to receive it (fig. 32). This swivel prevented the lid being slid downwards again to release the hooks. The same arrangement was used on the coffin of Neferuptah at Hawara, with the difference that the swivel seems to have been located in the head end instead of at the foot, so that the lid was fixed by sliding it downwards. Other anthropoid coffins are known with wooden dovetail tenons in place of metal hooks, but

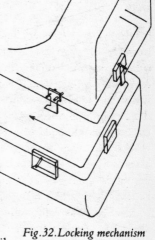

Fig.32.Locking mechanism of the coffin of Senebtisi

the method of operation is the same (fig. 33). To go to the trouble of fitting intricate locks on wooden coffins was really a waste of time, since a determined thief would simply smash the coffin open. The only persons who would have been prevented from stealing items from the mummy by such devices would have been the undertakers charged with the burial arrangements; they could not afford to risk breaking into the coffin, since they would leave evidence of their activities, but they may have been tempted to lift the lid and quickly remove a few pieces of jewellery from a coffin without a lock. In the Old Kingdom, locks had been put on stone sarcophagi, including those of kings Khafre and Menkaure. These mechanisms operated by the lid sliding across the coffin to engage in a groove on the far side, while two pins dropped from holes in the lid into similar holes cut to receive them in the edge of the sarcophagus (fig. 34).

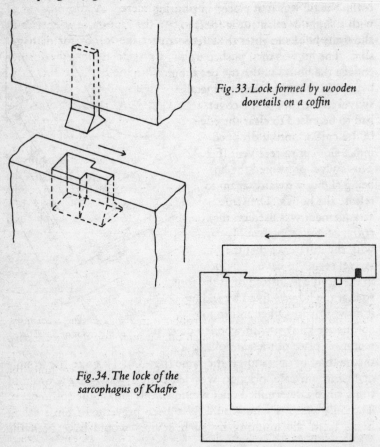

Fig. 33. Lock formed by wooden dovetails on a coffin

Fig. 34. The lock of the sarcophagus of Khafre

For the New Kingdom we have a wealth of information about tomb-robbing, and about the counter-measures taken to suppress it, from the written accounts of the Egyptians themselves. The important group of documents known as the Tomb Robbery Papyri give us more detail than we could ever have recovered from purely archaeological evidence, including the names of particular tombs which had been robbed, confessions of the thieves and the results of official inspections of the tombs. These accounts date to the Twentieth Dynasty, by which time the tombs of the kings of the Second Intermediate Period and the earlier part of the New Kingdom were already being plundered. A commission of high officials was set up to investigate the reports of robberies in the necropolis of Thebes, and to inspect the tombs for damage. The inspectors visited both royal and private tombs, the former including monuments from the Eleventh to the Eighteenth Dynasties. All but one of the royal tombs were found to be intact, only the tomb of King Sebekemsaf having been robbed. With the private tombs the situation was quite different, as the report in the Abbott Papyrus states:

The tombs and burial chambers in which rest the blessed ones of old, the citizenesses and citizens of the west of Thebes: it was found that the thieves had robbed them all, dragging their owners from their inner coffins and their outer coffins, they being left upon the desert, and stealing their funerary outfit which had been given to them, together with the gold and silver and the fittings which were in their inner coffins.[5]

The discovery of the true extent of tomb-robbing was complicated by personal rivalry between Pesiur, mayor of the city of Thebes on the east of the Nile, and Pewero, the mayor on the west, who was also the chief of police in the necropolis. Pewero did his best to discount any accusations of robbery in royal tombs, since any admission of the existence of such plundering would have exposed the failure of his own administration to keep it in check. However, bit by bit the truth was revealed; another papyrus contains the confessions made by the robbers of the tomb of King Sebekemsaf:

We went to rob the tombs in accordance with our regular habit, and we found the pyramid of King Sekhemre-shedtawy, the son of Re, Sebek-emsaf, this being not at all like the pyramids and tombs of the nobles which we habitually went to rob. We took our copper tools and we broke into this pyramid of this king through its innermost part: We found its underground chambers and we took lighted candles in our hands and we went down. Then we broke through the rubble that we found at the mouth of his recess, and found this god lying at the back of his burial-place. And we found the burial-place of Queen Nubkhaas, his queen, situated beside him, it being protected and guarded by plaster and covered with rubble. This also we broke through, and found her resting [there] in similar fashion. We opened their sarcophagi and their coffins in which they were, and found the noble mummy of this king equipped with a falchion; a large number of amulets and jewels of gold were upon his neck, and his head-piece of gold was upon him. The noble mummy of this king was completely bedecked with gold, and his coffins were adorned with gold and silver inside and out and inlaid with all sorts of precious stones. We collected the gold we found on the noble mummy of this god, together with[that on] his amulets and jewels which were on his neck and [that on] the coffins in which he was resting, [and we] found the queen in exactly the same state. We collected all that we found upon her likewise and set fire to their coffins. We took their furniture which we found with them consisting of articles of gold, silver and bronze, and divided them among ourselves. And we made into eight parts the gold which we found on these two gods coming from their mummies, amulets, jewels and coffins, and 20 *deben* of gold fell to each of the eight of us, making 160 *deben* of gold, the fragments of furniture not being included. Then we crossed over to Thebes.[6]

The quantity of gold mentioned by the thieves is equivalent to 14½ kg, an amount which some scholars have regarded as an exaggeration. There is no reason at all to suppose that this is so, in view of the weight of gold included among the burial-equipment of a minor king like Tutankhamun. Gold is, in any case, a very dense metal, and 14½ kg would not have constituted much bulk. A significant point also recorded in the papyrus is the fact that a large proportion of the thieves were artisans, with professions like stone-cutting or carpentry, which would have equipped them very well with skills needed for tomb-robbing. This particular gang had only recently turned their attention to royal tombs, but had been involved in robbing private tombs for some time. One of their number, a certain Amenpnufer, appears in another of the tomb-robbery papyri for investigation concerning the violation of the tomb of the Third Prophet of Amun, Tjanefer. On this occasion, Amenpnufer related the following events:

> We...went to the tomb of Tjanefer, who was Third Prophet of Amun. We opened it and we brought out his inner coffins and we took his mummy and left it there in a corner of his tomb. We took his inner coffins to this boat, along with the rest, to the district of Amenemope. We set fire to them in the night, and we made off with the gold which we found on them, and four *kite* of gold fell to each man...[7]

The burning of the coffins was a simple means of separating the gilding from the wood, since the gold would not be at all harmed by the fire. In this case the complete coffins were taken to a safe distance across the river and burnt, but on occasions the thieves state that they removed the gold by the same process actually in the tombs. Again, it is Amenpnufer who speaks:

> ...we brought away the inner coffins on which there was gold, and we broke them up and set fire to them by night inside the tombs.[8]

The documents reveal some of the methods used to gain entry to the tombs; a regular practice being the cutting of tunnels from tomb to tomb. In the Abbott Papyrus, it is stated that the tomb of Nubkheperre Intef was found to have an unfinished tunnel of $2\frac{1}{2}$ cubits in its north side, starting from the outer chamber of the later rock-tomb of a certain Iuri, overseer of offerings in the temple of Amun. Exactly the same process had been used in the successful attack on the burial-place of Sebekemsaf, entry having been made through a passage from the tomb of Nebamun, overseer of the granary under Tuthmosis III. The tomb-chambers of the necropolis of Thebes were so crowded together that even tunnels cut at random would probably hit something, and as we have seen, the plunderers often had sufficient information to enable them to dig towards a precise objective. This art of tunnelling has survived the centuries; when measures were taken by the Antiquities Service to safeguard the decorated tomb chapels in the early 1900s, tunnels were found to have been cut from the back of a dwelling in Qurna into four tombs. In 1924, thieves burrowed in similar fashion right into the antiquity store of the Metropolitan Museum of Art expedition at Thebes, having started the tunnel, in the traditional manner of their ancestors, from a nearby rock-tomb. Fortunately, the intruders succeeded only in entering a room full of empty boxes and broken pottery.

The robbers brought before the investigators of the Twentieth Dynasty were questioned about their activities and witnesses were called to confirm or contradict their stories. Both the accused and the witnesses were beaten as an aid to their memories. A typical interrogation runs as follows:

Examination. The citizeness Mutemwia was brought, the wife of the measurer Pewero. They said to her: 'What have you to say concerning Pewero, this husband of yours who brought away this silver while he was in your house?' She said: 'My father heard that [he] had gone to the tomb and said to me: I will not allow this man to enter my house.' She was examined again. She said: 'He never brought me his load.' She was examined again with the birch and the screw. She said: 'He stole this silver and put it in the house of the overseer of the chamber, Ruty, the husband of Tabeki, the sister of the measurer Pewero.'[9]

Often, the defendants were obliged to take an oath in the name of Pharaoh to tell the truth, and from these statements we learn something of the punishments handed out to those found guilty. A certain Paoemtaumt took oath saying:

As Amun lives and as the Ruler lives, if I be found to have had anything to do with any one of the thieves may I be mutilated in nose and ears and [be] placed on the stake.[10]

The phrase, 'placed on the stake', occurs throughout the papyri, and refers to the death penalty by impaling. Another punishment was banishment to Nubia, perhaps to join a garrison or quarry-gang there. The harshness of the penalties reflects the very serious nature of the crimes, for the thieves were not only taking away the funerary gifts of the dead but actually endangering their survival in the afterlife by destroying their bodies. It is also worth mentioning that it was not only tombs that were robbed by the treasure-seekers; papyrus British Museum 10053 contains details of robberies from the mortuary temple of Ramesses II, carried out by the temple staff themselves. The main objective of the thieves was the gold plating on the granite doorways of the temple, and they spent their time pulling this away piecemeal. But their activities were noted by the scribe of royal records, Setekhmose, who threatened to report them to the chief priest of Amun. Setekhmose, however, soon quietened down after he had been presented with two gifts of the stolen gold.

One of the most important developments in guarding the royal burial-places in the New Kingdom was the decision to construct the tombs in the lonely valley behind the cliffs of Deir el-Bahari, now called the Valley of the Kings. The first ruler to be buried here was Tuthmosis I, who employed the architect Ineni for the preparation of his tomb. Ineni boasts in his own inscriptions of the secrecy of this project, 'I supervised the excavation of the rock-tomb of his majesty alone, none seeing and none hearing...'[11] Secrecy was the prime objective of the Eighteenth Dynasty tombs, as a reaction away from the extremely obvious and vulnerable pyramids of earlier times. The entrances to the tombs were small and inconspicuous, located in odd angles and clefts in the rock, and the passage might be undecorated for some distance, to give the impression of an unfinished tomb. The early tombs have corridors which change their direction at some point along their length, but sepulchres later than the reign of Amenophis III usually have a straight axis. Included in the design of a number of tombs of both types is a system of creating an apparent end to the tomb, by continuing the corridor from below the floor of what seems to be the final chamber. In the plan of the tomb of Amenophis II shown in figure 35, room F would appear to be the end of the tomb, the stairway leading to the true sarcophagus chamber having been blocked and hidden behind plaster. Another well-known feature of the royal tombs, which has long been considered as a security device, is the deep pit which bars the passage before the antechamber. A recent theory has proposed that the pit had a mythological rather than a practical purpose, being intended to symbolize the tomb of the god Osiris, with whom the king was identified. However, since the sealed doorways behind the pit were decorated right across, to hide the presence of the door, it is quite likely that the pit also served as an obstacle to plunderers even though this may not have been its primary function. The ancient name of the chamber containing the pit was 'The Hall of Waiting', or 'The Hall of Hindering', but it is not clear who or what was being hindered. Another suggestion is that the shaft was intended to trap any storm-water which might flood into the tomb. This is not so unlikely as it might seem; rainstorms were considered to be products of the evil god Seth and the water would have to be kept away from a royal burial. Egyptian temples were equipped with elaborate drains for the same purpose.

It is very clear that the attempts of the Eighteenth Dynasty rulers to keep the location of their tombs a secret were a failure, and in the later tombs we find large, imposing facades, all hope of secrecy having been abandoned. At the same time, the sarcophagi used to contain the burial were increased in size, in the vain hope that the Pharaoh's body would be protected by a few tons of granite. It is a well-known fact that only one royal tomb in the valley survived almost intact to modern times, this being the famous tomb of

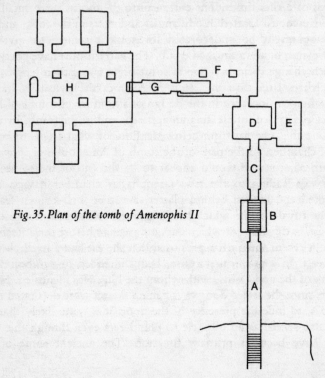

Fig.35.Plan of the tomb of Amenophis II

Tutankhamun. In fact, robbers had succeeded in entering the tomb, but they had been disturbed at an early stage in their activities. The ultimate preservation of this burial was a matter of pure chance, the entrance having been buried under tons of rock chippings from the cutting of the later tomb of Ramesses VI.

Although the royal tombs in the Valley of the Kings were looted, many of the mummies originally housed within them survived to the present day, thanks to the precautions taken by priests of the Twenty-First Dynasty. Since it had become quite clear that it was impossible to guard all the tombs safely, the High-Priests of Amun decided to collect and move the royal bodies to secret hiding-places. Several moves were necessary over a period of time, but the mummies finally came to rest in two locations: one group was placed in a side-chamber of the tomb of Amenophis II, while the rest were hidden in an old shaft of the Eleventh Dynasty at Deir el-Bahari, together with a number of burials of the priests of Amun. The latter hiding-place remained undisturbed until about 1875, when it was rediscovered by some modern descendants of the old tomb-robbers, and objects from the cache began to appear on the antiquity market. Of course, the burials were not equipped with all their funerary goods, which had been stolen prior to the moving of the bodies. The action of the high-priests had been a last desperate effort to save the mummies from destruction, giving up any hope of supplying and guarding a full set of tomb-furniture. The bodies, having been stripped of their wrappings by thieves in search of jewellery, had to be re-wrapped and in some cases supplied with new coffins in the Twenty-First Dynasty, and many of the bandages bear ink inscriptions giving the dates of the restoration of the burials. The simplicity of the final resting-place of the Pharaohs was in marked contrast to the lavish furnishings which must have been placed in their original tombs, but at least their bodies have remained substantially intact, which in Egyptian belief means that the spiritual existence of these rulers has not yet come to an end. The Deir el-Bahari cache was eventually located by the Antiquities Service in 1881, and the mummies were taken to the Cairo Museum, where they remain. They include some of the most famous rulers of the New Kingdom: Amosis I, Amenophis I, Tuthmosis I, Tuthmosis II, Tuthmosis III, Seti I, Ramesses II and

Ramesses III. From the tomb of Amenophis II, found in 1898, came the mummies of the owner and eight more kings, in addition to three female bodies and a boy. For some time the body of Amenophis II was left in his sarcophagus in the tomb, but an attack was made upon it by modern robbers and the authorities sent the mummy to Cairo to join the others. The only royal mummy still in its original tomb at the present day is that of Tutankhamun.

During the Twenty-First Dynasty, the priesthood of Amun were concerned about their own burials, in addition to those of former royalty. A large number of them – over 150 – were interred in another cache at Deir el-Bahari, discovered in 1891, while others were buried in smaller groups in the cliff-tombs of the same region. The excavation of some of these tombs affords interesting side-lights on the activities of plunderers. A tomb originally made for the burial of a princess Henttawi, daughter of the High-Priest Pinudjem, was closed only by a wooden door so that subsequent burials could be added. The first addition was the installation of the coffin and mummy of a princess Djedmutesankh, followed some time later by another Henttawi. The outer wrappings of the latter were intact but those on the other two mummies had been torn and cut in a search for valuables, and the bandages on the left hand of Djedmutesankh had been ripped aside to reach the finger rings. This vandalism had been partly hidden by pulling the outermost sheet of the wrappings back into place to cover the tangled cloth beneath. Such furtive concern to hide the theft, coupled with the fact that the second Henttawi had not been robbed, shows that her burial-party were responsible. But the matter was not yet over, for the tomb was opened again to add the coffin of a certain Menkheperre, and his undertakers cut the gilded faces from all three of the earlier coffins and covered the damage with sheets of linen. This same tomb was repeatedly opened in later times for yet more burials, the coffins being piled up on top of one another, until finally room had to be made for newcomers by throwing out older mummies into the pit. Sometimes the bodies were robbed even before they reached the tomb. The mummies of the second Henttawi and of a certain Nesitiset, who had been buried here subsequently, were found to have the outer bandages in good order but the deeper ones in considerable disarray. Eventually the archaeologists arrived at the layer in which there had been amulets and jewellery; the marks of these items were still visible in the resin, but the objects themselves had gone, stolen by the embalmers three thousand years before. It has also been known for members of the burial party to replace valuables by worthless substitutes, one recorded case being a box for jewellery, found sealed, but containing only rough chunks of wood.

A similar case of theft to that described above was found by the same team of American excavators in another tomb at Deir el-Baḥari. This sepulchre had been made in the Eighteenth Dynasty for the burial of Meritamun, whose enormous wooden coffin can be seen in the Cairo Museum, but the tomb was re-opened in the Twenty-First Dynasty when a certain Entiu-ny was brought there to be buried. The burial cortege entered the tomb carrying a large outer coffin, three coffin lids, the mummy within its inner coffin and other items of funerary equipment. Part-way into the rock passage the procession was halted by a deep vertical pit in the floor, rather like the pits in the royal tombs of the Valley of the Kings. The coffins and the body were placed on the floor while the party considered what to do. It seems that several members then went off to look for wood to bridge the pit, leaving a few people to guard the coffins. These individuals, sitting in the corridor beside the gilded coffins, were obviously prey to temptation; they quickly cut the gold-covered masks from the three lids, which were subsequently abandoned as they lay beside the edge of the shaft. The original burial in this tomb lay further back, beyond the obstacle which had halted the undertakers, but it was soon discovered that Meritamun, the daughter of Tuthmosis III, had not lain here undisturbed for long. A hieratic inscription on the front of the mummy read, 'Year 19, third month of winter, day 28. On this day examination of the king's wife Meritamun.' Inscriptions on the inner wrappings confirmed that the body had been re-wrapped in the Twenty-First Dynasty, during the reign of Pinudjem I. Finally, in the rubbish lying on the floor of the tomb, the excavators found the remains of the original bandages ripped off the mummy by the plunderers. There could be no doubt as to their ownership, since one bore a text in ink giving the name of Meritamun.

It is pleasant to record one piece of evidence to show that even the tomb-robbers possessed a sense of humour. A number of New Kingdom shafts in the Valley of the Kings had been used for the burial of animals, including baboons, dogs, ibises and ducks. These pits had, as usual, been searched by robbers, and the wrappings of the mummies had been torn. In one tomb, however, a dog and a baboon had been completely unwrapped by the intruders; they had then set the baboon upright on a piece of wood and stood the dog in front of it, so close that it seemed almost as though they were engaged in conversation. The fact that plunderers had the time to indulge in jokes says something about the state of security in the Theban necropolis.

After the development of rock-cut tombs for royalty in the Valley of the Kings, the inventive capabilities of the tomb architects seem to go into decline, as if they had given up the struggle to find new counter-measures to theft, and the valley continued as the royal cemetery in the Nineteenth and Twentieth Dynasties more because of tradition than security. In the Twenty-First Dynasty we find a new development, again for the tombs of royalty or persons of very high rank, while the poorer tombs took their chance with the limited protection their owners could afford. The new tomb design, which continued in vogue down to the Twenty-Sixth Dynasty, involved building the sepulchres within the precincts of a major temple, so that the tombs, instead of being hidden away in lonely places where robbers could work undisturbed, would always be under the eyes of the temple staff. This system was adopted for the royal burials of the Twenty-First and Twenty-Second Dynasties at Tanis, for the tombs of the divine votaresses of Amun at Thebes, and for those belonging to the kings of the Twenty-Sixth Dynasty at Sais. The latter tombs have never been found, but we are told by Herodotus:

> The people of Sais buried within the temple precinct all kings who were natives of their province. The tomb of Amasis is farther from the sanctuary than the tomb of Apries and his ancestors, yet it is also within the temple court; it is a great colonnade of stone, richly adorned, the pillars of which are wrought in the form of palm trees. In this colonnade are two portals, and the place where the coffin lies is within their doors.[12]

Tombs of this form were covered by brick or stone chapels for the continuance of the offering cult, while the sepulchres lay at a shallow depth below ground and were reached by pits. The shallowness of the burials was probably the enforced result of building the tombs in the flat ground of the Nile Valley, where the high subsoil water level prevented any attempt to dig deep shafts. At Medinet Habu, two of the chapels of the Divine Votaresses remain standing, but the royal tombs at Tanis have been destroyed except for their subterranean chambers. The latter necropolis contained the burials of kings Psusennes, Osorkon II, Amenemope and Shoshenk III, in addition to a co-regent named Shoshenk-Hekakheperre and a number of high-ranking private persons. Although some of these tombs had been entered by thieves, their plundering had not always been complete, and certain burials had escaped attention. The tomb of Osorkon II had been reached by breaking in through the roof, while an ingenious band of thieves had tunnelled into the chamber of Shoshenk III by cutting down below its floor, to emerge beside the sarcophagus (fig. 36). But the effectiveness of locating the royal cemetery in the temple area as a means of security is revealed by the wealth of spectacular funerary equipment discovered in the burial apartments of Psusennes, Amenemope, Shoshenk-Hekakheperre and other individuals of only slightly lower rank, among whom were the prince Hornakhte and the general Wendjebaendjed. Had the discovery of these burials not occurred during the Second World War it would probably have attracted the same amount of attention as did the finding of the tomb of Tutankhamun in 1922, yet even now the treasures of Tanis are but little known

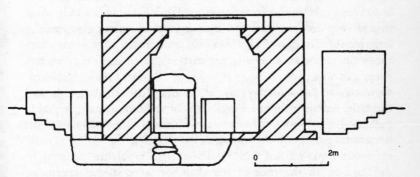

Fig.36. Robbers' tunnel under the tomb of Shoshenk III at Tanis

among the general public. Apart from the amulets and jewellery of gold, which are in themselves exquisite works, there are the superb silver coffins of Psusennes and Shoshenk-Hekakheperre, the latter with a remarkable falcon-headed mask. Within the coffins were separate face-masks of gold, that belonging to Psusennes being of similar style to the mask of Tutankhamun, but with surface decoration cut in the metal in place of elaborate inlays. The treasures were not all upon the bodies, for in the tomb-chambers there was also a quantity of highly decorative vessels in gold and silver, inscribed with the names of their owners, in addition to more mundane items of funerary equipment, such as shabti-figures, stone vases and bronze weapons. No one who visits the Cairo Museum to view the objects from the tomb of Tutankhamun should neglect to enter the nearby room in which the splendid items from the royal cemetery of Tanis are displayed.

The tombs of the Divine Votaresses of Amun at Thebes did not fare so well as the Tanite burials, although the date at which they were first robbed is unknown. They had been completely despoiled by the Ptolemaic Period, at which time some of the stone sarcophagi from these chapels were removed for re-use. On the subject of the re-use of coffins, it is worth mentioning that the occupants of the royal tombs of Tanis had provided for their own burials by the liberal re-employment of older sarcophagi, one of the coffins of Psusennes, for example, having originally been cut for king Merenptah of the Nineteenth Dynasty.

In the Twenty-Sixth Dynasty we at last reach the ultimate achievement in tomb protection, found, oddly enough, not in royal tombs, but in large private monuments of extremely wealthy individuals. The burial chamber was built at the foot of an enormous pit in the rock, nearly ten metres square and thirty metres deep, and was covered by a vaulted roof of stone. Once completed, there was no point of entry to the chamber from the large pit, and the only entrance for the installation of the burial was through a parallel shaft of much smaller size, which was connected by a short horizontal passage to the mouth of the chamber (fig. 37). The main excavation was refilled with sand above the sepulchre, right up to the surface. In the roof of the chamber were special apertures, closed by setting into them pottery jars, base downwards, held firmly in plaster (fig. 38). After completion of the burial ceremonies and the closing of the sarcophagus, which had, of course, been built into the tomb during construction, the last man to leave the chamber smashed the bases from the jars, letting through a cascade of sand from the pit above to fill all parts of the room. The party then retired up the small pit, which was subsequently filled in. Any robbers who might attempt to break into the tomb were bound to enter initially by the small shaft, the clearance of the main pit being far beyond their means, but on forcing a way through the blocking of the burial chamber they would have been met by a flood of sand tumbling down into the passage. If they had not encountered a tomb of this type before, they would have attempted to dig away the sand in order to clear a way forward, but as fast as they could

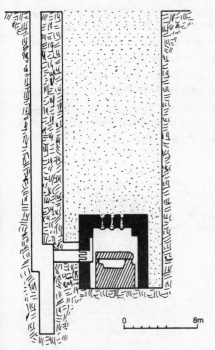

Fig.37.Section of a large shaft-tomb of the Twenty-Sixth Dynasty

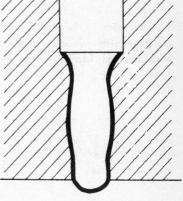

Fig.38.Pottery jar set in the roof of the burial chamber

dig more sand would fall in from the pit to replace what had been removed. To reach the burial was impossible without the complete excavation of the main shaft, a lengthy process, as archaeologists know to their cost. One of the finest examples of this kind of tomb is that of Amun-Tefnakhte at Saqqara, which, surprisingly, had all this elaborate protection to no useful purpose; although the burial was intact there was not a single object of any kind upon the body. More typical burials of the same type have been found covered with a whole series of amulets, made of gold and semi-precious stones. Considering the exceptional security offered by this tomb design, it is surprising to find that the style seems to be restricted to the Memphite necropolis. This is probably due to favourable local conditions at Saqqara and Giza, where there was a long history of the cutting of deep shafts, and also plenty of sand available for the filling. In addition to its use as an anti-theft device, sand was employed in these tombs for the lowering of the heavy sarcophagus lid, in a manner rather similar to that devised in the Thirteenth Dynasty for lowering the roofing blocks of the royal pyramids. The lid had square projections at the sides, which fitted into recesses in the walls of the chamber, so that the lid could be supported by wooden props resting on sand (fig. 39). The sand was released through small apertures into chambers cut at a lower level, allowing the lid to descend slowly into place.

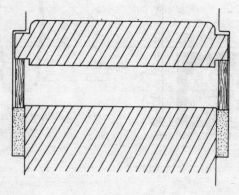

Fig. 39. Method of lowering the roof of the chamber

The burials of the final stages of Egyptian civilization produced no more significant technical innovations to counter the threat from plunderers, apart from some huge stone sarcophagi, which, as had frequently been demonstrated in earlier times, were no serious obstacle. Poor people of the Graeco-Roman Period were often buried in large communal tombs, stacked to the roof with mummies. Wealthier burials possessed more imposing funerary monuments, but the methods used in closing the tombs were the old standard procedures of filled shafts and masonry blockings, none of which was secure. In the long struggle between tomb-builders and tomb-robbers, the advantages had always lain with the robber. Almost as an expression of the futility of technical methods of achieving security, the Egyptians had always relied upon a second line of defence, that of magical protection, which became increasingly dominant in the Late Period. We have already seen how the statues and reliefs in a tomb could function by magic to sustain the deceased and ensure his continued existence, but there were also whole books of inscriptions intended to confer protection. The mythological content of these texts will be discussed in Chapter 6, but it is worth quoting here a typical protective spell from the Pyramid Texts, the earliest of the religious books: 'O Osiris the King, may you be protected. I give to you all the gods, their heritages, their provisions, and all their possessions, for you have not died.'[13] Other spells heap curses upon potential enemies of the king, or upon dangerous animals which might do him harm, especially snakes. The extent of magical texts intended to safeguard the dead is vast, but there is no evidence to show that tomb-robbers were the slightest bit deterred by their presence.

Magical protection by means of amulets was provided from very early times, but gradually became more and more extensive, to include not only individual amulets but also amuletic designs painted or carved upon the coffin. Certain amulets supplied only a general protective influence, but others were more specific in their function, those in the form of parts of the body having the power to restore the living faculties. Amulets were made in imitation of a great range of objects and were sometimes inscribed with a text relating to their purpose. The model of a headrest was supposed to prevent the head being taken from the corpse; the amulet of a snake's head protected the deceased against snakebite; and the symbol of a papyrus sceptre provided for the continued vigour of the limbs. Among amulets of more general protective nature were the Tyet, the Djed pillar, the eye of Horus and the Ankh (fig. 40). The

Fig. 40. Common amulets

latter is the Egyptian hieroglyph for 'life', and is probably the most familiar of all Egyptian amulets. Since we are here concerned only with the protection of the dead, the origin of amuletic forms and their mythological significance are reserved for Chapter 6. The heart was protected by amulets in the form of the organ itself, and also by the large stone carvings of the scarab beetle now known by the term 'Heart Scarabs'. These bore a text from the Book of the Dead intended to prevent spontaneous confessions which might weigh against the deceased in the final judgement. In Late Period burials, amulets in the form of small images of various deities are common. Very popular divinities over a longer span of time were the four sons of Horus, both as amuletic figures and represented upon coffins. The dead were also under the protection of the goddesses Isis, Nephthys, Selkis and Neith, who can occur upon coffins and sarcophagi, although the best examples of these goddesses in their funerary role are the four gilded figures from the tomb of Tutankhamun. Funerary deities in the decoration of sarcophagi are often accompanied by a text recording the words spoken by the god to the deceased, beginning, 'I have come to you in order that I may be your protection...' These words seem rather ironic upon the lid of a broken and empty sarcophagus, for which both technical and magical security had failed. The most amazing feature of Egyptian funerary practice is the fact that they continued to place valuables with their bodies, even though they must have realized that in so doing they were virtually ensuring the destruction of the mummy. As for those individuals who cleared an old burial from its tomb and then had themselves interred in the same chamber – often at the same time usurping the coffin and funerary goods of the previous occupant – how they expected their bodies to escape a similar fate is hard to imagine.

Permanent security could only exist for burials which were known to contain no objects of value. This is amply proved by Coptic Christian cemeteries from the third century A.D. onwards; since the new religion required no grave-goods, the burials have remained undisturbed. In the whole matter of tomb protection, the Egyptians were trapped between their belief that the body had to remain intact and the desire to provide it with goods, and they were not prepared to discard one requirement in order to safeguard the other.

PRESERVED FOR
ETERNITY

The early attempts of the Egyptians to preserve the dead have already been described in a previous chapter, but we have yet to examine the development of embalming subsequent to the Old Kingdom. For an overall picture of mummification techniques we depend on the account given by Herodotus, writing in the fifth century B.C. By this date the art of embalming had declined considerably, but it is nevertheless quite likely that much of the description given by Herodotus is coloured by the careful methods of the New Kingdom, the tradition of which was still preserved in memory even if no longer so fully carried out in practice. Herodotus describes three alternative methods of embalmment differing in complexity and expense. The most elaborate process involved the removal of the brain tissue through the nostrils, extraction of the viscera through an incision in the flank, cleansing and anointing the interior of the body and re-closing it by stitching across the cut. After all this, we are informed, the corpse was covered with natron for seventy days, before being washed and wrapped. Herodotus was mistaken over this point; in fact, the whole process of mummification took seventy days, as we know from Egyptian sources, and the treatment with natron occupied only a part of this time. It was long thought that the body was immersed in a bath of natron in solution, but recent studies have shown that the material was really employed in the form of a dry powder.

Experiments with animal corpses have demonstrated that while powdered natron will dehydrate tissue very effectively, the same material in solution fails to have any such effect and the corpse quickly disintegrates into an unpleasant mess. The most recent commentary on the description supplied by Herodotus points out that the words employed in the Greek text support the view that dry natron was heaped over the body.

The second method of embalming in the Greek historian's account consists of the injection of oil at the anus, combined with external treatment with natron. After a period of time the oil was released, bringing away with it the dissolved remains of the internal organs. It is unlikely that any kind of oil would have had this effect, although the viscera may well have decomposed spontaneously and flowed out with the oil. Some bodies were almost certainly treated in this manner, since they lack the embalmer's incision in the flank, and the same process seems to have been employed in the mummification of certain Apis bulls.

In the final process listed by Herodotus, which he states to be the most economical, the body was simply cleansed and dried with natron. Probably it was then wrapped in linen, but Herodotus does not mention this. The archaeological evidence shows that there was considerable variation in embalming technique at different periods, and, in support of Herodotus, not all mummies were eviscerated. A group of mummies belonging to Eleventh Dynasty princesses, found in their tombs at Deir el-Bahari, all lacked the abdominal incision, and it seems that they may have been treated with resin injected at the anus, or had received no internal treatment whatsoever. On investigation of the bodies, decayed remains of the organs were found still within the abdomen and thorax, although there was evidence of extensive decomposition. Probably the extent of the mummification process had been limited to dehydration with natron and some attempt to preserve the outer tissues with oil or resin, the remains of which could be detected upon the bodies. Surface decomposition had caused the loss of the epidermis, together with the hair and the nails. At this date no attempt was made to remove the brain, this refinement being an innovation of the New Kingdom. The bodies of the princesses had been wrapped while still in a pliable state, the marks of jewellery worn by the Princess Ashayt being impressed in the flesh, but despite this, the wrapping had not been done swiftly enough to prevent the entry of insect larvae.

Another group of burials which had received even more brief attention from the embalmers is that of the soldiers of King Nebhepetre Mentuhotpe, victims of battle, who had been brought back to Thebes for burial at Deir el-Bahari. There were about sixty bodies, all wrapped in linen but in a poor state of preservation. No true embalming had been attempted, but the presence of a large amount of sand adhering to the remains suggests that the corpses may have been temporarily buried in sand as an economical method of drying prior to their being wrapped. In this case the bodies would have been subjected to similar conditions to those in Predynastic graves, and the degree of preservation resembles that of burials from such tombs. This simple method of achieving some degree of preservation may well have been more common in the preparation of poor burials than is generally recognized.

More frequently, the bodies of the Middle Kingdom were treated in a manner not dissimilar to that used for wealthy burials of the late Old Kingdom, involving the removal of the viscera through a slit in the abdomen and the packing of the body-cavity with linen. Indeed, the presence of receptacles for the internal organs in tombs of the Twelfth Dynasty shows that bodies were regularly eviscerated, even though few of the mummies themselves have survived. By this date, these containers had assumed the form of four stone or pottery jars with a stopper in the likeness of a human head, as a development from the vessels with plain lids of the Old Kingdom. Such vases are normally referred to as 'Canopic jars', and by extension, the same term is applied to any other kind of container for viscera, whether it be a box of wood or stone, or a miniature coffin. The word 'Canopic' originates in a Greek tradition about the pilot Canopus, who was believed to have been worshipped in the form of a vase with a swollen body and a human head. More details on the development of Canopics, with a discussion of the inscriptions upon them, will be included in the following chapter.

An intact Eleventh Dynasty mummy unwrapped in modern times is that of a nobleman called Wah, who died and was buried at Thebes in the reign of King Sankhkare Mentuhotpe III. The soft organs below the diaphragm had been removed from the body through the usual incision, but the embalmers had expended far more time over the wrapping of the corpse than over the treatment of the actual tissue. Masses of linen were used around the body, amounting to some 375 square metres in all. The bandaging did not consist only of narrow strips of cloth; there were also wide sheets and thick folded pads of linen, the latter used as packing to fill out the outlines to a suitably plump appearance. Jewellery and amulets occurred at intervals below the wrappings, and every so often the layers of cloth had been coated with resin. The inner bandages, which were not to be visible, were stained in places with traces of the same resin from the dirty fingers of the embalmers. There were also other signs of carelessness, a dead mouse and a lizard having been accidentally wrapped in with the mummy. Some of the sheets of linen bore the date of manufacture in black ink, a not uncommon feature of mortuary linen, and eleven pieces were marked with the name of Wah.

From the same area of Thebes came the discovery of a cache of embalmers' materials, again of the Eleventh Dynasty, representing the leftovers from the mummification of a certain Ipy. Such deposits are not rare; they date from all periods and they were normally placed a short distance from the tomb to which they belonged. It is possible that this refuse, since it might contain fragments of tissue from the deceased, had to be buried near the tomb to ensure that the body should be complete in the next world. Burial of the material in the tomb itself may have been impossible, if the products of embalming were considered ritually impure, and so the Egyptians compromised by placing the deposits in the vicinity of the burial. On the other hand, it has also been suggested that the material was buried to prevent anyone acquiring a small fragment of the deceased and utilizing it for the purpose of malevolent magic against him. The deposit of Ipy included cloth, excess natron, oils and sawdust, as well as the actual embalming table. This consisted of a board with four wooden blocks set across it to support the body, all stained with the oils used in the process. The table had been broken up into its constituent boards in order to fit it into the small rock-cut chamber in which the items were accommodated. All the fluid and powdered materials had been collected in sixty-seven pottery jars, which had been carried up in several trips by means of a wooden yoke with rope slings for the vessels. On dumping the last of the jars, the bearers simply left them in their slings and abandoned the yoke in the chamber.

Two mummies of early Middle Kingdom date from Saqqara had received fairly elaborate preparation, the viscera having been removed and the bodies packed with linen. The eyes had been filled with plugs of the same material and the nostrils had been closed with resin. The body of the lady Senebtisi at Lisht, belonging to the Twelfth Dynasty, had likewise been eviscerated and packed, in this case with a mixture of sawdust and linen. Resin-soaked cloth had been used to seal the embalming incision and the remains of the soft organs were found wrapped in linen inside the four Canopic jars.

A highly detailed examination of two mummies from a Twelfth Dynasty cemetery at Rifa was carried out at the Manchester Museum in 1906. Unfortunately, both bodies had been virtually reduced to the skeletons, with only shreds of tissue remaining on the bones. Some of the viscera, at any rate, had been removed, for their decayed remnants were found in two of the Canopic jars. An interesting point was the fact that the skin around the fingertips had been cut and tied down, to prevent loss of the nails as the epidermis peeled off under treatment. This technique became standard practice in mummies of the New Kingdom.

For the Second Intermediate Period we lack information about mummification techniques, very few bodies having been preserved. One famous mummy of the late Seventeenth Dynasty, now in the Cairo Museum, is that of King Seqenenre, which exhibits fearful damage to the head inflicted by blows from an axe and other weapons. These combined injuries must have been fatal, although it has been suggested that they were received in two separate attacks, and the assumption has been made that the king died in battle against the Hyksos invaders. While this may well be the correct interpretation, we must bear in mind that the facts tell us only that King Seqenenre died as the result of wounds received from a battle-axe of Asiatic type. Probably as a consequence of the circumstances of the king's death, the embalming of the corpse seems to have been somewhat hastily carried out. The viscera had been extracted through a cut in the left side of the abdomen and the cavity was filled with linen, but no treatment of the badly damaged head was attempted, the brain having been left in place. Most of the flesh has disappeared from the mummy, leaving a skeleton within a covering of decayed skin. An interesting burial of the same period, but of far humbler status, was discovered by Petrie in a cemetery at Qurna. The body had been very carefully wrapped in many layers of bandages, but the preservative treatment had been largely ineffective, practically all the soft tissues having decomposed to leave only the bones remaining.

Significant advances in mummification were made in the Eighteenth Dynasty, and the Egyptians at last managed to achieve a better degree of preservation for their dead. Removal of the brain was first practised during this period, and the embalming techniques must have been similar to those described by Herodotus as the most expensive method of treatment. To remove the brain from the skull a chisel was inserted into the nostril, in oider to break through the ethmoid bone into the cranial cavity, thereby enabling the tissue to be extracted piecemeal by means of an iron probe. Despite the difficulty of this operation there is no doubt that it was regularly accomplished, since many mummies possess the break in the ethmoid bone and have little or no brain tissue remaining in the cranium. The empty skull was often filled with resinous material after removal of the brain. Experiments in modern times have shown that the brain was not pulled out in fragments with a hook, as has often been stated, but was extracted by virtue of the adherence of semi-liquid tissue to the iron probe, aided by rapid softening caused by decomposition. It is also possible that the embalmers may have deliberately introduced water into the cranial cavity to promote the liquefaction of the cerebral matter, in which case it would eventually drain out through the nostrils by gravity if the head was in an upright position. In rare cases the brain might be removed by some other method, as in the mummy of Amosis I, where the operation had been carried out through an incision in the neck, thereby giving access via the foramen magnum to the brain cavity. In accomplishing this feat the embalmers succeeded in losing the atlas vertebra. The skull of the king was refilled with linen, which had been steeped in resin before insertion.

Much of our knowledge of embalming in the New Kingdom is derived from a study of the royal mummies, which no doubt must have received the best possible treatment of their time. The wife of Amosis I, Queen Ahmose-Nefertari, died at an advanced age and had lost much of her natural hair. The embalmers rectified this state of affairs by placing twenty strings of twisted human hair over the head, to which longer plaits were attached, in addition to weaving other plaits into the remaining natural hair of the head. A similar process had been used somewhat earlier in the case of the mummy of Queen Tetisheri, of the late Seventeenth Dynasty. Both the hands of Ahmose-Nefertari, together with part of her right forearm, had been broken off, almost certainly the work of tomb-robbers anxious to remove bracelets from the wrists. A vertical incision had been made in the left side of the abdomen in order to extract the viscera, the cut having been sealed after the operation by plugging with resin-soaked linen and covering with a metal plate. The mummy of Amenophis I, successor of Amosis, had been re-wrapped in the Twenty-First Dynasty when the High-Priests of Amun at Thebes restored and concealed the royal bodies. Since the wrappings are in excellent condition this mummy has never been unwrapped in modern times, but X-ray examination has been carried out. A profile view X-ray photograph revealed that the level of the head was considerably lower than that of the cartonnage mask which covers it, the face of the mummy in fact lying under the chin of the mask.

Some doubt had always surrounded the identification of the mummy of Tuthmosis I. Maspero believed that a mummy from the Deir el-Bahari cache was that of the king because of the similarity in the appearance of the head to Tuthmosis II and Tuthmosis III. While there can be no doubt that this mummy was

embalmed by techniques current in the Eighteenth Dynasty, it
now seems unlikely to be Tuthmosis I, X-ray examination having
shown that the age at death was less than twenty years, instead of
the fifty years one would expect from historical evidence. Who-
ever this mummy represents it is certainly to be dated prior to Tuthmosis II because of the position of the arms, which are extended
with the hands over the genital region. This attitude succeeded the
laying of the arms straight down the sides of the body, current at
the start of the dynasty, but in turn gave way to a custom of
placing the arms in a crossed position on the chest. This latter
style lasted until the end of the Twentieth Dynasty, after which
there was a return to the extended position.

The mummy of Tuthmosis II displays some interesting features
apart from the crossed position of the arms mentioned above. The
surface of the skin is covered with raised marks, also evident in
the later mummies of Tuthmosis III and Amenophis II, but it
is not clear whether these are the result of some disease or simply
an effect of the treatment undergone by the body during embalmment. Tomb-robbers had damaged the body severely, the arms
having been broken off and the right leg hacked away by a blow
from an axe, in addition to numerous violent cuts into the trunk
which succeeded in demolishing almost the entire abdominal wall.
Despite this damage a small part of the embalming incision remains visible. The nostrils had been sealed with linen soaked in
resin and the latter material had also been used to close the ears.
According to the usual practice of the New Kingdom, care had
been taken to preserve the finger and toenails, which in this
mummy were neatly trimmed. The usual method of saving the nails
was to secure them with binding so that they did not fall off with
the loss of the epidermis, but some mummies had tubular finger-
stalls of metal placed over the nails for the same purpose. With
Tuthmosis III a new custom was introduced in the manner of cutting the abdomen for the extraction of the viscera. In earlier mummies this incision had always consisted of a vertical slit in the left
side, but the cut in the body of Tuthmosis III and his successors
down to the close of the Twentieth Dynasty was made at a lower
level, sloping diagonally from the hip bone towards the pubic

region (fig. 41). In the case of Tuthmosis III the incision had been cleverly re-sealed by stitching. Owing to the extensive damage caused by plunderers the body had to be consolidated in the Twenty-First Dynasty with four wooden splints, three of which were bound under the wrappings and one outside. Despite the great maltreatment of the body it was still possible to determine that the arms had been laid in a crossed position on the chest, the right hand having been fixed in its location by tying it to a piece of wood. It is very likely that the hands of royal mummies laid in this position originally held the emblems of royalty, that is, the sceptre and the flail, such as were found with the body of Tutankhamun. These items of regalia were probably made of gilded wood and have not survived the depredations of the tomb-robbers. The body-cavity of Tuthmosis III was filled with linen and the skin had been darkened by the use of resins during mummification.

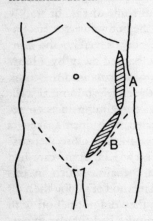

Fig.41.Location of the embalming incision:
(A) pre-Tuthmosis III (B) post-Tuthmosis III

It is quite evident that by the mid Eighteenth Dynasty the Egyptians had solved many of the problems connected with the preservation of a corpse, as demonstrated by the state of the royal mummies. The condition of the skin, flesh, hair and even the eyelashes of certain mummies is quite remarkable, and no doubt the general appearance of the bodies would have been even more impressive had it not been for the destruction wrought by tomb-robbers. These high standards of preservation were generally maintained throughout the New Kingdom and attained a peak of achievement with the development of new techniques in the Twenty-First Dynasty. Certain individual mummies of the New Kingdom present features of interest, the minor variations in treatment from one body to another showing that the embalmers were experimenting with the mummification process in the hope of achieving even better preservation. A common feature of Eighteenth Dynasty mummies is the dark appearance of the skin, noted in the case of Tuthmosis III above and also evident on the body of Tuthmosis IV. The application of resins to the skin seems to have been intended to insulate the tissues from moisture which would promote decay. The body-cavity of Tuthmosis IV was filled with linen and resin according to the standard practice, but more elaborate techniques were used for the mummy of Amenophis III, the skin of the arms, legs and neck having been filled out by means of resin packing. This material had been introduced under the skin and moulded to the form of the limbs, so that on drying the body would have retained its natural contours and would not have suffered the severe shrinkage noted in earlier mummies. The use of filling materials under the skin of the limbs became common in the Twenty-First Dynasty, when mud and sand were employed for this purpose, but the use of resin in the mummy of Amenophis III represents an unusually early attempt to counter the problem of shrinkage. Unfortunately, the body had been damaged and the broken fragments re-united by means of linen binding. Some confusion seems to have attended this re-assembly of the body, the interior of which was found to contain human toe and arm bones, together with the leg bones of a bird.

The mummy of Tutankhamun, in contrast to the splendour of his funerary equipment, was relatively poorly preserved, the libations which had been poured over it at the burial ceremony having destroyed large areas by slow combustion. This was not the fault of the embalmers, who probably did their job adequately, but of over-enthusiastic mortuary priests.

One of the most striking royal mummies of the Nineteenth Dynasty, in view of the remarkable preservation of the head, although the rest of the body had been extensively damaged, is that of Seti I (plate 16). This mummy was embalmed by the same processes as those of the Eighteenth Dynasty, but the succeeding Pharaoh, Ramesses II, received a somewhat more refined treatment, which overcame the problem of excessive darkening of the skin. The embalming incision in the body of Ramesses II was longer than usual in order to allow for easier access to the abdomen. Some hair remained on the head, although it had turned yellow, and both the ears and nose had been sealed by resinous material. The mummy of Merenptah, badly damaged by robbers, had been completely eviscerated and treated with a layer of balsam. The embalming incision had been covered by a plate of some kind, now missing, only the impression remaining in the resin. In the case of the body of Siptah the abdomen had been packed with dried lichens instead of the usual resinous linen, and the same is true of the later mummy of Ramesses IV. Siptah suffered from a deformed foot, identified by some as a 'club-foot' condition, but by others as a possible result of poliomyelitis. The cheeks of the mummy were filled with linen to help retain the shape of the face, and the incision in the abdomen had been re-sealed by stitching. Both of these techniques became customary in later mummies, although isolated examples of sewn embalming wounds are known in the Eighteenth Dynasty. Plunderers had broken off the right hand of Siptah, probably to remove a bracelet, but the restorers of the Twenty-First Dynasty had carefully replaced the hand in position, attaching it to the arm by means of two wooden splints bound with linen. The body of Seti II had also been rewrapped, but in the bandages were found two complete tunics of linen, with neck- and arm-holes, together with some fragments of other garments and excess bandages. These were probably left over from the original outer wrappings of the mummy and were simply bound in under the new coverings in the Twenty-First Dynasty.

A curious feature was discovered in the mummy of an unidentified woman from the cache in the tomb of Amenophis II. On the sole of each foot was tied a bundle of linen, that on the right foot containing the remains of the epidermis mixed with natron, while the package on the left foot held fragments of viscera. These tissue fragments had been placed with the mummy in order to render it complete. Although not precisely dated, the body must belong to the late Nineteenth or early Twentieth Dynasty.

The body of Ramesses III has not been completely stripped of its inner coverings, but X-ray examination has revealed figures of three of the four sons of Horus inside the thorax. Such figures, normally made of wax, were to become common in Twenty-First Dynasty mummies. The mummy of Ramesses III is the earliest to have been fitted with artificial eyes in order to increase the lifelike appearance of the face. In this mummy and others of the Twentieth Dynasty the hands are not clenched but are laid flat on the shoulders, with the arms crossed over the chest. Of the remaining royal mummies of the Twentieth Dynasty, that of Ramesses IV had artificial eyes formed of small onions placed in the sockets, the mummy of Ramesses V had been packed with sawdust and Ramesses VI was so damaged that the fragments of his mummy had been tied to a wooden board for support. Certain marks on the skin of the abdomen and face of Ramesses V suggest that he may have suffered from smallpox.

During the Twenty-First Dynasty the Egyptians reached their greatest achievements in mummification, owing to the use of a variety of new techniques. Chief among these was the widespread employment of packing materials beneath the skin in order to re-create the plump appearance of the body. In the case of an early mummy of the dynasty, that of Nodjmet, wife of the High-Priest of Amun, Herihor, the restoration of the form of the limbs had been accomplished by the addition of sawdust bound in linen to the exterior, but in later mummies the packing was normally introduced under the skin. The face of Nodjmet had been packed through the mouth, artificial eyes of stone had been inserted, and false eyebrows of human hair had been applied to replace the real eyebrows lost under natron treatment. The arms were extended by the sides as now once again became the fashion, although the mummies of the High-Priests and Priestesses of Amun have the hands over the pubic region. Many mummies of the Twenty-First Dynasty have been examined and all testify to the care taken by the embalmers in the preparation of the corpse. They also tried to make the body as complete as possible, and the internal organs, formerly stored separately in Canopic jars, were now returned to the body-cavity after treatment, protected by images of the four sons of Horus (plate 17). Bodies could also be repaired; the mummy of an old woman had leather patches sewn on to the skin to cover the marks of bed-sores. Mummies were painted yellow or red and artificial eyes were regularly inserted into the sockets. The complete packing of a corpse required more cuts in the skin than the single incision in the abdomen. Through the latter slit, the embalmer could only push material up into the neck and down into the legs. The feet had to be filled later through cuts across the heels. To pack the trunk efficiently, the skin had to be separated from the underlying muscular tissue to allow the introduction of material beneath the skin of the chest and back. Additional cuts were made at the shoulders for the packing of the arms. The substances used for packing varied, and included resin, fat, soda, linen, sawdust, mud and sand. In some cases the face was over-filled, giving it a swollen appearance, or even causing it to burst open. The abdomen was often packed twice during mummification; a temporary filling of linen was inserted during the treatment of the corpse with natron, to aid drying of the tissues, and this was later removed and replaced by the final packing material.

Although the results of these elaborate processes are quite remarkable, the embalmers' trade must have been a particularly gruesome occupation. How the embalmers themselves could have entertained any belief that these corpses, however well prepared, would serve as homes for the immortal spirits of their owners is difficult to comprehend – perhaps they did not. The fine standards of this age lasted through the Twenty-Second Dynasty, but in subsequent periods there was a steady decline. In some instances there was still an attempt to pack the corpse, but it was carelessly done, and the embalmers seem to have spent most of their energies upon fine bandaging. The viscera were replaced in the body down to the Twenty-Fifth Dynasty but thereafter it became more usual to wrap the organs in linen and deposit them between the legs of the mummy, or to preserve them in Canopic jars. A regular feature of many Late Period and Ptolemaic mummies is the extensive use of a black, pitch-like substance as a consolidant. This is conveniently described as bitumen although the name is not, strictly speaking, correct. Indeed, the term 'mummy' is a derivation of the Arabic word for 'bitumen' or a 'bituminized thing'. The material was used freely in both human and animal mummies of the later stages of Egyptian civilization and, although it rendered the corpse very solid and heavy, it was not very effective in achieving true preservation of the tissues (plate 18). When the bitumen-soaked linen has been removed from a mummy of this type, very little apart from the skeleton remains. There can be no doubt that the use of this substance enabled large numbers of bodies to be processed quite rapidly, apart from the time spent upon bandaging and ritual. It is clear, however, that many corpses had to wait for some time before receiving attention, for the signs of advanced decomposition are often very evident. Maggots and beetles are very frequently observed in mummies, sometimes embedded in the resin or bitumen poured into the cavity. Recent experiments on rat corpses have shown that insect larvae are capable of surviving within a body even during treatment with dry natron. The problem of rapid decomposition before embalming explains the disordered state of some Ptolemaic mummies, which seem literally to have fallen to pieces before the embalmers began work. As a result, parts of bodies were lost, or mixed up with pieces from other corpses. Mummies are known in which the bones of several individuals have been wrapped up together to make up a single skeleton, while any parts which had gone missing were replaced by bits of pottery, mud, linen or wood. One apparent child mummy from Nubia had the skull of an adult woman, together with some of the vertebrae, the ribs, half the pelvis and some leg bones, but the bones of the other leg had belonged to two different male skeletons. Mummies in this sort of condition are quite common, and they may have elaborate and intricate bandaging, which belies the chaos within. Corpses were occasionally adjusted to suit the size of a coffin; one example had been reduced in bulk by discarding the shoulders and arms, and breaking the femora so that part of each leg could be thrown away. A possible explanation for incomplete bodies, apart from simple decomposition and carelessness, is that they may represent the remains of individuals who had been drowned in the Nile and partly devoured by crocodiles. In the Ptolemaic Period such fortunate persons were deified and accorded special reverence, so that their remains would certainly have been gathered for burial. Coffins and sarcophagi of drowned persons can be identified by the occurrence of the epithet 'The Praised One' before the name of the owner.

Mummies of the Graeco-Roman Period have most elaborate bandaging, consisting of many layers of linen wound around the body to form patterns where the folds overlapped. Diamond-shaped patterns were popular (plate 20), often with gilded studs at the centre of each panel. Mummies were further embellished by the regular addition of gilded covers for the fingernails, and, in the case of women, for the nipples. In other examples, less common, the entire head could be gilded directly over the skin.

On the operation of the embalming industry Egyptian sources are rather unhelpful, concentrating on the ritual aspects of the process. More information of a technical nature is available from Greek documents, but there may well have been some differences between the organization current in the Graeco-Roman Period and that of earlier times. We know both from Egyptian texts and from Herodotus that the process of mummification took seventy days, but this represents the total period between death and burial, the actual embalming taking only a part of this time. The seventieth day is given in the demotic story of Naneferkaptah as the day of placing the corpse in its coffin, and the same tale records day 35 as the day of wrapping. Since other demotic texts mention the issuing of cloths to the lector priests before the thirty-fifth day, these cannot be the linen bandages for the final wrapping of the mummy, but must have been for some other purpose, perhaps for swabbing or temporary packing. The work of the embalmers was carried out in the *Wabet* and the *Per-nefer*, which in most cases would have been temporary structures close to the necropolis. The body was taken into the *Wabet* on day 4, by which time it seems that it would already have been dried. Probably this initial stage was carried out in the open, the bodies being laid on mats and covered with natron. After dehydration, the corpse was washed free of excess salt with Nile water, as recorded by Herodotus. This washing may have been a highly ritualized operation, since it was believed to symbolize the mythology of the rising of the sun from the Nile and the subsidence of the inundation waters. A vignette in tombs or on coffins of the New Kingdom, showing

Fig. 42. Scene of the ritual lustration of the deceased

the figure of the deceased sitting above a large vessel, bathed in a purifying stream of water poured from above, is a conventional illustration of this rite (fig. 42). The ceremonial aspect of mummification was of great importance to the Egyptians and was the main reason why the process took so long to complete. A purely mechanical embalmment and wrapping could have been accomplished in a far shorter time. Some insight into the ritual side of the affair is given by a text preserved in two separate papyri, one in Cairo and the other in the Louvre. Although both papyri belong to the Roman Period it is likely that they were copied from earlier originals. The text contains directions to the embalmers concerning different stages in the preservation of the corpse, beginning with the anointing of the head, followed by similar treatment for the rest of the body. After this come instructions for dealing with the viscera and for the application of oil to the back. The subsequent passage appears to be a reminder to the operators, rather than a specific direction, to avoid tilting the body towards the head end, since this would cause the fluids with which the corpse had been treated to run out. At each stage in the proceedings, the papyri supply the requisite formulae to be recited by the priests. From this point the text continues with the following directions:

1. The nails and toes are to be gilded before wrapping and finger-stalls are to be placed in position. This instruction reflects the Roman date of the text, for gilding the nails was a practice not developed until very late times. To accompany this stage, the embalmers are told to recite a spell concerning the restoration to the corpse of the use of hands and feet.

2. A final anointing of the head, followed by wrapping in specified numbers of bandages impregnated with oil or resin. The recitation deals with the restoration of the senses and mentions the provision of amulets.

3. The treatment of the head is now complete and the priest recites that the deceased may pass on to the next world, and that he will never again be deprived of his head. The latter statement is a very ancient one derived from the legend of the dismemberment of Osiris.

4. The hands and arms receive further wrapping, and protective amulets are supplied.

5. More instructions concerning the wrapping of the hands and their treatment with oil or resin.

6. In this final stage the legs are treated and wrapped in linen bearing drawings of protective deities. The recitation confirms that the deceased has regained the use of his legs.

It is interesting to note that these texts contain no reference to the initial drying of the body, which must have been done before any of the stages described here. Possibly different groups of embalmers may have worked on a single body, each responsible for only a part of the mummification. A demotic text in Leiden contains a promise by a group of Memphite embalmers to hand over a corpse to a second group within four days or to pay a fine. The period of four days may well be significant, since it probably represents the time taken for the dehydration of the body. In the Graeco-Roman Period it is known that embalmers worked in teams or professional guilds; those teams responsible for the evisceration and drying of bodies were referred to in Greek as 'slitters' and 'curers', after the terms for curing fish. A link

1. View across the Nile Valley from the desert

2. Naturally preserved Predynastic burial

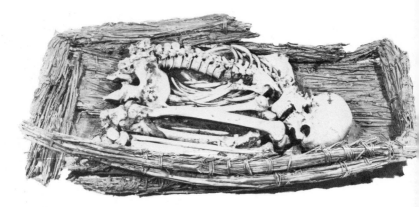

3. First Dynasty burial in a basketwork coffin

4. Linen-wrapped arm from the tomb of King Djer, with bracelets in position

5. First Dynasty palace-facade mastaba

6. Funerary meal in a Second Dynasty tomb

7. The funeral procession, from the funerary papyrus of Hunefer, Nineteenth Dynasty

8. The ritual of Opening the Mouth, from the funerary papyrus of Hunefer, Nineteenth Dynasty

9. (left) An example of a false-
door stela of the Old
Kingdom

10. (above) Set of copper models
from the tomb of the priest
Idy, Sixth Dynasty

11. (below) New Kingdom
tomb-painting of a pond
surrounded by trees

12. Wooden model of servants making bread and beer, Eleventh Dynasty

13. Wooden shabti-figures of King Ramesses VI

14. Tunnelled limestone portcullis in a First Dynasty tomb

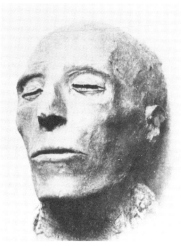

15. Old Kingdom sarcophagus as found, with the lid wedged open by plunderers

16. Head of the mummy of Seti I

17. Amuletic figures of the four sons of Horus, Twenty-First Dynasty

18. Ptolemaic mummies as left by plunderers

19. The Judgement of the Dead, from the funerary papyrus of Ani,
   Nineteenth Dynasty

20. (*left*) Elaborate bandaging of a Roman-age mummy

21. The Fields of Offerings, from the funerary papyrus of Ani, Nineteenth Dynasty

22. Hypocephalus inscribed for Neshorpakhered, Ptolemaic Period

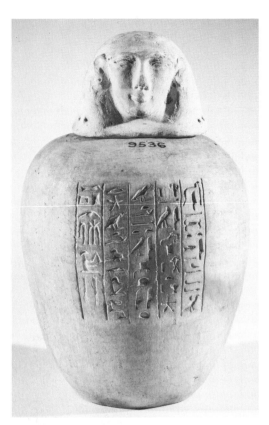

23. Pottery Canopic jar of the Eighteenth Dynasty, inscribed for Ahmose

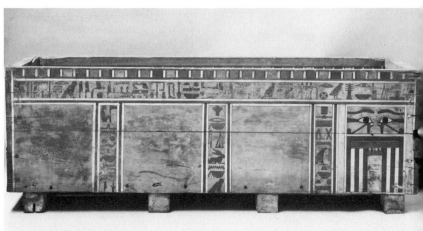

24. Wooden coffin of Seni, Twelfth Dynasty

25. Inner and outer gilded coffins of Henutmehit, Eighteenth Dynasty

26. Anthropoid coffin in Tjentmutengebtiu, Twenty-First Dynasty

27. The deified King Amenophis I, from a coffin of the Twenty-First
   Dynasty

28. Vaulted coffin of Her, late Twenty-Fifth Dynasty

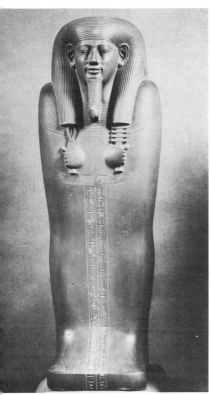

29. Schist sarcophagus of the vizier Sisebek, Twenty-Sixth Dynasty

30. The goddess Nut on the lid of the coffin of Soter, Roman Period

31. Mummy portrait in coloured wax, Roman Period

32. Stela recording the burial of a Buchis bull in Year 19 of Ptolemy VI

33. Bronze figure of the Apis bull, Late Period

34. Bronze figure of an ibis, Late Period

35. Mummified cat from Abydos, Roman Period

36. Simple pit-grave at Abydos, Predynastic Period

37. Stone mastaba of the Fifth Dynasty, showing the entrance to the chapel

38. Entrance to a rock–cut tomb chapel of the Twelfth Dynasty

39. Chapel-tomb of the Divine Votaress, Amenirdis, Twenty-Fifth Dynasty

between mummification and the preservation of fish is found much earlier in the tomb of Khabekhet at Deir el-Medina, where a painted scene shows Anubis, the embalmer-god *par excellence*, attending to the mummification of a large Nile fish, which is resting upon a bier like any human mummy (fig. 43). The embalming priests took upon themselves the roles of the gods in carrying out their duties, and sometimes wore masks in the appearance of the appropriate divinities. A mask of this type with the face of a jackal in impersonation of Anubis is preserved in the museum at Hildesheim; it is equipped with eye-holes under the chin to enable the wearer to see out.

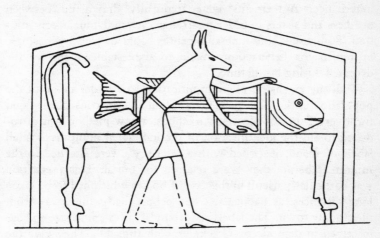

Fig.43. Anubis embalming a fish

More information on the rituals associated with mummification is given in two papyri from Thebes, known as the Rhind Papyri, in which a total of seventeen ceremonies are mentioned. Each rite was held in connection with a separate part of the body, these being the seven openings of the head, the four viscera, the two legs, the two arms, the chest and the back. These documents agree with our other sources over the seventy-day period for the completion of the whole process. Graeco-Roman texts sometimes contain promises to complete the burial within a specified time. At this late epoch, the arrangement of a burial could become a fairly involved legal issue, with official receipts and contracts being exchanged between the various parties concerned. This may well have been the case in earlier periods but the documentary evidence has not survived. In Roman times the main point of concern for the relatives of the deceased seems to have been the cost of the funeral, and just how this should be shared among members of the family. Not only did the expense of mummification and the services of the mortuary priest have to be considered, but also the tax which was levied for each interment. In some cases the children of the departed would be required to provide for the funeral expenses under a clause in the will before they could claim their inheritance. Agreements were frequently drawn up between brothers and sisters in order to arrange each individual's contribution. Sometimes, the funeral expenses could be paid by a temple in return for benefactions made to the establishment by the deceased during his lifetime.

With the extension of mummification to a wider range of the population in the Graeco-Roman Period and the consequent rapid turnover of the embalmers workshops, a new method was introduced to aid the identification of the individual mummies. Small labels of wood, inscribed with a brief text, were attached to the mummies before they were released for burial. This precaution was particularly useful in the case of bodies which had to be taken long distances, as happened when people died while away from their home town. The labels are around 12 × 5 cm in size and are inscribed in demotic or Greek, or both (fig. 44). They give the name and age of the deceased, sometimes with the names of his parents. In the communal tomb-pits, where bodies were stacked without coffins or any funerary equipment, the labels would have

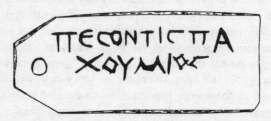

Fig. 44. Wooden mummy label inscribed in Greek for Pesontis, son of Pachomios

been the only means of identification. Some labels provide rather more than the basic details and request that the body should be buried in a particular necropolis. One Greek papyrus records that a certain Senpamouthes sent her mother's body to her brother, who presumably was to arrange the burial. The text states that the corpse could be identified by the label on its neck, and by the fact that it possessed a pink shroud with the name written over the abdomen.

Deposits of leftover embalming materials have already been mentioned earlier in this chapter in connection with burials of the Eleventh Dynasty. Such dumps are by no means rare in later periods, being especially common in the region of Deir el-Bahari at Thebes, where one deposit was mistakenly identified as an embalmers' workshop. Some of this material probably did constitute the refuse of such establishments, but, more often, the caches were associated with nearby tombs. At Deir el-Bahari were buried embalming materials of various periods from the Middle Kingdom to Graeco-Roman times. An Eighteenth Dynasty deposit contained the leftovers in pottery vessels, each marked in ink with the name of its contents and also with the names of the two embalmers involved. Late burials were accompanied by embalming refuse left in shallow holes close to the graves, the excess natron and stained linen being sealed in pottery containers. In another case the disposal of the material had been more careless, and the substances had simply been dumped in an old coffin. The deposits at Deir el-Bahari were associated with the tombs of private individuals, but in the royal burial-ground at the Valley of the Kings the leftovers of the embalming materials of Tutankhamun were found. These items lay in a shallow pit not far from the tomb, and included linen bandages and pots containing bags of natron and chaff. But in addition to the embalming relics there were also in the deposit the remains of the funerary banquet, eaten by the persons who attended the burial of Tutankhamun. The bones from the pottery jars in the cache showed that the meal had been quite lavish; there were bones from a cow, a sheep or goat, nine ducks and four geese. The pottery dishes on which the food had been served were also found in the pit, together with numerous wine-jars, water containers and drinking cups. Most of the vessels had been deliberately broken in order to pack them away in the larger pots. Another interesting feature was the discovery of floral collars, also packed in the jars, originally worn by those present at the feast. Not all the collars had survived, but from the presence of eight drinking cups and the same number of water jars it has been proposed that eight persons attended the meal. After the conclusion of the proceedings and the packing of the remains, the

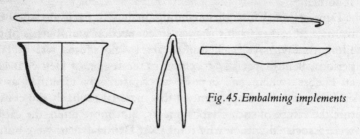

Fig.45. Embalming implements

Fig.46. Scenes of mummification from the tomb of Tjoy at Thebes

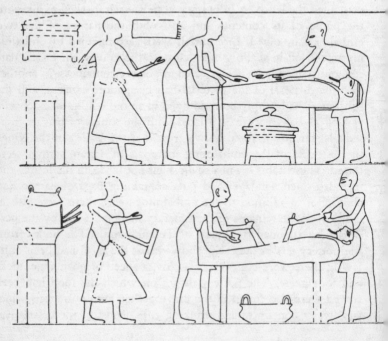

floor was swept clean with two brooms, which were also found in the deposit. The remnants of the banquet constitute a major difference between this cache and those of private individuals at Deir el-Bahari, in which only embalmers' refuse occurs. Unfortunately, no other royal deposits have yet been found to provide a comparison.

In certain Late Period tombs the embalming instruments were left in or near the burial chamber. The reason for this practice is the same as that which prompted the gathering up of embalming materials: to ensure that the deceased entered the next world in a complete state, not deprived of even a speck of flesh which may have remained on the implements. A good selection of such tools was discovered in the tomb of a certain Wahibre at Thebes. Among them were an enema, a pair of forceps, a knife and a long hook, the latter having been used to extract the brain (fig. 45). Some embalming tools were also found with the burials of the sacred Buchis bulls at Armant.

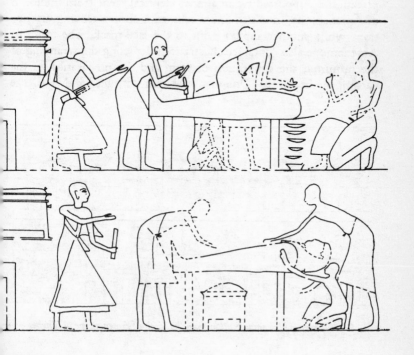

Egyptian pictorial representations of the mummification process are not common, reflecting the scarcity of informative texts on the subject. A few tombs, however, contain scenes depicting the work in the embalming shop, although in a rather conventional fashion. In the Theban tomb of Tjoy, of the Nineteenth Dynasty, there are four scenes of mummification illustrating different stages of the process (fig. 46). The two better-preserved vignettes show the bandaging of the mummy, which is supported horizontally on blocks, and the brushing on of hot resin. Two workmen apply the resin from small vessels which they hold in their hands. A larger bowl with two handles, shown beneath the body, may have contained the stock of the material, and a similar bowl to the left is perhaps being heated to the required temperature. The scenes on the right are considerably damaged and the exact nature of the operations cannot be determined. It may be that the mummy in the upper register is already in its anthropoid coffin, since one man appears to be carving an inscription on it with a chisel. This interpretation is supported by an almost identical scene from the tomb of Amenemope, in which one workman is shown carving inscriptions while another applies paint to the face-mask. The tomb of Amenemope also contained illustrations depicting the wrapping of the mummy, the application of resin and the preparation of the cartonnage headpiece. One man is shown with his hand in a large

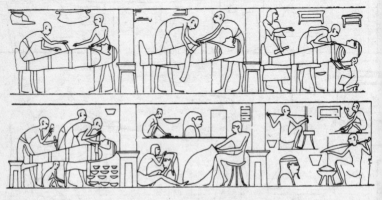

Fig.47.Scenes of mummification from the tomb of Amenemope at Thebes

pottery jar, which may have been used to store embalming materials (fig. 47). It is worth noting that the mummy is shown in each scene as though it were already complete, despite the fact that it is supposed to be at different stages of preparation. This is because of the Egyptian artistic convention, which ruled that objects should be drawn not as they appeared, but in such a manner as to leave no doubt over their identity.

The study of ancient Egyptian human remains has benefited greatly in recent years from scientific advances in medicine, especially in the application of X-ray photography. The value of this method of study was recognized very early on by Petrie, who published an X-ray photograph of the limbs of a wrapped body from Deshasha in 1898. Prior to the discovery of X-rays, the detailed examination of a mummy involved the removal of the bandages and consequent destruction of the mummy as a coherent specimen. Not only does X-ray examination leave the body intact, it also reveals considerably more about the individual than can be deduced from a visual inspection of the bones and tissues. Recent developments in the use of X-rays include three-dimensional photographs and tomography, the latter being a technique by which views of previously inaccessible areas can be obtained.

The examination of Egyptian mummies by X-rays has been carried out sporadically over many years, often with only a single body as the subject of study. Although an individual specimen can reveal interesting features, far more valuable for the general assembly of knowledge are those studies which have included the investigation of a whole collection of mummies in a single project, thereby providing a mass of data for statistical analysis. Much of the information gained is of interest for the study of the physical anthropology and health of the ancient population, and, as such, is not directly relevant to Egyptian funerary beliefs and practices, which are the concern of this book. However, it is worth giving a brief summary of the medical details revealed by the X-raying of mummies, if only to show the capabilities of the technique. A survey of over 130 mummies in European museums provided evidence of arthritis, arrested growth during adolescence and occasional calcification of the arteries. These conditions have also been found in the royal mummies of the New Kingdom, which were subjected to an extensive programme of X-ray investigation between 1967 and 1978. Numerous bone fractures were observed in the bodies, but practically all of them had occurred after death as the result of careless embalming or the handiwork of tomb-robbers. From the royal mummies there were examples of ankylosing spondylitis (in Amenophis II), poliomyelitis (in Siptah) and scoliosis (in Meritamun and Ahmose-Neferιari, as well as in the non-royal Thuya). Recent work in Manchester, using larger X-ray equipment than is normally available for the study of Egyptian mummies, has demonstrated the presence of parasites in certain bodies, including guinea worm and, possibly, bilharzia. One very common feature in radiographs of mummies is the marked opacity of the intervertebral discs, which is thought to be an effect of the embalming process rather than the result of disease.

Radiology of the jaws and teeth has revealed much about the dental health of the Egyptians. Particularly interesting is the fact that they were not troubled much by dental caries, owing to the lack of sugar in their diet. Their chief dental problems were extreme wear of the teeth, caused by the gritty nature of much of the food, and periodontal disease, that is, destruction of the bone in which the teeth are set. In older individuals the gradual attrition of the teeth often exposed the pulp cavity and led to the formation of abscesses. All levels of Egyptian society were affected by these conditions, including royalty. King Ramesses II, in particular, must have suffered from considerable dental pain in his old age.

Scientific information from Egyptian human remains can sometimes provide material of significant historical or archaeological value. In the first place, the many X-rays which have been carried out have served as a check on our knowledge of the variations in embalming technique at different periods, revealing details such as the position of the arms, presence or absence of viscera or brain tissue, and the insertion of packing materials, artificial eyes and amulets. Estimates of age at death can be particularly interesting in the case of the mummies of known individuals, especially members of the royal family, because the medical estimate can be compared with evidence from historical sources to see whether or not the two agree. Some of the proposed ages at death for the royal mummies have, in fact, been surprisingly low, and are difficult to reconcile with historical facts. A possible explanation for this state of affairs may be that some of the mummies are incorrectly identified, having been mixed up during the restoration of the burials in the Twenty-First Dynasty, or the criteria for deciding the age of the bodies from scientific examination are insufficiently accurate. An interesting case is that of the body of a woman from the cache in the tomb of Amenophis II, unidentified by any inscription and long known only by the term, 'The Elder Woman'. According to the X-rays, this would appear to be a misnomer, as the age has been evaluated at between twenty-five and thirty-five. This would be no problem had the body remained anonymous, but another investigation succeeded in identifying the Elder Woman as Queen Tiye, by matching the hair of the mummy with the lock of hair of Tiye found in the tomb of Tutankhamun. The identification confirmed what had already been suspected from the similarity of the mummy to that of Thuya, mother of Tiye. However, historical evidence requires an age at death for Tiye of somewhere in the region of fifty years, even at a low estimate, and just how this fact is to be reconciled with the medical estimate of twenty-five to thirty-five years has not been explained.

A variety of scientific techniques other than radiology have been applied in recent years to the study of Egyptian mummies, including the determination of blood-groups in order to establish family relationships, and the use of the electron microscope for the examination of small tissue fragments. Although a certain amount of interesting information has been obtained, these techniques involve the removal of samples from the corpse and can, therefore, be used only in the case of unwrapped mummies. As there are many mummies already stripped of their bandages in various collections around the world, it is preferable that such tests should be carried out upon these, rather than to undertake the unwrapping of additional specimens.

The mummies of ancient Egypt have excited public interest to a great degree, perhaps because this method of preparing corpses for burial is so far removed from the customs of western culture. However, it is desirable that general interest should be based on some knowledge of the purpose of mummification, or at least on an admiration of the technical achievements of the ancient embalmers, instead of being generated by simple curiosity about old human remains. Such admiration is occasionally found in unlikely places, as in the following quote from a Coptic text, recording the thoughts of a hermit and his son about a large number of mummies in a rock-tomb at Thebes. It is noteworthy that on this occasion the ascetic Copt treated the mummies with far more respect than was generally shown by the early Christians towards the relics of the older Pharaonic civilization:

And it happened that on a day when my father was still with me in the mountain of Djeme that my father said to me, 'My son, rise up, follow me and I will show you the place in which I repose, so that you may visit me and bring me food and water to drink to sustain my body.' And we came to a place that was in the form of a door which was wide open. And when we had entered that place, we found it had been hewn out of the rock. Now there was a large number of bodies that had been mummified in it, so that if you were merely to walk outside that place you would be able to smell the sweet smells which emanated from these bodies. And we took the coffins and we piled them one on top of the other. The wrappings in which the first mummy was enveloped were of royal linen; and its stature was large, and the fingers of its hands and its toes were bandaged separately. And my father said, 'How many years ago is it since these people died, and from what nomes do they come?' And I said to him, 'It is God only who knows.' And my father said to me, 'Get thee gone, my son. Dwell in your monastery and take heed to yourself; this world is a thing of vanity and we may be removed from it at any moment.'[1]

THE EGYPTIAN
AFTERLIFE

Our knowledge of the Egyptian concept of the next world is derived almost entirely from inscriptional evidence and consequently we understand very little about Egyptian beliefs in this sphere for the earliest period. The Predynastic cultures may well have believed that continued existence after death resembled earthly life, to judge from the everyday objects supplied in graves, and indeed this remained a popular belief in later times. Certainly the servant-burials around the tombs of royalty or of high officials in the First Dynasty show that there was an expectation that the life-styles of master and servant would continue unchanged after death. During the Old Kingdom, a distinction becomes apparent between the kind of afterlife to be followed by royalty and that reserved for ordinary persons, and this division must have begun some time earlier, although just how early is not clear. It should be pointed out at this stage that the Egyptians did not necessarily hold a single view of the next world at any one time, but, because of their reluctance to abandon old ideas, were quite capable of maintaining two or more conflicting opinions at once. This is already apparent in the Pyramid Texts, our major source of information on the mortuary religion of the Old Kingdom, in which the views expressed concerning the afterlife of the king may vary considerably in different spells, depending upon whether they were early or more recent in origin.

The Pyramid Texts were designed specifically for royalty and the vision of the next world which they contain was entirely closed to lesser individuals. The best that private persons could hope for was to continue to exist after death in much the same way as they had lived on earth. The king, on the other hand, was destined to join the gods with whom he was at least equal, while some texts assert that he was even their superior. One of the earliest beliefs contained in the Pyramid Texts states that the king would become one of the circumpolar stars, regarded as a symbol of permanence because they are never seen to set when viewed from Egypt. The stellar concept of the afterlife probably accounts for the location of the earliest pyramid temples on the north side of the Third Dynasty step pyramids, and, as mentioned in Chapter 4, certainly determined the orientation of the entrances towards the north in all pyramids of the Old Kingdom. In later spells of the Pyramid Texts the king is said to join Re, the sun-god, in his daily journey across the sky. This fresh opinion was inspired by the great importance which the cult of Re acquired during the Fifth Dynasty. Typically, the Egyptians continued to align the pyramid entrances towards the circumpolar stars, despite the fact that the king was no longer to travel there, but was to spend his afterlife in the boat of Re. The gods were regularly considered to travel in boats, reflecting the standard means of transport in ancient Egypt. Spell 469 refers to the king taking his place in the solar bark:

I am pure, I take my oar to myself, I occupy my seat, I sit in the bow of the boat of the two Enneads, and I row Re to the West.

Another passage contains references to the conflicting stellar and solar versions of the afterlife in a single sentence, the two concepts being conveniently linked by assuming that the king would travel in the company of both the sun and the stars:

Be pure; occupy your seat in the bark of Re; may you row over the sky and ascend to the distant ones; row with the Imperishable Stars, navigate with the Unwearying Stars, receive the freight of the Night-Bark.[1]

Less prominent beliefs appear throughout the Pyramid Texts; the dead king is identified with a whole series of divinities, or is stated to be chief of the gods, but is at the same time under their protection; in addition, he might traverse the sky with Orion or pass through the underworld with Osiris. The lack of a consistent viewpoint did not trouble the Egyptians, whose theology was well able to accept the identification of king or god with several entities at the same time.

A further important element in the Pyramid Texts is the identification of the dead king with Osiris, later to become the supreme god of the dead. In legend, Osiris had been a good king of Egypt, but he had been treacherously slain and dismembered by his brother, Seth. Isis, wife of Osiris, had retrieved the scattered fragments of her husband's body and restored it to life by magic, and Osiris assumed his new place as king of the dead in the netherworld. However, Seth had seized the kingship of Egypt and thereby denied it to Horus, son of Osiris and Isis. It was left to Horus to defeat Seth, avenge his father, and claim his rightful inheritance, a task in which he eventually succeeded. This story is one of the most fundamental tales of Egyptian religion, and allegorical references to it are widespread in Egyptian literature. Its importance in funerary belief stems from the fact that any dead king was considered identical to Osiris, while the heir to the throne and the ruling king was the embodiment of Horus. As will be explained later, identification with Osiris did not remain a royal privilege in subsequent periods, as the royal funerary inscriptions were exploited by private individuals. Numerous spells in the Pyramid Texts refer to the king as Osiris, either directly or in metaphor. Of the three major beliefs represented in the pyramids, that of a stellar afterlife was to lapse into obscurity, but the solar and Osirian concepts were to remain strong for the duration of the Dynastic period.

As a result of the collapse of central authority during the First Intermediate Period, the old religious texts for the protection of the king were usurped and adapted for more widespread use, particularly upon the wooden coffins of the Eleventh and Twelfth Dynasties. The revised texts so created are now known as the Coffin Texts because of this use. Basically, they provided guarantees of perpetual survival after death similar to those granted to the king by the Pyramid Texts. Some of the new spells compiled for the Coffin Texts form the antecedents of certain passages in the Book of the Dead, the great funerary work of the New Kingdom. Many individual sections of the Coffin Texts possess their own headings which state the purpose of the spells concerned. There are standard incantations to avoid total oblivion, with headings like, 'Spell for not perishing in the land of the dead' or 'Not dying a second death'. The latter title refers to the fear of losing the life beyond the grave, the so-called 'second death' being the complete destruction of all trace and memory of a person upon earth. Other spells are more specific in content, and include the following titles: 'Spell for eating bread in the realm of the dead', 'To repel a snake and to repel crocodiles' and 'Not to rot and not to do work in the realm of the dead'. There are also a large number of transformation spells by which the deceased could assume the form of various divinities or animals. Spell 290 contains the ultimate assurance in this respect, for it concludes with the words: 'The man shall be transformed into any god the man may wish to be transformed into'. As in the earlier Pyramid Texts, there are conflicting opinions upon the final destination of the spirit, which might go up to the sky to join the boat of Re or could dwell in the netherworld with Osiris, although the latter view was now becoming increasingly dominant. The floors of some Middle Kingdom coffins bear texts and illustrations from a work known as the Book of the Two Ways, which describes alternative routes to the abode of the dead and served as a guide to the deceased on the journey.

The transference of funerary inscriptions from the walls of pyramid-chambers to the interior of coffins had broken the royal monopoly of such texts, but far more widespread distribution amongst the ordinary people was brought about by the New Kingdom development of writing the religious texts upon papyrus. A roll of papyrus could be quickly prepared and was easily available to persons of no great wealth and, from the New Kingdom, burials were regularly equipped with the necessary magical texts upon such scrolls. These texts, a further development of the earlier funerary inscriptions, constitute the important Book of the Dead, in which a large number of separate chapters were included. The Book of the Dead was to remain the most important single funerary book right down to the Ptolemaic Period, but it underwent a number of revisions during its long history. The best versions of the chapters belong to the Eighteenth and Nineteenth Dynasties; in later times the contents of individual papyri were often composed of selected chapters or a miscellaneous collection of spells.

Early copies of the Book of the Dead are written in vertical lines of hieroglyphs with the chapter titles and some other significant points highlighted by the use of red ink in place of the usual black. The papyri soon came to be illustrated by small vignettes in black outline, inserted into the text at appropriate points. Later on, particularly in the Nineteenth Dynasty, the vignettes were painted in colours and became small works of art in their own right (plate 19). However, the increasing attention devoted to the illustrations was matched by a decline in the standard of the text, and many of the beautifully coloured funerary papyri bear inscriptions which are full of mistakes. By the Twenty-First and Twenty-Second Dynasties the vignettes were sometimes inserted in places where they had no relevance to the accompanying text, and the choice of what to include or omit in a papyrus was largely a matter of individual taste. In the worst cases, earlier chapters were re-copied in the reverse order by error, or any odd sections of text would be amalgamated to fill the spaces between the vignettes, without any care being taken to adhere to the standard chapters. At this date some of the papyri were inscribed in hieratic, although hieroglyphs always remained popular for funerary texts. A major revision of the Book of the Dead took place in the Twenty-Sixth Dynasty, involving the re-establishment of some order in the chapters and a return to the simple outlined vignettes. Although papyrus copies of the Book of the Dead were by far the most popular means of taking these important funerary spells into the tomb, it should be noted that certain chapters could be inscribed upon tomb-walls or coffins. That the ancient Egyptians themselves did not comprehend much of the content of the spells is shown by the frequent errors which occur in the writing, but the actual meaning of the texts was of secondary importance; it was their effect which mattered. The roll of papyrus with its inscriptions and vignettes was regarded as the means of reaching the next world in safety, avoiding all the obstacles which barred the way.

It should be noted that the term 'Book of the Dead' is a modern one; the Egyptians themselves referred to these texts as the 'Chapters of Coming Forth by Day'. This title alludes to the power of the inscriptions to enable an individual to emerge from the tomb after death. The Egyptian concept of the underworld included a whole series of traps and pitfalls for the unprepared, which could only be evaded if the spirit of the deceased knew the correct procedure to follow and the appropriate speeches to recite at certain points on his journey. These answers were all contained in the chapters of the Book of the Dead, and all the deceased had to do in order to reach his goal was to follow the instructions laid down in the papyrus. There was never really any doubt concerning the success of the soul in making the journey, because the papyri always record that the individuals for whom they were written overcame all difficulties and eventually reached the domain of Osiris. Travelling to the next world was very much like taking an examination with prior knowledge of all the questions and a supply of prepared answers in one's possession. Belief in the efficacy of magical spells to influence events was central to Egyptian funerary religion, and was an offshoot of the strong belief in the power of the written word, which we have already noted in the offering cult.

An important element in the transfer to the next world was the judgement of the deceased, described in chapter 125 of the Book of the Dead. By the second half of the Eighteenth Dynasty this concept had become so strong that an introductory section to the Book of the Dead was provided, containing a large illustration of the final judgement, together with hymns to Re and Osiris. In this test, the conduct of the individual upon earth was assessed by weighing the heart in a balance against the feather of Maat, goddess of truth and justice. Plate 19 shows a fine vignette of this scene, from the papyrus of a scribe named Ani. The deceased enters on the left, with his wife, bowing down as they come into the judgement hall. Around the figures is written a speech of Ani, consisting of an appeal to his own heart not to betray him. The heart itself appears in the left-hand pan of the balance, with the feather of Maat on the right; the actual weighing is carried out by the jackal-headed Anubis and the result is recorded by Thoth, scribe of the gods. Behind the latter figure crouches the monster Ammit, a creature with the head of a crocodile, foreparts of a lion and hindquarters of a hippopotamus. His name means, 'Eater of the Dead', and his function was to devour the hearts of those who failed to pass the test. In fact, his services were never required, because all the papyri record a favourable verdict. Thoth reports the outcome of the judgement to the assessor-gods, shown at the top, and their reply is given in the inscription above the figure of Anubis:

Words spoken by the Great Ennead to Thoth, who dwells in Hermopolis: 'What you have said is true. The Osiris scribe Ani, justified, is righteous. He has committed no crime nor has he acted against us. Ammit shall not be permitted to prevail over him. Let there be given to him of the bread-offerings which go before Osiris, and a permanent grant of land in the Fields of Offerings, as for the followers of Horus.'

In this vignette only a selection of the major divinities are shown presiding over the judgement, but chapter 125 states that the examination took place in the presence of forty-two assessors, each of whom had to be addressed in turn by the deceased. This spell makes it quite clear that the person under test was not expected to await the decision of the gods meekly, but to be effusive in the proclamation of his righteousness. He effectively demanded access to paradise as a right rather than a privilege, and there is no trace in his statements of any sense of repentance for misdemeanours on earth. The address to the gods on entering the judgement hall is termed the 'Negative Confession' by Egyptologists, because various sins are denied in turn, but it is really a somewhat misleading name, since the deceased does not confess to anything; instead, he simply enumerates his virtues:

'I have not acted evilly towards anyone; I have not impoverished associates; I have not done evil instead of righteousness; I do not know what is not [correct]. I have not committed sins. I have not set tasks at the start of each day harder than I had set previously. My name has not reached the Pilot of the Bark. I have not reviled the god. I have not robbed the orphan, nor have I done what the god detests. I have not slandered a servant to his master. I have not made anyone miserable, nor have I made anyone weep. I have not killed, nor have I ordered anyone to execution. I have not made anyone suffer. I have not diminished the food-offerings in the temples, nor have I damaged the bread-offerings of the gods. I have not stolen the cakes of the blessed. I have not copulated [unlawfully], nor have I indulged in fornication. I have not increased nor diminished the measure: I have not diminished the palm. I have not encroached on fields. I have not added to the weights in the balance. I have not taken milk from a child's mouth. I have not driven herds from their fodder. I have not snared birds for the harpoons of the gods; I have not caught the fish of their [lakes]. I have not stopped the flow of water at its seasons; I have not built a dam against flowing water. I have not extinguished a fire in its time. I have not [failed to observe] the days for [offering] haunches of meat. I have not kept cattle from the property of the god. I have not opposed the god at his processions.'

After this tirade of self-righteousness, the deceased continues with a statement of his purity and asserts:

No evil shall befall me in this land in this Hall of the Two Truths, because I know the names of the gods who exist in it, the followers of the Great God.[2]

The very elevated moral standards revealed by the statements in the address to the gods may have served as an underlying force for righteous conduct in ancient Egypt. It is clear that everyone knew the correct way to act, and even if they might fall short of the righteous path from time to time, the very existence of such knowledge would tend to preserve a tolerant society. The Book of the Dead recognized the fact that people were not faultless and attempted to protect them from the consequences of their sins by magical spells. The long passage quoted above is introduced by the words, 'What to say when arriving at the Hall of the Two Truths, purging the deceased from all the evil he has done'.[3] This statement is an open admission that the person under judgement had not been entirely free from guilt, but it also reassures him with the guarantee that his faults will not come to the notice of the assessors, provided he recites the formulae correctly. In addition to the general declaration of innocence made by the deceased, he was also required to address each of the forty-two assessor-gods in turn by their names. Knowing the names of deities or demons on the route to the next world was essential if the journey was to be completed in safety, because the Egyptians believed that to know someone's name was to have power over them. All the names which it would be necessary for a person to know in order to reach the netherworld were detailed in the chapters of the Book of the Dead. These names were not only those of divinities: even the architectural features of the different gates and halls which had to be traversed possessed their own names:

'We will not allow you to enter past us,' say the jambs of this door, 'unless you say our name.' Accurate Plumb-bob is your name. 'I will not allow you to enter past me,' says the right lintel of this door, 'unless you say my name.' Pan for Weighing Truth is your name. 'I will not allow you to enter past me,' says the left lintel of this door, 'unless you say my name.' Offering of Wine is your name. 'I will not allow you to pass over me,' says the threshold of this door, 'unless you say my name.' Ox of Geb is your name. 'I will not open for you,' says the bolt of this door, 'unless you say my name.' Toe of his Mother is your name.[4]

This question-and-answer session is carried out at various points in the Book of the Dead, and the soul is only permitted to pass on after he has supplied the correct responses to all the questioners. Some parts of the interrogation seem to go into extremes of detail, as in the following passage, where the traveller is required to know the correct magical names of his own feet:

'I will not allow you to tread on me,' says the floor of the Hall of the Two Truths. Why, pray, I am pure? 'Because I do not know the names of the feet with which you tread on me. Say them to me.' Flames of Ha is the name of my right foot; *Wnpt* of Hathor is the name of my left foot. 'You know us; enter then in over us.'[5]

Many chapters of the Book of the Dead refer to gates, halls or districts through which the soul had to pass, each guarded by a fierce divinity who had to be addressed by name (fig. 48). This concept of separate divisions in the netherworld is encountered again in other funerary texts, which will be described later. As in the earlier Pyramid and Coffin Texts, some chapters of the Book of the Dead are concerned with the need to protect the corpse from the attack of noxious creatures, or to re-establish the living faculties. Chapters 21 and 22 provide the deceased with a mouth, chapter 25 gives him the power of memory, while several chapters guard against the removal of the heart from the body. The opinion of the texts over the final destination of the soul is divided, having taken over this confusion from the Pyramid and Coffin Texts.

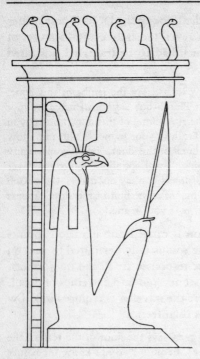

Fig.48.One of the gates from the Book
of the Dead, with its guardian

Certain sections adhere to the old philosophy that the soul was
intended to join the boat of Re and sail around the sky with the
god, but more emphasis is laid upon the alternative viewpoint of
a permanent home for the spirit in the domain of Osiris. This abode
was known by the names 'The Fields of Offerings' and 'The Fields
of Reeds', and was a place in which the souls of the dead lived a
utopian existence in a land of plenty. This vision of paradise was
modelled upon the land of Egypt itself, and the illustrations in the
funerary papyri show the Fields of Offerings intersected by the
irrigation channels typical of the Egyptian countryside. In this
domain the deceased carries on the same agricultural tasks as upon
earth, ploughing, sowing and reaping the crops in the fields
between the canals (plate 21). However, the duplication of Egyptian agricultural life was not quite identical, because in the land of
Osiris everything had been made considerably better than on earth.

Pests did not exist, the wheat grew to a height of five cubits, the ears being two cubits in length, and the barley was seven cubits high, with ears of three cubits. Since the length of the cubit was about 53 cm, it is clear that the Egyptians expected rich harvests in paradise. It was to carry out the cultivation of these crops that shabti-figures were provided, enabling the deceased to enjoy the benefits of the harvest without having to do any work. This was the ancient Egyptian view of paradise, a parallel world to the Nile Valley, in which everything was for the best and perpetual life was assured under the benign authority of Osiris. Perhaps the great popularity of this view of the next world was due to the attraction of a home in a land which was essentially familiar, owing to its similarity to the Egypt of the living. This concept offered a bright future of comfortable existence, rather than the strange and gloomy progress through the sky and the underworld proposed for the solar afterlife in the boat of Re. The optimistic view of life beyond the grave is summarized by the rubric to chapter 99 of the Book of the Dead:

If this chapter is known [by the deceased] he shall come into the Fields of Reeds, and bread, wine and cakes shall be given to him at the altar of the Great God, and fields and an estate [sown] with wheat and barley, which the Followers of Horus shall reap for him. He shall eat of that wheat and barley and his limbs shall be nourished by it, and his body shall be like the bodies of the gods, and he shall emerge into the Fields of Reeds in any form whatever he likes, and he shall appear there regularly and continually.

Papyrus rolls inscribed with personal copies of the Book of the Dead were placed in the tomb at the time of burial, and were often laid between the legs of the mummy in its coffin. From the Third Intermediate Period, it became customary to place the roll within a hollow wooden figure of the composite divinity Ptah-Seker-Osiris, whose presence in the tomb was considered beneficial to the resurrection of the corpse. Not all Books of the Dead were specially prepared from the outset for a particular individual; we know that it was possible to buy 'off the shelf' copies in which spaces had been left in the text for the name of the purchaser to be inserted; mass-produced coffins could be purchased in the same way.

Study of the funerary religion of the ancient Egyptians sometimes offers explanations for apparently purposeless objects found
in tombs. For example, chapter 137A of the Book of the Dead
states that the text, in order to be really effective, should be
inscribed upon four model bricks of clay, which were then to be
walled up in recesses in the walls of the burial chamber. Such
inscribed bricks have actually been found, their purpose, so the text
informs us, being to repel the enemies of Osiris from the tomb.
Religion could also have profound effects upon the architecture of
tombs, especially those of royalty. The pyramids of the Old Kingdom were regarded in the solar religion as a concrete symbol of
the descending rays of the sun, up which the dead king would
mount to the sky. At the same time, certain passages of the
Pyramid Texts show that the pyramid could also represent the
primeval mound, that is, the first piece of land to appear from the

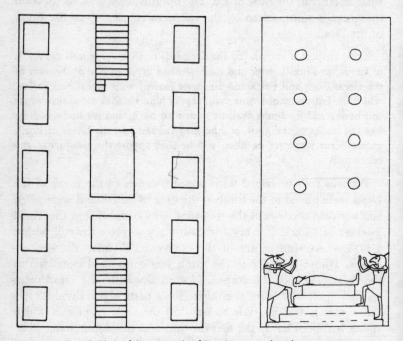

*Fig.49.Plan of the cenotaph of Seti I compared with an ancient
illustration of the tomb of Osiris*

inert ocean in the Egyptian view of the creation of the world. By the New Kingdom, the increasing importance of the Osiris cult, coupled with the identification of the king with the god, led to the royal tomb being made as a model of the tomb of Osiris himself. This is seen in its best form in the cenotaph of Seti I at Abydos, which fulfils all the requirements of an Osiris-tomb. The structure was underground, covered by a mound, which probably had a sacred grove of trees upon it, and the subterranean building possessed columns and a sarcophagus chamber on an island surrounded by water. Figure 49 shows the similarity between this structure and the Egyptian view of the tomb of Osiris, derived from an illustrated funerary papyrus. Of course, this cenotaph was deliberately built as a close model of the Osiris-tomb, to serve as a funerary monument for both the dead King Seti and the god in the main cult-centre of Osiris. In the Valley of the Kings at Thebes it was impossible to duplicate all these features, but the basic resemblance in the layout of the burial chamber was retained. In addition to its Osirian connections, the burial chamber also symbolized the entire cosmos, the roof representing the sky and the floor the earth, and this symbolism was confirmed by the addition of appropriate decoration. Even in the Old Kingdom, the roofs of pyramid-chambers were covered with stars in paint or relief, to imitate the night sky. The New Kingdom royal tombs have ceiling decoration which includes star maps with groups of stellar divinities and religious books concerned with the daily birth of the sun. The sarcophagus usually stood upon a separate block of stone – set into the floor of the chamber – which was intended to represent the primeval mound. Placing a burial either upon or beneath a symbolic copy of this mound was considered of great importance for the resurrection of the body, owing to the spontaneous appearance of life upon the original mound of the creation myths.

The funerary texts of royal tombs during the New Kingdom were inscribed on the walls of the tombs themselves, instead of being written on papyrus as was the usual custom for private persons. Private tombs often contain scenes of everyday life, but these are excluded from the royal monuments in favour of a whole series of different religious inscriptions. The Book of the Dead, strangely enough, is not very prominent among these texts, most of which are concerned with the general theme of the progress of the sun through the day and night. By day the sun travelled across the sky, illuminating the land of Egypt and ensuring stability and order, but at night the god had to pass through the underworld, on a dangerous and difficult journey, to reach the next dawn (fig. 50). The fate of the dead king was associated with that of the sun-god, and the forces of evil, which might attempt to hinder the progress of the solar boat during the hours of darkness, were regarded as a threat to the king himself. A convenient link was made between the solar and Osirian views of the afterlife by assuming that the sun-god was effectively dead during the night, and therefore was identical both to Osiris and to the dead king.

Fig.50. The boat of the sun-god

The major books which follow this story are termed 'The Book of Gates', 'The Book of What is in the Underworld' and 'The Book of Caverns'. The last-named consists of six divisions, but the others divide the journey through the underworld into twelve sections, corresponding to the twelve hours of the night. In all three compositions the sun-god confers life upon those who dwell in the underworld, with the exception of the enemies of Re and Osiris, who are exterminated. Each book ends with the rebirth of the sun at dawn. The god descended into the underworld as Atum and re-emerged from the eastern horizon at Kheperi, 'he who comes into existence', represented in the scenes by the scarab beetle. The Book of Caverns shows the scarab pushing along the disk of the sun, just as a real scarab beetle may be seen pushing the ball of dung in which it lays its eggs (fig. 51). The emergence of new beetles from a seemingly lifeless ball of dung was the reason why the scarab became so closely linked with resurrection in Egyptian belief.

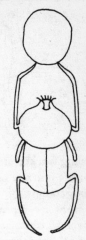

Fig. 51. The scarab with the disk of the sun

In both the Book of Caverns and the Book of Gates is a scene depicting the Judgement Hall of Osiris, which was reached by the sun-god in the middle of the night. Other parts of the underworld were populated by all kinds of mysterious beings, who could be either good or evil. The former rejoiced at the approach of the sun-god and his retinue and aided him in his journey by overcoming the evil-doers and rendering them ineffective. One of the chief opponents of Re was the serpent Apopis, who had to be slain or immobilized (fig. 52). In the seventh division of the Book of What is in the Underworld we see the Apopis-serpent defeated by the knives of four goddesses, who are described by the caption: 'They are of this form, carrying their knives, and they punish Apopis in the underworld every day.'⁶ The eventual fate of all the opponents of Re was complete destruction, their bodies and even their souls

Fig. 52. The defeat of Apopis from the Book of What is in the Underworld

Fig.53.Burning the enemies of Re and Osiris

being hacked up and burnt in pits of fire (fig. 53). The outcome of the journey of the solar bark was a foregone conclusion, like the judgements of the Book of the Dead, because the inscriptions emphasize repeatedly that Re, Osiris and the dead king triumph over all obstacles to emerge again into the day. During the hours of daylight the underworld was totally dark and inert, and the gods who dwelt in it were considered to be dead, awaiting the return of the sun to grant them another brief period of life and light. In order to increase the mysterious nature of the texts, the Egyptians often wrote the columns of hieroglyphs in the reverse of the usual order, the so-called 'retrograde' inscriptions, or in cryptograms. At some points in the inscriptions we find a hieroglyphic label stating, 'found destroyed'. This shows that the scribe was copying the text from an earlier version which was damaged in places, and the use of this caption marks for us those points where the scribe could not see what to copy. This feature is more common in the Late Period versions of the same texts, by which time rather more had been lost. The texts are also full of errors, due to the miscopying of individual hieroglyphic signs or the accidental omission of certain passages. During the Late Period these funerary books were inscribed upon the walls of tombs, or, more frequently, on stone sarcophagi, but they were no longer restricted to monuments of royalty. Just as the Pyramid Texts had been usurped by commoners, so the royal funerary inscriptions of the New Kingdom were adopted by wealthy private individuals of the Late and Ptolemaic Periods. The Book of What is in the Underworld occurs more frequently in the Late Period than that of Gates or Caverns, and exists on sarcophagi of both royal and private persons. Papyrus copies are also known.

These texts are not the whole of Egyptian funerary literature by any means, but, with the Book of the Dead, they are the most important. From royal tombs and sarcophagi of the New Kingdom we also have copies of the Book of Night and Day, concerning the birth of the sun from the goddess Nut, the Book of Aker, the earth-god, and the Book of the Divine Cow. The great number and extent of the funerary compositions of Egypt show how important it was considered to be that no soul should go into the next world without being fully prepared, and the inscriptions reveal an interesting combination of religion and magic to achieve this end. Amulets attached to the mummy could be rendered effective by the recitation of spells from the Book of the Dead, and the objects themselves were sometimes inscribed with the same texts. This practice was carried out according to instructions given in the Book of the Dead itself; at the conclusion of chapter 159, for example, we find the note: '[This chapter] shall be recited over a *wadj*-amulet of green felspar upon which it has been inscribed, and the *wadj*-amulet shall be placed on the neck of the deceased.'[7] Instructions with spell 162, intended to provide warmth to the head, state that the text should be written on a piece of fresh papyrus and placed under the head of the mummy. In Late Period times this papyrus was mounted on a circular piece of cartonnage to form a more permanent object, of the type now known as hypocephali (plate 22).

Most amulets worked on the principle of sympathetic magic; that is, the belief that an image of an object or creature could act for or against the item represented, depending on the spells associated with its use. This kind of magic appears elsewhere in Egyptian life, particularly in anti-foreigner rites, in which images of Egypt's enemies would be maltreated or destroyed. We have already noted how amulets in the form of parts of the body could restore the living functions by this power of imitation but, equally, amulets representing certain objects of power could in the same manner confer that power upon the deceased. An example of the latter type is the amulet of the royal crown, which bestowed on the mummy the authority which it represented. Many amuletic forms were derived from images of gods, or of items associated with particular deities. The *wdjat*-eye is a good illustration. This common amulet represents the eye of Horus, which had been torn out and broken up in combat with Seth. It was later restored by Thoth, and consequently acquired the name *wdjat*, 'the healthy [eye]' (fig. 54A). Also associated with divinities were the *Tyet* symbol (fig. 54B), representing protection by the blood of Isis, and the scarab, which was the image of Kheperi, the deity of resurrection. Other amulets were derived from the hieroglyphic signs for such words as 'good', 'eternity' or 'truth'.

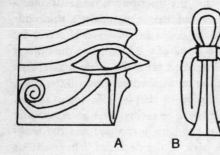

Fig.54.(A) *The eye of Horus*
(B) *The* Tyet *symbol of Isis*

A   B

Some chapters of the Book of the Dead specify the materials of which certain amulets were to be made, for it seems that the use of the correct material was thought to have magical benefits. Green felspar, rock-crystal and haematite were popular, but vast numbers of amulets were also manufactured in the cheaper green-glazed composition. The magical properties of wax figures were particularly marked; they were employed for images of the four sons of Horus and also for the earliest shabti-figures.

The Egyptian belief in the ability of any image or representation to possess magical powers sometimes manifests itself in extraordinary ways. In the hieroglyphic script were a large number of signs illustrating animals, some of which, such as scorpions or snakes, were decidedly unpleasant. If these signs were employed in the inscriptions of a burial chamber or coffin, what was to prevent them from coming to life by magic and harming the deceased? Even the less dangerous creatures could be a problem if they should happen to consume the food-offerings intended for the tomb-owner. At certain periods the Egyptians took care to guard against this danger by carving hieroglyphs which were deliberately left

incomplete to deprive them of the power of life. This practice
occurs already in the Pyramid Texts and is more common in the
funerary inscriptions of the Middle Kingdom. Figures of snakes
were incomplete, animals and birds were carved without legs, scorpions lack their stings and hieroglyphs showing human beings are
reduced to only the head and arms. An example of these so-called
'mutilated hieroglyphs' from the coffin of Princess Nubheteptikh-
ered is given in figure 55. The prevalence of magic in funerary
belief is also demonstrated by the fact that objects placed in the
tomb were sometimes deliberately broken in order to 'kill' them
before they went to accompany the deceased.

Fig.55.Mutilated hieroglyphs

The deities associated with death and burial were very numerous, even if we exclude the vast armies of semi-divinities found in
the underworld as depicted in the funerary books of the New Kingdom royal tombs. Osiris, king of the dead, appears everywhere in
mortuary inscriptions, but there are also many invocations to more
local necropolis-gods, including Hathor, Mertseger, the deified
King Amenophis I and Sokar. Anubis, as the embalmer-god, and
Wepwawet, another jackal-headed divinity, were a regular part of
funerary religion. Although Isis and Nephthys were not exclusively related to mortuary contexts, their role as divine mourners
means that they appear regularly in tomb-inscriptions or on
coffins. A number of funerary deities are associated together in
the mythology surrounding the Canopic jars, in which the viscera were preserved. In Chapter 2 we saw how the earliest true
jars for viscera appeared in the Old Kingdom, but these vessels had
simple convex lids and lacked the religious formulae inscribed on
their later counterparts. In the Middle Kingdom, the jars had stop-
pers in the form of human heads, representing the owner, and after
the Eighteenth Dynasty we encounter lids with heads appropriate

to the four sons of Horus, guardians of the
entrails: Imset had a human head, Hapy
a baboon head, Qebhsenuef a falcon
head and Duwamutef a jackal head
(fig. 56). In theory, each god
protected a specific organ, Imset
looking after the liver, Hapy the
lungs, Qebhsenuef the intestines
and Duwamutef the stomach.
Despite the absence of the
different heads on jars prior to
the Nineteenth Dynasty, we
know that these same deities
were linked with the Canopics
because of the occurrence of
their names in the texts.
In addition, the jars were
identified with the goddesses Isis,
Nephthys, Neith and Selkis,
whose names are likewise found
in the inscriptions. These texts
show that the embalmed contents
of the vases were not simply under
the protection of the four sons of
Horus, but were actually identified
with them: 'O Isis, may you
take care over Imset who is
within you! The revered one before
Imset, the King of Upper and Lower Egypt, Aw-ib-re.'[8]

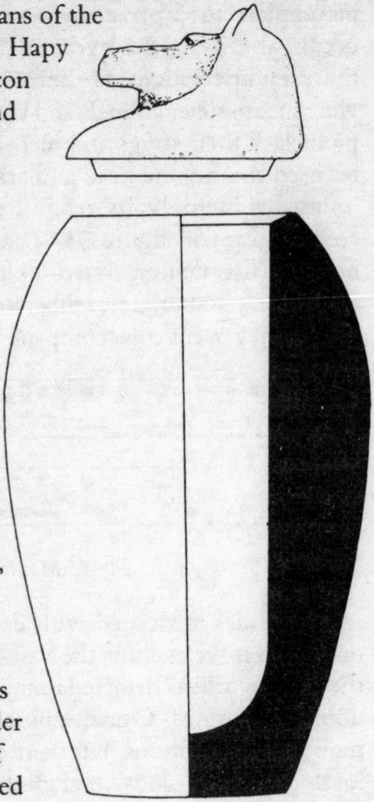

*Fig.56.Canopic jar with the
head of Duwamutef*

Each of the four sons of Horus was always associated with the
same goddess: Isis protecting Imset, as in the above example,
Nephthys with Hapy, Neith with Duwamutef and Selkis with
Qebhsenuef. The length and content of the inscriptions varies on
different jars, but the basic message is the same. In many cases the
texts were regarded as speeches made by the goddesses of the Canopics, and by the Late Period these often appear in a form which
shows very well the roles of the different Canopic divinities:

Words spoken by Neith: 'I spend day and night of every day in making protection for Duwamutef who is within me. The protection of the Osiris, the commander of the army Neferibre-emakhet, son of the commander of the army Psamtik-sineith, born of Tadinubhotpe, justified, is the protection of Duwamutef, because of the Osiris commander of the army Neferibre-emakhet, son of the commander of the army Psamtik-sineith, he is Duwamutef.'[9]

Canopic jars were manufactured in a variety of materials, including stone, wood, pottery and glazed composition (plate 23). Not all were functional; during the Twenty-First Dynasty the viscera were returned to the body after treatment, but a set of Canopics was often provided in the tomb for purely traditional reasons. In similar fashion, jars were sometimes placed with mummies even when no evisceration had been carried out. Occasionally, we find elaborate substitutes for the conventional jars, such as the miniature golden coffins for viscera found in the tomb of Tutankhamun. The Canopic jars could be enclosed inside a box of wood or stone, the exterior surfaces of which were sometimes used for supplementary inscriptions invoking the usual protective gods and goddesses of the viscera. Stone Canopic chests, often with plain surfaces, have been found in many royal pyramids of the Old and Middle Kingdoms (fig. 57). In the unfinished pyramid of the Thirteenth Dynasty at south Saqqara, both the Canopic box and sarcophagus had actually been cut out in one piece with the floor of the burial chamber. In the New Kingdom, the royal Canopic chests became more decorative, with inscriptions and relief-work on the exterior, sometimes with blue pigment in the hollows of the carving. These boxes were often made of alabaster and had figures of the goddesses

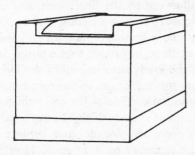

Fig.57. Stone Canopic chest of the Middle Kingdom

Isis, Nephthys, Neith and Selkis in relief at the corners, with their wings extended to enclose and protect the contents. Private Canopic chests were most frequently made of wood, with four internal compartments to accommodate the four vessels. The Middle Kingdom boxes are simple rectangular affairs with flat lids, but in later times a new style arose, consisting of a container in the form of a shrine mounted upon a sledge base. This type is sometimes illustrated in the funerary procession as depicted in tomb-scenes or papyri of the New Kingdom and later (fig. 58).

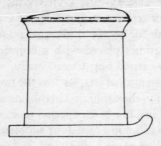

Fig.58.Canopic box in the form of a shrine

It is in the paintings of the burial ceremonies that we find certain very ancient rituals which stem from religious beliefs handed down from the beginning of Egyptian history. A number of wall-scenes in tombs of the Old Kingdom and later show episodes from a kind of pilgrimage made by the funeral cortege to various cult-centres, most of them in Lower Egypt. Brief mention of this journey has been made during the description of an ancient Egyptian burial in Chapter 3, but we have now to explain the origin and religious significance of this pilgrimage. In Middle and New Kingdom tombs the ritual is heavily influenced by the Osiris cult, and one of the places visited by the funerary boat is Abydos, but the Old Kingdom versions show that the pilgrimage was not originally connected with Osiris. In fact, the scenes allude to the burial rites of the ancient rulers of Buto, the Predynastic capital of the Delta, and refer back to a time before the unification of the country as a single state. It seems that the burial cortege of the early chiefs of Buto had visited the main religious centres of the Delta, notably Sais and Heliopolis, but sometimes also Mendes and Behbeit el-Hagar, before returning to the cemetery of Buto itself. Here the dead ruler was greeted by dancers, representing his ancestors, who in the later tomb-scenes appear as the Muu, the ritual dancers of the necropolis. The representations in private tombs are an echo of this ancient royal mortuary tradition, re-interpreted and applied to the burial of ordinary individuals. Reliefs in Old Kingdom mastabas show the funeral barge landing at Buto and Sais to be met by a lector-priest and the Muu. The towns are indicated by the symbols of their religious buildings; Buto is represented by a row of vaulted shrines interspersed by palm trees, while Sais is shown

 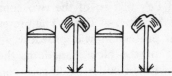

Fig. 59. The emblems of Sais and Buto

by the two flagstaffs which stood before the temple of Neith in the city (fig. 59). The shrine of Buto, known as the Per-Nu in Egyptian, was an extremely important symbol and came to be regarded as the national shrine of Lower Egypt.

In the later tomb-scenes of the New Kingdom, the true significance of these representations was forgotten, and they were perpetuated merely as a mortuary tradition. The drawings of Sais and Buto, originally shown on separate registers, were often amalgamated into a single group by the artist. In figure 60, taken from the Eighteenth Dynasty tomb of Rekhmire at Thebes, the flagstaffs of Sais have been linked by error to create a door, with the palms and shrines of Buto placed above.

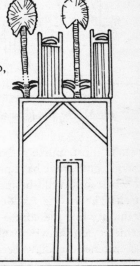

*Fig. 60. Combined emblems of Sais and Buto
from the tomb of Rekhmire at Thebes*

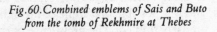

The connection of the pilgrimage with the old royal burial ceremonies of Buto had been completely forgotten, and it was instead
associated with Osiris, with the addition of his main cult-centres
of Abydos and Busiris to the list of places visited. The ritual
dancers, the Muu, now met the funeral procession at the necropolis
wherever it happened to be, and were considered only as acces-
sories to the burial rites, their origin in the royal ancestors of Buto
having been lost in the passage of time. The hieroglyphic labels on
the tomb-scenes preserve a link with the origin of the ritual,
because even in the New Kingdom they retained their archaic character. Groups of figures are labelled 'The People of Dep', or 'The
People of Pe', that is, of the two contiguous settlements which
made up the town of Buto. The presence of these individuals in
the burial procession was probably a complete mystery to the
Egyptians of the New Kingdom; they simply carried on the
tradition without understanding its content. Figure 61 shows the
conventional manner in which the visit to Sais and Buto was
depicted in the New Kingdom.

Fig.61. The visit to Sais and Buto from the tomb of Paheri at El-Kab

It is most unlikely that these religious pilgrimages were ever
carried out; as we have noted previously, the mere presence of the
tomb-scenes could be just as beneficial to the owner as the ritual
itself. The visit to Abydos was occasionally acted out in symbolic
fashion while the corpse was being ferried across the Nile to the
cemetery on the west bank, and it is possible that some of the older
ceremonies may have been similarly mimed. The prevalence of the

old representations is a good example of the Egyptian liking for continuity with earlier religious customs, especially in the sphere of funerary belief, and the lack of true understanding of the rites only added to their mystery and appeal.

In keeping with the usual Egyptian line of thought, the pilgrimages were considered to have been made by boat, travelling along the Nile channels through the Delta. The presence of boats in this ritual may be a partial explanation for the burial of full-sized boats close to some Egyptian tombs, particularly certain royal pyramids of the Old and Middle Kingdoms. The significance of these boats has been a matter of some discussion, because they could be linked with a number of different religious concepts. Either they are solar boats representing the bark of Re, in which the king would travel after death, or they might be connected with the ritual pilgrimage to Buto, or they could simply have been intended as a means of transport for their owner. Although the boats of the pyramid age may have been of a solar character, this is unlikely to be true of much earlier boats buried alongside First Dynasty mastabas of nobles at Saqqara and Helwan, because the solar cult had not attained any great importance at that time. Probably the correct interpretation is that the boat-burials do not originate from any single concept, but are the result of a mixture of beliefs, in which both the solar religion and the earlier funerary rituals of Buto are represented.

A remarkable feature of Egyptian funerary religion is its complexity, which developed as new beliefs were incorporated without older ones being discarded. The funerary inscriptions of the Book of the Dead are a typical example. We have seen how spells were required to pass individual obstacles on the way to paradise, despite the fact that the Egyptians had already included certain wide-ranging spells offering safe passage to the next world in a single package. It would have simplified matters greatly to have discarded all the superfluous individual spells and to have reduced the entire Book of the Dead to a single-line guarantee of safe access to the netherworld, but it was not in the Egyptian character to do so. This inability to rationalize a mass of duplicate material into a simpler and more efficient form can be seen in other aspects of the culture, a prime example being the retention of hundreds of phonetic signs in the language when they could have been replaced by an already extant alphabet of twenty-four signs. On the other hand, the same inability to adopt rapid changes contributed greatly to the stable and resilient nature of Egyptian civilization, and was probably the reason why it lasted so long.

7

COFFINS AND SARCOPHAGI

In an earlier chapter, some mention was made of the first attempts of the Egyptians to protect the body from the filling of the grave by enclosing it within a container of some kind, usually a simple affair of basketwork or wood. From these humble beginnings there developed a progressive series of more elaborate coffins, varying in style and decoration at different periods. The development of coffins and sarcophagi as the ultimate receptacles of the corpse was greatly affected by religious belief, and the coffins themselves soon acquired their own religious symbolism. The entire coffin, but more especially the lid, came to be identified with the sky-goddess Nut, who is often depicted on the interior. When the goddess is shown on the underside of the lid, the latter is to be interpreted as symbolically equivalent to the sky. On the floor of the coffin the figure of Nut is sometimes replaced by Hathor or Sokar, as divinities of the necropolis. By the time of the Old Kingdom, the religious symbolism of the sarcophagus was firmly established, as is clear from certain passages in the Pyramid Texts:

Nephthys has collected all your members for you in this her name of 'Seshat, Lady of Builders'. [She] has made them healthy for you, you having been given to your mother Nut in her name of 'Sarcophagus'; she has embraced you in her name of 'Coffin', and you have been brought to her in her name of 'Tomb'.[1]

The wooden coffins of the Early Dynastic Period, the first true coffins to appear, were made in both short and long versions for contracted and extended burials respectively, the latter gradually becoming the standard form. These coffins were made of small bars and planks of wood, held together by dowelling, a mode of construction which persisted until the latest times. The relative scarcity of good timber in the country made the Egyptians very economical in their woodworking, and they would much rather patch a coffin together from small pieces than resort to the wasteful carving of large beams. The Early Dynastic coffins had their own symbolism, often being made with recessed sides in the so-called 'palace-facade' design, common on the brick mastabas of the period (fig. 62). This is really a house facade, derived from primitive reed buildings, and its appearance on a coffin was an expression of the identification of the coffin with the dwelling of the deceased. The recessed panelling is by no means restricted to coffins of early date; it occurs sporadically on both wooden coffins and stone sarcophagi of all periods. This type of decoration was often combined with the use of a slightly vaulted lid, copied from the shape of the roofs of early buildings. Each deep recess on the side of a panelled coffin was intended to represent a doorway, and as such it provided an exit for the *Ka* of the occupant. In the Middle Kingdom, a door of the same type was shown entirely in paint on the flat surface of the coffin.

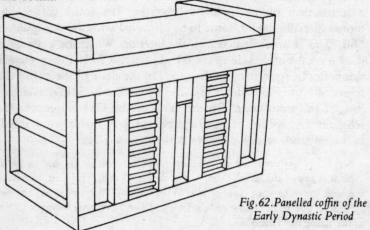

Fig.62.Panelled coffin of the Early Dynastic Period

From the Late Predynastic Period to the Old Kingdom a number of poor burials were made in large pots, as a substitute for a more expensive coffin. The body could be placed either inside the pot or beneath an inverted vessel, but in both cases the corpse had to be very tightly contracted. Sometimes one pot was used to contain the burial and another was placed on top as a cover. During the Old Kingdom, pot-burials could be protected by a corbelled structure of mud-brick, and in some of the poorest graves the pottery container was omitted, leaving the body covered by the brickwork alone.

The earliest stone sarcophagi, belonging to the Third Dynasty, are somewhat rough affairs in private tombs, consisting of a rectangular box of white limestone with plain sides and a slightly vaulted lid. Some finer examples have been recovered from royal burial-places, including the pyramid complexes of Djoser and Sekhemkhet. From subterranean galleries on the east side of the Djoser pyramid came a well-made sarcophagus of alabaster, hollowed from a single block, in the usual manner, again with a curved top.

Fig.63.Section of the sarcophagus of Sekhemkhet

The sarcophagus of Sekhemkhet is atypical, having a rising panel in one end instead of a conventional lid (fig. 63). During the Old Kingdom the tombs of royalty and of wealthy private individuals regularly possess very fine sarcophagi, their wealth being reflected in the enduring nature of the material or the quality of the decoration, which often takes the form of palace-facade panelling. The high nobility were, of course, only imitating royal practices in the use of elaborate stone sarcophagi, and there is some evidence to show that the provision of a fine sarcophagus was something which the king could order as a favour. The nobleman Uni, who lived in the Sixth Dynasty, records in his biographical inscription:

I asked the majesty of my lord that there might be brought for me a sarcophagus of white limestone from Tura. His majesty caused the seal-bearer of the god and a crew under his direction to ferry over in order to bring for me this sarcophagus from Tura. He returned with it, in a great transport-boat of the Residence, together with its lid...[2]

Lifting the cover of a stone sarcophagus was facilitated by two projecting bosses of stone at each end, which seem generally to have been left rather than being trimmed off after completion of the task. The bosses are quite large and are a regular feature of Old Kingdom sarcophagi, especially the finer examples. This may be due to the better-made lids being equal in length to the coffin, making some provision for lifting desirable; in many rough sarcophagi the bosses are absent, but the lid itself overlaps the coffin slightly at each end. The sarcophagi of poorer tombs continued to be made of limestone, many examples being left rough and un-inscribed on their exterior surfaces, with the chisel-marks of the stonemasons clearly evident. The texts on better-finished stone coffins of the Old Kingdom are normally quite brief and their content is generally restricted to a record of the name and titles of the owner. Wooden coffins were used to contain the body inside the larger sarcophagi of stone, the former being simple rectangular boxes with flat lids. Old Kingdom wooden coffins were made of irregularly shaped planks, which very often could not be joined without leaving numerous odd gaps. These deficiencies were filled by cutting small pieces of wood to the exact shape of the hole, fitting in the patch like a piece from a jigsaw, and fastening it in position with wooden pegs. The drawing in figure 64 shows this method of construction in one side of a typical coffin. The ends of the planks at the corners of the box were cut to a 45° mitre, so that the jointing of the corner could be effectively carried out. Once again, the fixing consisted of dowels. Old Kingdom coffins could be inscribed or painted, sometimes on both interior and exterior.

In addition to the name and titles of the owner, the interior decoration could include a conventional list of offerings, such as also
occur on the tomb-walls.

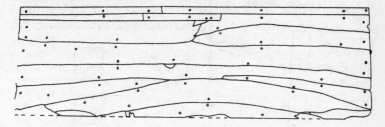

Fig.64.Construction of an Old Kingdom wooden coffin

The rectangular style of coffin with either a flat or vaulted top
was still in regular use in the Middle Kingdom, although considerable development in the construction and decoration had taken
place. Some of the poorer examples remained essentially similar to
their Old Kingdom antecedents, with the same patchwork of
rough boards, but the large coffins of the wealthy Middle Kingdom
nobles were of far superior construction, consisting of broad planks
of imported timber with straight joints running in level horizontal
lines along the sides. The neat appearance of this form of manufacture is shown in figure 65. Fine coffins like this were decorated
inside and out with paint applied directly to the wood; the rough
coffins of poorer individuals were often decorated on the exterior
alone, over a layer of plaster to conceal the irregular construction.

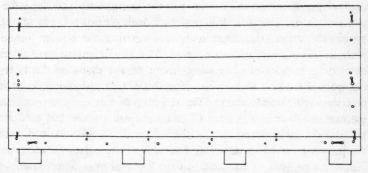

Fig.65.Construction of a Middle Kingdom wooden coffin

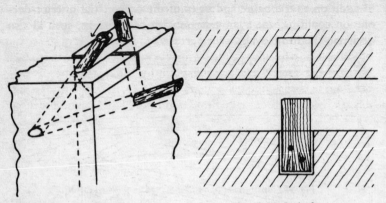

Fig.66.Dowels at the corner joint
of a Middle Kingdom coffin

Fig.67.Method of creating
a tenon joint

At the corners the mitred joints were stopped short of the ends of
the planks, where an overlapping tenon was cut to allow for more
secure dowelled fixing (fig. 66). As well as dowels, cord binding
and the occasional tenon joint were used to attach the planks,
although by no means so frequently. The tenons were not carved
from the wood; instead, a mortise was cut in the edge of both
planks, and a separate piece of wood was fixed in one slot to form
a projecting tenon (fig. 67). As in the stone sarcophagi of the Old
Kingdom, the lids of large wooden coffins were lifted by means
of a circular boss at each end. The wooden lids being so much
lighter in weight have only a single boss, which, unlike its stone
equivalent, was normally sawn off after completion of the interment. Rich burials were equipped with multiple coffins, one fitting
within the other, the outer coffin substituting for a stone sarcophagus. The decoration of good Middle Kingdom coffins is
extremely important, including many of the elements formerly
carved upon the tomb-walls. The outside of the finest type is
inscribed with horizontal and vertical lines of text in a conventional
pattern, as shown in figure 68. At the head on the left side are
painted the two sacred eyes, either alone or in combination with
a representation of an elaborate doorway of the palace-facade type.
The arrangement of the texts on the exterior was determined by
the position of the body, which was laid on its left side so that the

painted eyes on the coffin were immediately in front of the face of the occupant. These eyes, representing those of the god Horus, conferred protection upon the deceased and enabled him to see out of the coffin, while the painted doorway supplied him with a means of entry and egress. The starting-point for the inscriptions was the head of the corpse, the texts running away from this corner in both directions to the foot, as indicated on figure 68. Around the upper

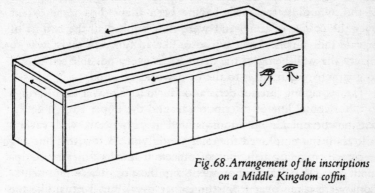

Fig.68.Arrangement of the inscriptions on a Middle Kingdom coffin

edge is a long horizontal inscription containing a conventional prayer for offerings and concluding with the name and titles of the owner. The vertical texts on the sides can be of two types: either a series of short phrases, each one complete in a single line, invoking divinities on behalf of the deceased, or a continuous text running on from one line to the next, taken from standard funerary inscriptions. These are the regular texts found on a great number of coffins; there are, of course, some exceptions with more varied and complex inscriptions.

The wooden inner coffin of Seni in the British Museum is a good example of the best type of Middle Kingdom decorated coffin. The three vertical columns of inscription shown in the photograph (plate 24) are to be read as a single running text, and they contain a spell adapted from the older Pyramid Texts: 'Your mother Nut has spread herself over you, she has caused you to become a god, and your enemies do not exist, O Seni!'³ The sky-goddess Nut is here identified with the lid of the coffin, as mentioned previously in this chapter. An additional link between the coffin lid and the sky is given by the decoration of the underside, showing the boat of the sun-god traversing the heavens. The floor of the coffin, on the other hand, represented the underworld and is painted with religious texts and vignettes illustrating different sections of that mythological region. These inscriptions, together with those on the lower areas of the sides inside the coffin, are written in the hieratic script and belong to an important group known as the Coffin Texts. They were derived from the earlier royal inscriptions of the pyramids, the spells having been adapted to some extent over the course of time, and were now applied to the coffins of private individuals. Their purpose, like all funerary texts, was to ensure the well-being of the deceased in every possible sense, and to guarantee his transfer to the next world as a god.

The remaining interior decoration includes a prayer for offerings in a horizontal line of inscription around the upper edge, like the text on the outside but often painted in finer detail, with several colours being employed for each hieroglyph. Below this line is a register containing paintings of objects from the funerary equipment and other items of amuletic significance. These representations were taken over from the earlier royal burial ritual like the Coffin Texts and do not accurately reflect the true possessions of a private individual. On the best coffins each item is labelled with its name.

Stone sarcophagi with rather similar decoration are known from tombs of the Eleventh Dynasty at Thebes, although they are not common. The sarcophagi of the princesses of the dynasty, found in their tombs at Deir el-Bahari, are somewhat different, having more varied decoration in which scenes of daily life are included. These sarcophagi are also unusual in having been constructed from separate slabs of limestone, fastened at the corners, instead of being monolithic. Sarcophagi of hard stone were employed for the royal tombs of the Twelfth and Thirteenth Dynasties, most examples having the traditional vaulted cover with raised ends. The sides of these coffins are sometimes plain but others have palace-facade panelling around the lower part, giving way to a flat surface above (fig. 69). On the plain area at the head end of the left side are the two amuletic eyes. Private stone sarcophagi with plain or panelled sides and vaulted lids occur in rich tombs of the Twelfth Dynasty,

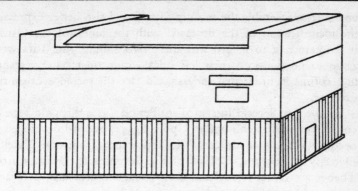

Fig.69.Panelled sarcophagus of the Middle Kingdom

notably at Riqqa and Illahun. The workmanship of some Middle Kingdom sarcophagi is remarkable; two examples from private tombs at Illahun had errors which could only be detected by the most painstaking measurement. Even greater accuracy of cutting was found in the sarcophagus of Sesostris II, in which the deviation of the edges from true parallel alignment, or of the sides from exact planes, is so small as to be virtually non-existent. Most sarcophagi, however, have not been sufficiently well examined to detect whether this degree of accuracy exists or not.

During the Middle Kingdom it became fashionable to provide a close-fitting mask to cover the head and shoulders of the mummy, with the face and wig represented in paint or even in gilding. These masks were made of linen strengthened with plaster, a material now generally known as cartonnage. This fabric could be moulded in three dimensions before the plaster set and so provided an opportunity for the careful modelling of the face, enabling a lifelike portrait to be fitted to the mummy inside the coffin. It is also in the Middle Kingdom that the first anthropoid coffins appear, some special examples with intricate locking devices having been already discussed in Chapter 4. Two fine anthropoid coffins were found at Rifa by Petrie; they are made of wood and elaborately painted, although the inscriptions are restricted to a single vertical line down the front. The adoption of the anthropoid form was an important step, since the coffin could be made to resemble the mummy itself, and also better expressed the identification of the deceased with the mummiform Osiris. It is interesting to record that these two coffins from Rifa were again found lying on their left sides within their outer rectangular coffins in order that they should face the sacred eyes on the exterior.

By the late Second Intermediate Period the anthropoid type of coffin was well established in Upper Egypt, but had developed to become somewhat different in appearance from the Twelfth Dynasty prototypes. Coffins of the Seventeenth Dynasty from Thebes are rather heavy and bulky, and are generally decorated with a pattern of feathered wings enveloping the case. This decoration is so characteristic that the name for coffins in this style is *rishi* - a derivation of the Arabic word for 'feather'. The feathers were intended to represent the wings of the goddesses Isis and Nephthys who, in the form of kites, were considered to be the divine mourners of the dead. Figures of the goddesses in this role appear frequently on coffins and sarcophagi of later periods, and they are also depicted in funerary papyri. The best *rishi* coffins were made for royalty, with the feathered decoration completely covered in gold-leaf instead of being rendered in paint. One example in the British Museum, belonging to King Nubkheperre Intef, has a substantial part of the original gilding preserved and is fitted with inlaid eyes. The cover of this coffin has been cut from a surprisingly large piece of wood, involving considerable waste in the process, instead of being patched together from small pieces in the more usual way. A few other examples of the wasteful carving of timber are known from the Second Intermediate Period. Certain rough coffins for private burials at Thebes were hollowed out from tree-trunks, but these normally retained much of the original shape of the trunk, and cannot be described as anthropoid. Child-coffins were also dug out from solid pieces of wood; they were of rectangular shape with a flat board as the lid. These coffins are usually devoid of decoration and are not very common. The more elaborate *rishi* coffins were made in sections and bear inscriptions in addition to their feathered decoration. This motif does appear on some coffins of later date, but in a more developed style. *Rishi* coffins of the late Second Intermediate Period are in any case easily distinguishable from later anthropoid coffins by their relatively poor modelling to the human form.

During the New Kingdom, the anthropoid coffin became standard, but the styles of decoration varied quite widely. The tendency from the New Kingdom down to the Late Period was for coffins to be ever more crammed with painted scenes and texts, all of a religious nature. Early Eighteenth Dynasty coffins are fairly simple; they represent the mummy in its outermost wrappings with the bandages across the body and down the front shown as painted bands upon a white background (fig. 70). These provided a convenient space for inscriptions, which could run in opposite directions from the middle towards the edges. Most early Eighteenth Dynasty coffins do not have any indication of the hands, but on the coffins of the queens Ahmose-Nefertari and Ahhotpe the hands and arms are shown in relief, grasping sceptres in the form of the *ankh* symbol. These two coffins are also of interest in having a kind of shawl over the shoulders, carved in the wood and originally inlaid with semi-precious stones. In place of the multiple bands of text they bear only a single column down the centre at the front. The enormous coffin of Meritamun, found at Deir el-Bahari, was also of this type, except that the hands held papyrus

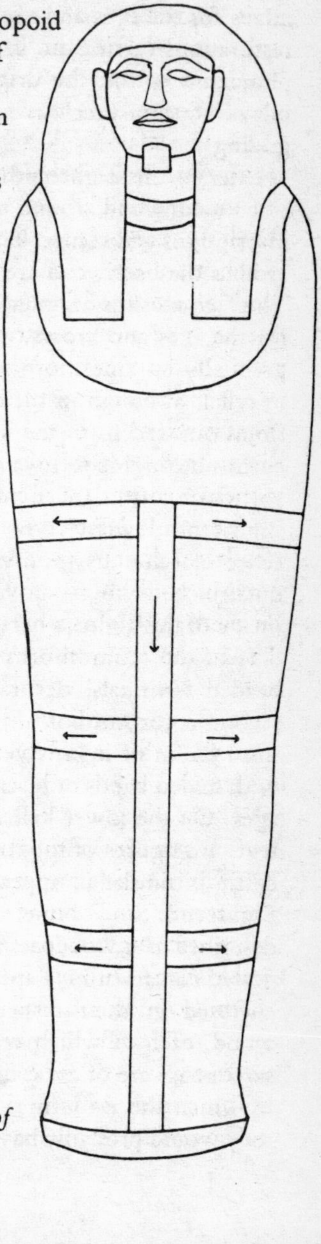

Fig.70.Bands of inscription in imitation of mummy bandages, Eighteenth Dynasty

sceptres in place of the *ankh*. This coffin was found to have blue paint in the relief carving of the shawl and was equipped with glass inlays for the eyes and eyebrows. All these details, however, were restorations carried out in the Twenty-First Dynasty to an already plundered coffin; the original decoration had possessed superior inlays of semi-precious stones combined with extensive surface gilding.

Later in the Eighteenth Dynasty the spaces between the bands of text along and around the coffin were used to contain additional inscriptions and scenes. The coffins were skilfully built to fit closely around the body, and are a good copy of the mummiform shape. The face-mask is an integral part of the coffin, often having inlays for the eyes and brows, and the whole framed by a heavy wig. It gradually became more common for the hands to be represented in relief, although in the case of multiple coffins they were sometimes omitted from the innermost, as exemplified by the nests of coffins belonging to Iuya and Thuya, parents of Queen Tiye. These particular coffins are an interesting group for illustration of the later Eighteenth Dynasty type. Already they show the increasing occurrence of religious motifs; the lids bear figures of a vulture with outstretched wings above the goddess Nut, or, alternatively, an image of the goddess herself with spread wings. Around the shoulders of the mummiform coffins are broad necklaces with falcon-headed terminals, decorated with coloured inlays. The first and second coffins of both Iuya and Thuya have elaborate gilding; the third coffin of Iuya is very large, covered with pitch interspersed with gilded bands of inscriptions in imitation of the mummy bandages. On the lower half of the latter coffin, between the bands of text, are figures of the four sons of Horus, also in gilt-work. This coffin is similar in appearance to the stone sarcophagi of the late Eighteenth and Nineteenth Dynasties, and should really be described as a wooden sarcophagus rather than a coffin. The three nested coffins of Iuya and the two belonging to Thuya were finally enclosed in their respective massive rectangular sarcophagi of wood, each of which was mounted on a sledge base. These two sarcophagi are of great interest, since they are the actual containers in which the mummies were transported to the tomb, although they would probably have been mounted upon more sturdy sledges for the journey. The one belonging to Iuya has the traditional vaulted top with raised panels at the ends, while Thuya's sarcophagus possesses a different form of lid, sloping down from one end to the other, in the manner of the roof of a shrine. Both are ornamented with bands of gilding and representations of the four sons of Horus with other divinities (figs. 71,72).

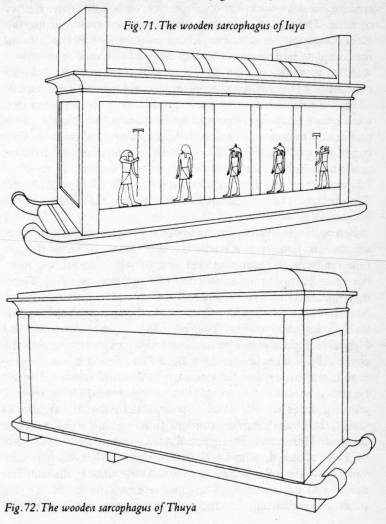

Fig.71. The wooden sarcophagus of Iuya

Fig.72. The wooden sarcophagus of Thuya

Although the majority of coffins for private burials were decorated in paint, the use of gilding was by no means uncommon. A chantress of Amun in the temple of Karnak at Thebes, named Henutmehit, had two very fine anthropoid coffins almost completely overlaid with gold, both of which can be seen in the British Museum (plate 25). In addition to these coffins, the body was covered by an openwork cover of cartonnage, embellished with figures of gods. The use of cartonnage was greatly extended during the New Kingdom, being employed not only for face-masks but also for complete body-cases. The popularity of this type of container was due to its being relatively cheap and far more close-fitting to the outline of the mummy. Furthermore, the white plaster surface of the case provided an excellent ground for painted decoration. Cartonnage body-cases could either be made in two halves, like a coffin, and bound together through holes along the sides, or they could be laced up at the back. The decoration of New Kingdom cartonnage body-cases is very elaborate, and includes a variety of religious elements. To take a relatively simple example from the Twenty-First Dynasty, illustrated in plate 26, the scheme of the decoration is as follows:

Below the jewelled collar is painted a winged scarab, representing the sun-god, spread across the upper chest. Beneath this are four registers of decoration, the first of which contains a scene depicting Horus bringing the deceased, a priestess called Tjentmutengebtiu, into the presence of the four protective goddesses, Isis, Nephthys, Neith and Selkis. Above the figures are short label-texts giving their names. The following register shows Isis and Nephthys at the sides, with outstretched wings extending over the cover. Above them hovers the winged disk of the sun, a very common motif throughout Egyptian art. In the third register, Isis and Nephthys appear yet again, but this time in ordinary human form, standing on either side of an elaborate *Djed* pillar, the symbol of Osiris. The fourth register contains an interesting scene depicting the gods Horus and Thoth pouring a stream of lustration-water over the deceased, who kneels between them. The water is conventionally shown as a chain of *ankh* and *was* symbols, the emblems of life and dominion, as a graphic reference to the revivifying powers of the lustration. Under this last register is a large vulture and a horizontal band of text containing prayers for food-offerings.

Other New Kingdom body-cases can show considerable differences from this pattern, and it seems that a number of styles were in use at the same time, the final choice resting upon the preference of the owner. Both coffins and body-cases seem to have been available for purchase from stock, examples being known with their decoration complete except for spaces which have been left in the texts for the addition of the purchaser's name. With certain other coffins, a difference in the style of the inscription shows clearly that the name has been added some time after the rest of the painting.

The development of the wooden coffin during the New Kingdom was largely a matter of changes in decoration rather than structure. As mentioned above, the simple bands of text of the early Eighteenth Dynasty were soon supplemented by additional inscriptions and scenes in the intervening spaces; after this stage, by the Twenty-First Dynasty, the original bands are very much reduced in width and become little more than convenient register-divisions between the individual vignettes. The position of the inscriptions becomes more flexible, the old single column down the front of the coffin often being replaced by two columns some distance apart with scenes in between. These changes are well shown by the series of coffins from the burials of the High-Priests and Priestesses of Amun at Thebes. The increasing number of vignettes led to a corresponding extension of the repertoire of subjects included, and it would take a great amount of space to describe all the variations. The most frequent pattern consists of several registers showing offerings being presented to divinities, who are either standing or seated within shrines. Winged figures, whether the goddess Nut, scarabs, cobras, falcons or vultures, are a regular feature. Osiris, chief god of the dead, together with Isis and Nephthys as divine mourners, figures prominently among the divinities. This is only the decoration of the cover; additional scenes and texts were painted all over the sides and back of the coffin, illustrating yet more shrines containing gods and goddesses, or mythological scenes taken from standard funerary books.

The paintings on the inside of the coffin are often just as fine in execution as those on the exterior. Generally, the floor of the coffin bears a large figure of either Nut, Isis or Osiris, the latter being replaced on occasion by his emblem, the *Djed* pillar. Sometimes these subjects are dropped in favour of a representation of the deified king Amenophis I, or of Hathor, both regarded as protectors of the Theban necropolis (plate 27). Smaller figures of divinities, such as Nekhebet and Wadjet, goddesses of Upper and Lower Egypt respectively, may occupy the remainder of the floor area. Certain private coffins of the Twenty-First Dynasty substitute four or five registers of scenes for the large central figure, and include vignettes of the deceased offering to the gods or receiving ceremonial purification. The interior surfaces of the sides bear yet more deities, among whom the four sons of Horus make frequent appearance. The underside of the lid was often painted plain white or black, although a few examples, such as the coffin of Pinudjem I, were inscribed with extracts from the Book of the Dead. This custom became more popular in the Twenty-Second to Twenty-Fifth Dynasties.

Stone sarcophagi were used for royal burials throughout the New Kingdom, but they were rarely employed by private individuals until the Nineteenth Dynasty. The first anthropoid sarcophagi for non-royal persons appear in the late Eighteenth Dynasty, such as those made for the Viceroy of Kush, Merymose, who was given an inner and outer sarcophagus of black granite. The former is in good condition and may be seen in the British Museum. It is inscribed on the lid with bands of text in low relief, arranged in the familiar mummy-bandage pattern, like the wooden coffins of the Eighteenth Dynasty. On the sides of the lower half are standing figures of the four sons of Horus, and the gods Thoth and Anubis, with appropriate recitations. The speech of Qebhsenuef reads:

Recitation by Qebhsenuef: 'I have come in order that I may be your protection. I gather together for you your bones, I draw together for you your members, I have brought for you your heart and I have placed it in position.'⁴

The sarcophagi of Merymose are truly mummiform and very skilfully worked. During the Nineteenth and Twentieth Dynasties numerous high officials were buried in anthropoid sarcophagi of hard stone, but these are often quite bulky with rather crudely formed lids. Most examples continue to reproduce the appearance of the wrapped mummy, but a few unusual sarcophagi represent the deceased in the official dress of daily life.

The royal sarcophagi of the New Kingdom exhibit numerous features of interest, and show a progressive development. The earliest form, well illustrated by the sarcophagus prepared for Hatshepsut as queen, is a direct copy in stone of the rectangular wooden coffins of the Middle Kingdom, complete with the amuletic eyes and vertical columns of text on the exterior. All the corners, both inside and out, are cut to a sharp right angle, and the lid consists of a simple flat slab with a very slight rebate underneath. The upper surface of the lid is decorated with a large cartouche, which appears also on other royal sarcophagi down to the reign of Tuthmosis III. Very similar in type is the stone coffin, probably made for Tuthmosis II, found unfinished in tomb 42 of the Valley of the Kings. On the upper surface of the cover are four stone loops used for lifting the slab on ropes. These attachments would have been cut away had the coffin ever been finished. The development proceeds in the two sarcophagi made for Hatshepsut as king, with the adoption of a convex profile for the upper side of the lid and the rounding of the interior angles. In the earlier of the two coffins, later altered for the burial of Tuthmosis I, only the corners between the sides and floor are curved, but the later sarcophagus has all the interior corners rounded. This is also the first of the royal sarcophagi to possess a rounded end at the head, making the receptacle actually copy the form of the royal cartouche. Another feature of both these sarcophagi is the bevelling of the angles on the outside, which becomes more evident under subsequent kings. With Tuthmosis III we reach the first instance of a truly vaulted lid, being convex above and concave underneath to allow more room inside the sarcophagus for the inner coffins. Later sarcophagus lids were even more arched, for the same reason. Tuthmosis IV had a very large sarcophagus of essentially the same type, made of quartzite like all the preceding Eighteenth Dynasty examples. Only the lid of the granite sarcophagus belonging to Amenophis III is preserved and it is interesting to note that it bears the amuletic eyes on its upper surface. Presumably these had been transferred from the left side of the coffin, their standard location in all earlier sarcophagi, in order to adapt, somewhat belatedly, to the fact that the body no longer faced to the left but rested on its back looking upwards. In other respects, the decoration of the sarcophagi from the reign of Hatshepsut down to Amenophis II shows remarkable uniformity as to the positions of the individual deities and texts. The left side bears the eye-panel, to the right of which is a figure of Hapy, one of the four sons of Horus. On the other side of the amuletic eyes stand Anubis and Qebhsenuef, accompanied by columns of inscription. The right side of the sarcophagus bears representations of Imset, another form of the god Anubis and Duwamutef, running in that order from head to foot. On the rounded head end of the coffin is the goddess Isis, while Nephthys is shown at the foot. The inscriptions show a gradual development; those on the earliest sarcophagus, that of Hatshepsut as queen, consisting only of reworked extracts from the older Pyramid or Coffin Texts. In the subsequent sarcophagi increasing use is made of the new funerary composition known as the Book of the Dead, which became the most popular mortuary text of the New Kingdom.

During the Amarna period the steady evolution of the stone sarcophagus was upset, and as a consequence we find a different type in the tombs of Tutankhamun, Ay and Horemheb. This consists of a rectangular box with a cornice along the top edge, such as might be found on a shrine. The new style provided scope for a change in decoration; a figure of a goddess being carved in relief at each of the four corners, with outstretched wings extending along the sides. The goddesses are Isis, Nephthys, Neith and Selkis, the four traditional protective goddesses of the dead, individual gilded figures of whom were found in the tomb of Tutankhamun.

In the Nineteenth and Twentieth Dynasties the royal tombs at Thebes were equipped with heavier outer sarcophagi, usually of granite, and sometimes decorated with an image of the king in high relief upon the lid. In certain tombs the rectangular sarcophagus was set down into a pit in the floor of the burial chamber, which was then covered by a granite lid. Inner anthropoid sarcophagi of alabaster were employed, that belonging to Seti I having been found in a good state of preservation, except for the lid, which had been broken to fragments. This sarcophagus was transported to

England by Belzoni, and is now in Sir John Soane's Museum at Lincoln's Inn Fields, London. It consists of a fine anthropoid chest, covered with texts and scenes from the Book of Gates, the incised hieroglyphs having been originally inlaid with blue pigment. On the interior of the base is a large figure of the goddess Nut surrounded by religious inscriptions. The lid was fixed in place by means of copper tenons, which engaged in slots in the edges of the coffin. King Merenptah seems to have possessed a similar anthropoid sarcophagus of alabaster, although the only piece to have survived is a small fragment of the foot. The inscriptions upon royal sarcophagi of the Nineteenth and Twentieth Dynasties were more varied than those of the preceding dynasty, and include sections from a number of religious compilations. A discussion of the different types of mythological beliefs represented by these texts is given in Chapter 6.

Stone sarcophagi continued to be used for royal burials during the Twenty-First and Twenty-Second Dynasties, the majority of examples coming from the cemetery of Tanis. But private sarcophagi, which were reasonably common in the rich tombs of the Nineteenth and Twentieth Dynasties, tend to disappear and be replaced by wooden coffins. Even the stone sarcophagi of royalty were not quarried under the rulers of the Twenty-First or Twenty-Second Dynasty, but were usurped from earlier tombs and re-inscribed for their new owners. In consequence, the forms of the Tanite sarcophagi are not representative of the continued development of the type but illustrate sundry New Kingdom or even earlier sarcophagi, gathered together from various sources. Eight of the thirteen sarcophagi from Tanis had already been used in earlier tombs and the original inscriptions were not always completely removed. Among the names of the original owners were King Merenptah of the Nineteenth Dynasty, a private individual of the Middle Kingdom called Ameny, and a priest called Amenhotpe, who had been buried at Thebes in the New Kingdom. In other cases, the sarcophagi had been hollowed out of various architectural elements of nearby temples, which were exploited as a useful source of ready-cut stone. The coffin of Shoshenk III was cut from an architrave of the Thirteenth Dynasty, and the lids for three other sarcophagi were reworked from statues. Among the sarcophagi of

Tanis were examples of the plain rectangular box, anthropoid forms and the New Kingdom style of royal coffin with the rounded head end. The fine silver coffins which were placed within these sarcophagi have already been mentioned in Chapter 4. Throughout the New Kingdom, the stone sarcophagus in the royal tomb was designed to accommodate a set of coffins, sometimes resting upon a low bier. The anthropoid coffins were made of gilded wood or precious metal, and the complete set is best exemplified by the well-known coffins of Tutankhamun.

Private burials of the Twenty-Second to Twenty-Fifth Dynasties continued to employ the anthropoid coffins of wood and carton-nage which had come into vogue during the New Kingdom. Some changes in style occur: the hands, for example, are shown in relief on coffins until the Twenty-First Dynasty but become less common in later periods, when the front of the coffin reverts to a smooth appearance. The painted decoration is frequently more crowded and detailed than in the Twenty-First Dynasty, and the addition of texts from the Book of the Dead on the interior becomes a regular practice. One common feature of coffins belonging to this age is the appearance of a large painted *Djed* pillar upon the back, occupying most of the central part, although even this popular device could on occasion be replaced by lines of text. The front of the coffin often bears a representation of the mummy lying upon a bier, visited by the winged *Ba*, or soul. Beneath the couch the four Canopic vessels are normally shown. In addition, the front surface was painted with a winged figure of Nut across the chest, several columns of inscription down the centre, and subsidiary texts running horizontally towards the sides. The latter are normally associated with figures of deities, to whom the texts make reference. On the interior, the Book of the Dead texts underneath the cover could be inscribed around a figure of the goddess Nut, or the same deity might occur on the floor of the coffin. In the latter position she is sometimes replaced by Hathor, or, more rarely, by Osiris or Sokar. These are only a few of the regular themes found on coffins of the Third Intermediate Period; many variations exist, a number of coffins retaining the style of the New Kingdom, with simple bands of text. In nests of coffins, the decoration of the outer case might differ considerably from that of the inner, and it seems that much was left to personal taste. One point worth noting is the increasing prominence given to the god Re-Horakhty-Atum, who is regularly invoked in the offering formula in place of Osiris, who was formerly accorded this position.

The construction of coffins in the Twenty-Second to Twenty-Fifth Dynasties shows little development, the general rule being for narrow planks of wood to be shaped as required and pegged together. One area which caused some difficulty was the arched top over the head; if cut from a single block this involved considerable wastage, and as a result the arch was normally made up from small sections, again fastened by dowelling (fig. 73). The lid was attached to the coffin in the manner which had been in use since the beginning of anthropoid coffin development, that is, by means of tenons fixed in slots in the lid engaging in a further set of slots in the base, to be locked by pegging from the side. Significant

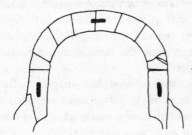

Fig. 73. Construction of the canopy
of an anthropoid coffin

changes in coffin design did not occur until the late Twenty-Fifth Dynasty, to be continued under the Twenty-Sixth, largely due to the deliberate archaism of the age. The most obvious development was an alteration to the form of the outer coffin. This had formerly been a larger version of the inner body-case, that is to say, it was anthropoid in shape but somewhat oversized and heavy. The new fashion replaced this outer coffin by a rectangular box with a vaulted top and high corner-posts, in fact, very much like certain coffins of the Middle Kingdom (plate 28). This style must have had great appeal in the upsurge of archaism, since it goes back to earliest times, being essentially the same as First Dynasty coffins except for the omission of the panelling along the sides. The shape is also seen in the form of the superstructures of First Dynasty mastaba-tombs, and symbolizes the tomb as a dwelling-house. As an inner container to be placed within these new-style coffins the anthropoid body-case, either in wood or cartonnage, was retained.

Interest in the resurrection of earlier customs extended far beyond the limited field of coffin development, covering the whole range of religious and funerary art. Recessed brick construction was revived in large tombs at Thebes, sculptures and reliefs were modelled on earlier prototypes and ancient religious texts were recopied. During this period, the pit of the Step Pyramid of Djoser at Saqqara was cleared and the burial restored. This was a considerable undertaking, and involved the driving of a new tunnel in the rock from the south side of the pyramid to the original Third Dynasty pit. At this stage the pit was full of rubble, all of which was removed to gain access to the burial chamber, after the construction of a wooden framework at the top of the pit to support the masonry of the pyramid. Nowadays, when visitors enter the Step Pyramid they do so through this passage of the Twenty-Sixth Dynasty and not by the dangerous and crumbling Third Dynasty tunnel from the north (although even the later entrance is only accessible with special permission).

The scenes and texts upon the revived box-shaped coffins remained exclusively religious in content. Often there are rows of divinities in vaulted shrines along either side, accompanied by texts from the Book of the Dead. An archaizing feature is the reappearance of the sacred eyes on the exterior, sometimes in their old location on the left side, but more frequently on the head end of the coffin. The paintings on the lid are of mythological character, often including a vignette showing the progress of the boat of Re.

At this period there was a marked revival in the use of stone sarcophagi, in private as well as in royal tombs. The sarcophagi of the Napatan rulers Anlamani and Aspelta are purely Egyptian in their inspiration, decorated with figures of the four sons of Horus and fully inscribed in Egyptian hieroglyphs. Both these stone coffins are rectangular in shape with a vaulted lid and high corner-posts, and they possess a very abbreviated copy of palace-facade panelling along the lower part of their sides. The sarcophagi from tombs of private individuals in Egypt are more frequently anthropoid in form, and consist of grey or black schist. They often have ponderous covers bearing a face-mask of rather flat appearance. A few are more finely carved, and appear to be modelled upon the best style of the New Kingdom, and it has been suggested that the two different forms represent the products of Lower Egypt and Thebes respectively. The Lower Egyptian type, with broad faces, normally have heavy wigs and, in the case of sarcophagi for men, are equipped with the false beard. A wide necklace with falcon-headed terminals extends around the shoulders, with sometimes a winged figure of the goddess Nut below. The inscriptions often cover all the remaining area of the lid, arranged in vertical columns, sometimes with figures of the four sons of Horus or other funerary deities at the sides. On the lower section of the coffin, however, there is frequently only a single line of text, running around the upper part just below the lip. The inscriptions on both lid and coffin are taken from the Pyramid Texts of the Old Kingdom, copies of which had been made to satisfy archaistic taste. The finer Theban style of sarcophagus was better cut to the anthropoid or mummiform shape, with a more realistic face-mask. The wig, beard and broad collar are worn, and the hands are sometimes carved in relief, grasping the amuletic *Djed* and *Tyet* symbols (plate 29). Across the chest is the figure of Nut with inscriptions extending below over the length of the cover. The coffer can either be free of all decoration or inscribed down the back.

Inner body-cases of wood or cartonnage were not always used in conjunction with the anthropoid sarcophagi of the Twenty-Sixth Dynasty. Two burials at Saqqara were each found without any inner coffin, the wrapped mummies having been laid directly in stone sarcophagi of the heavier Lower Egyptian type. Possibly this style of sarcophagus was regularly employed without any additional coffins, since the hollowing of the interior is often quite limited, leaving a great thickness of stone at the sides and base. Not all the sarcophagi of the Twenty-Sixth Dynasty are anthropoid or semi-anthropoid in type, a few being similar to the shape of the New Kingdom royal sarcophagus, that is, a deep rectangular chest with the head end rounded. However, there is a tendency for these late examples to have sides which do not run parallel, but converge slightly towards the foot (fig. 74). This feature is even more pronounced in sarcophagi of the Thirtieth Dynasty and of the Ptolemaic Period. One Twenty-Sixth Dynasty sarcophagus in the British Museum is of this type, belonging to an official called Hapmen. This monument is of particular interest in having not only the shape of a New Kingdom royal sarcophagus but also identical decoration. A comparison of the texts with earlier stone coffins shows quite clearly that the whole sarcophagus was deliberately copied from that of King Tuthmosis III of the Eighteenth Dynasty. The arrangement of the texts and scenes is the same as that on the earlier coffin, and yet differs completely from that of contemporary

Fig. 74. Plan showing the form of a stone sarcophagus of the Twenty-Sixth Dynasty

sarcophagi, indicating that the tomb of Tuthmosis III must have been accessible in the Twenty-Sixth Dynasty and was entered for the specific purpose of copying the sarcophagus. The private sarcophagi of the Late Period generally usurp earlier royal privileges in the choice of the texts with which they are inscribed, but rarely is the appropriation so blatant as this direct copying of the sarcophagus of a past ruler. Other non-anthropoid sarcophagi of the Late Period are those belonging to the divine votaresses of Amun at Thebes, the known examples being of rectangular shape. The stone coffins of Nitocris and Ankhnesneferibre had representations of their owners on the lids, the former bearing a figure shown full-face in very high relief, while the latter was carved with a low-relief representation in profile. The sarcophagus of Ankhnesneferibre is covered with inscriptions derived from the Pyramid Texts.

The rectangular wooden coffin with a vaulted top, revived in the Late Period, remained in use through the last of the dynasties and on into the Ptolemaic Period. During the latter age they were sometimes modified to have a gabled cover in place of the rounded vault, but the basic shape remained the same (fig. 75). This style did not by any means replace the anthropoid coffin, which was in any case retained as an inner container. .Certain individuals, however, still preferred to be buried in nests of two or three anthropoid coffins, the outermost of which sometimes imitated the appearance of a stone sarcophagus. In the case of a set of coffins the outer one always had to be quite large, and some examples from the Thirtieth Dynasty are extremely ponderous and bulky. They are covered with scenes and texts from the Book of the Dead, but the painting is poor in comparison with earlier work. Traditional themes of decoration persisted into the Ptolemaic Period, with the representations becoming more and more debased as their real significance was forgotten. Both anthropoid and rectangular coffins were used during the Graeco–Roman age, the latter sometimes being made in imitation of a shrine, by replacing the high corner-posts at one end with a decorated panel surmounted by a moulded cornice of wood. At either side were placed model columns to copy the monumental columns of a shrine facade (fig. 76). In the Roman

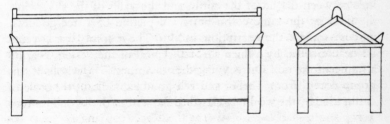

Fig.75.Gable-topped coffin of the Graeco-Roman Period

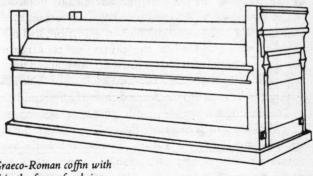

*Fig.76.Graeco-Roman coffin with
one end in the form of a shrine*

Period, around 100 A.D., these coffins were made with the line of separation between cover and base much lower than in earlier times, so that the original lid became the bulk of the structure, and the remainder of the coffin consisted of little more than a flat board upon which the body could be placed (fig. 77). Both the base-board and the cover were elaborately painted with the current versions of traditional Egyptian motifs, but these had departed greatly from their earlier style owing to the foreign influence now pervading the country. Among the representations on the exterior of this type of coffin we find the boat of Re, various funerary divinities, and the *Ba* bird visiting the mummy. The interior painting is sometimes more impressive and shows greater mixing of Egyptian and Graeco-Roman traditions. On the underside of the lid belonging to the coffin of Soter, in the British Museum, is a remarkable portrait of the goddess Nut in the fashion of a Graeco-Roman lady (plate 30). Around the figure are the signs of the zodiac, the presence of which again reflects the old symbolic link between the lid of the coffin and the vault of the sky, while the floor of the same coffin bears a depiction of a tree-goddess, who is named in the inscriptions as Mut. The mummy was covered inside the coffin by a linen shroud, typical of the period, bearing a figure of the god Osiris with other divinities. The whole of this group comes from Thebes and is a good example of the style of coffin used by the wealthier classes at the start of the second century A.D.

During the later dynasties and the Ptolemaic Period there was an expansion in the use of stone sarcophagi, with anthropoid or

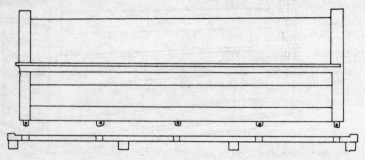

Fig.77. Roman coffin consisting of base-board and cover

mummiform styles being the most popular. The very heavy semi-anthropoid sarcophagi of the Twenty-Sixth Dynasty, with their short extracts from the Pyramid Texts, are replaced by less massive mummiform coffins of basalt, schist or limestone, the last being by far the most common. These coffins were inscribed with texts from the Book of the Dead, amounting to only a few vertical lines down the cover on the poorer examples, although wealthier sarcophagi of the Ptolemaic Period possess additional texts and representations of divinities. The anthropoid sarcophagi were made quite close-fitting to the mummy, and both halves often have a rabbeted edge so as to ensure a good fit between lid and coffin. Their manufacture had evidently become a much cheaper process than in earlier times, for limestone sarcophagi were now produced in large numbers and used by persons of no great rank, especially at centres such as Akhmim and Abydos. The close-fitting stone sarcophagus was used independently of a wooden inner coffin, the mummy being covered only by sections of decorated cartonnage.

Another class of stone coffin used at this period consists of a group of much larger polygonal chests, hollowed out from a monolithic piece of granite or similar hard rock. Most examples of this type belong to the Thirtieth Dynasty and the early Ptolemaic Period and they are found only in the tombs of royalty or high-ranking officials. These sarcophagi are descended from the royal sarcophagi of the New Kingdom, both in their shape and in their decoration. They are basically rectangular with a rounded end at the head, but the opposite sides converge towards the foot. This polygonal effect was heightened by the form of the lid, which usually has three long panels at different angles, tapering to the foot, with sometimes a complex arrangement of concave sections at the rounded head end. The long panels may be either flat or concave, as shown by the drawings in figure 78. These are the usual styles, but

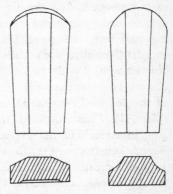

Fig. 78. Plans and sections of the lids of Late Period stone sarcophagi

a few sarcophagi perpetuate older traditions by making use of the simple vaulted lid. Sarcophagi of this type are extensively inscribed, usually with the funerary text known as the Book of What is in the Underworld, although extracts from the Book of the Dead can occur on the lid. One of the largest examples of this type is the green breccia sarcophagus made for Nectanebo II, now in the British Museum. This sarcophagus was never used, since Nectanebo fled from Egypt to escape the Persians, and the vast stone coffin was employed in later times as a ritual bath in a mosque at Alexandria.

The hollowing of sarcophagi in hard stone would have been a lengthy operation, carried out by means of drilling, chiselling and, probably most of all, by simply pounding the rock. Some sarcophagi show the marks of damage suffered at an early stage in the manufacturing process, before the decoration had been added. The stone-cutters seem to have been reluctant to abandon the work at this stage, and consequently we find the inscriptions have occasionally been cut down into rough breaks in the stone. Heavy sarcophagi of this kind died out during the Ptolemaic Period and were subsequently made only for the burials of sacred animals, particularly the bulls and cows of Armant. The anthropoid stone coffin lasted somewhat longer, but itself gradually fell out of use.

Wooden coffins had remained in use throughout the Graeco-Roman Period and they were supplemented by the employment of cartonnage body-cases. Cartonnage was extensively used at this date to make individual coverings for the head, chest, abdomen, legs and feet, each panel being heavily decorated with religious motifs. Complete body-cases also occur, usually with a considerable amount of gilding. Among the Greek settlers in Egypt a new custom arose, replacing the cartonnage face-mask by a flat portrait of the deceased, executed in coloured wax upon a wooden panel (plate 31). These so-called 'mummy-portraits' are purely Hellenistic in style, and the greater number come from the Graeco-Roman cemeteries of the Fayum. The body-cases themselves retain Egyptian motifs, including scenes of the corpse being prepared by Anubis or visited by the *Ba*. Figures of Isis and Nephthys as divine mourners occur regularly, together with other prominent divinities like Horus and Thoth. As an alternative to wax portraits, plaster head-pieces were employed during the first three centuries A.D. The early examples were hollow and fitted over the head, but later they were made solid and placed on top of the face, giving it the impression of being slightly raised. Petrie believed that mummies of this age, once prepared and equipped with portrait or mask, were kept in the houses of relatives for some time prior to burial. Although this view cannot be proved, it at least seems likely that mass burials took place from time to time.

In contrast to the lavish gilding found on these Roman body-cases, the poor cemeteries of the same period have very little in the way of embellishment. Many of the poorest burials were placed in communal underground chambers, the pitch-soaked mummies being stacked up to the roof without coffins or protection of any kind. In other cemeteries, such as the Roman burial-ground at Medinet Habu, the mummies were placed in pottery coffins as an economical substitute for wood. Coffins of pottery, as distinct from the use of large domestic pots for burials, are known from the Twenty-First and Twenty-Second Dynasties, especially in the Nile Delta region. The Roman pottery coffins are of several types, some consisting of a conventional box with a flat lid, while others have a lid extending only half the length from the head – the body would have been slid in downwards from the top. This form is generally referred to as a 'slipper-coffin'. One coffin had been made in a single piece as a long, narrow box, with the only opening being a hole in the head end, sealed after insertion of the body. In another grave, the coffin had been made from three pieces; these consisted of a pottery vessel at either end with a tubular section in between, all fastened together by cord binding.

At this period, in the third and fourth centuries A.D., we see the final stages in the slow abandonment of the old Egyptian tradition. The mummy wrappings still bear painted representations of Anubis and other gods, but new customs, such as the burial of the dead in everyday garments, or the use of a flat wooden board upon which to lay out the corpse, are features which link the latest pagan burials with those of the early Christian cemeteries. The spread of the new religion dealt the final blow to the continuance of ancient

Egyptian funerary practices, and the great series of coffins and sarcophagi, developed over more than three thousand years, came to
an end, no doubt aided by the extreme impoverishment of most
burials of the period.

8

SACRED ANIMAL
CEMETERIES

To the general observer, one of the most peculiar features of
ancient Egyptian civilization is the regular appearance of deities
in animal form, or with animal heads upon human bodies, in reliefs
and paintings. To understand the reasons for the presence of animal
divinities it is necessary to examine briefly the origins of Egyptian
religion. The beliefs of the early Egyptians grew out of supersti-
tions and traditions of the individual communities which settled in
the Nile Valley long before the emergence of a unified state. Each
village or town possessed its own local gods, and, despite attempts
to rationalize the mass of deities into some kind of order, the local
nature of Egyptian religion persisted right through to the latest times.
On tomb stelae the visitor is frequently asked to recite the formula
of offering, 'as surely as you love your local city-gods'. Amalgam-
ating these many deities into a state religion led to a number of
difficulties, but some order was produced by associating the various gods and goddesses into family groups, usually triads, with
one member being the child of the other two. For example, we
have Amun, Mut and Khonsu at Thebes, or Ptah, Sekhmet and
Nefertem at Memphis. But the fact that many of the divinities
originated in very early forms of worship, while others were of
more recent origin, means that the Egyptian gods cover a variety
of levels in the development of thought, with early and later concepts existing side by side. The different stages can be detected
quite clearly in the types of gods: animal deities belong to one of

the most primitive strata; a later development was to anthro-pomorphize the bodies and leave only the animal head; fully anthropomorphic gods, like Amun or Ptah, represent a still more advanced philosophy. Other gods may be described as cosmic deities: the sun, moon, earth and the Nile fall into this category. Many civilizations have gone through the same process of adapting their idea of a deity to fit the developing intellect of the time; the special feature in Egypt is the fact that the early beliefs were not replaced by the new ones – instead, the two were merely added together. A similar reluctance to discard the old in favour of the new was responsible for the persistence of local divinities. The important god Horus, for example, was a national deity combining a number of different forms, but never completely replacing them, and consequently we find references from all periods to Horus of Behdet, Horus of Pe, Horus of Nekhen and others.

The origins of animal worship must go back to a very early time, when the creatures themselves were the objects of religious devotion, and different animals may have been the local fetish or totem of individual regions. Later on, the animals serve only as rep-resentatives of particular gods and they are sacred because of their association with the divinity, not in their own right. Consequently, it is incorrect to say that the Egyptians of the Dynastic Period worshipped animals; in fact, they worshipped specific gods and goddesses who happened to have links with certain animal species. Even those gods who were normally represented in fully human form had their own sacred animals. Amun is a good example, with the ram and the goose as his animal representatives, while his wife the goddess Mut was linked with the vulture. Provision was made at many of the temples for the animals of the god to be kept in captivity within the sacred precincts. In some temples only a single animal would be kept, like the Apis bull in the temple of Memphis, but other cults required the accommodation of large numbers of animals, which might be ibises, baboons, hawks, crocodiles, rams or cats. A bronze ritual vessel in the British Museum is inscribed with the name of a man called Hor, who was Priest of the Living Baboons in the temple of Khonsu at Thebes. Whether a temple kept one animal or a large number depended upon an important distinction between two different kinds of animal cult, for in

certain cases a single animal was selected to be the divine representative on the basis of special markings, whereas in other
circumstances all members of a species were considered worthy of
particular reverence. The difference is clearly demonstrated by a
comparison of the cult of the Apis bull, as an example of the former
type, with the ibises of the god Thoth, which must have been kept
in thousands. Of course, this difference in the numbers of animals
involved in a cult had a direct effect upon the form of burial provided for the animals concerned; in one case there was only a single
burial to be provided for a creature of great veneration; in the other
it was necessary to supply more modest resting-places for large
numbers of individuals. Those cults in which a single animal was
chosen as the divine representative were of great importance, by
virtue of the special nature of the animal, which placed it apart
from other members of its species. The burial of such a creature
was a lavish affair, provided for by royal direction. The interment
of animals in entire-species cults, on the other hand, was far more
simple, often carried out at the expense of private individuals.

Without doubt, the most important of all the cults was that of
the Apis bull, and this is reflected in the elaborate nature of the
tombs of the bulls at Saqqara (plate 33). Although the oldest known
burials date from the New Kingdom, the cult of the Apis is known
to go back to the First Dynasty, and it is possible that earlier tombs
may still await discovery. The known tombs of the bulls, discovered by Mariette in 1851 and 1852, are of two types, the earlier
burials being individual structures and the later ones, after the reign
of Ramesses II, being linked by galleries in the rock. At present,
only the western section of the galleries is accessible, where the
sacred bulls were interred from the Twenty-Sixth Dynasty down
to the Ptolemaic Period. This burial-place is generally referred to
as the 'Serapeum', a term derived from the name of the Greek god
Serapis, who was linked with the Apis bull. However, despite the
apparent similarity between the full title of the deceased bull,
'The Osiris-Apis', and 'Serapis', the two names do not seem to
be related etymologically. The Serapeum is one of the most impressive ancient monuments of Saqqara and is a regular feature of
tourist itineraries, but it must be remembered that the appearance
of the galleries in antiquity would have been far more striking than

they seem today. Not only have the sarcophagi been opened and robbed, but a large amount of the fine limestone casing which originally covered the inner surfaces of the burial vaults has been removed.

The main passage of the later gallery runs for nearly two hundred metres beneath the desert surface, with the vaults themselves ranged along the sides at a lower level, so that one looks down on to the lids of the sarcophagi (fig. 79). These vast stone chests have

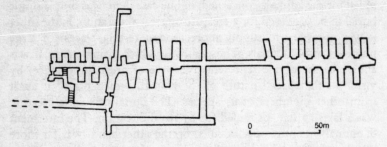

Fig.79.Plan of the Late Period vaults in the Serapeum

been hollowed out from individual blocks of granite to provide a final resting-place suitable for the god. In the earlier galleries of the Serapeum, containing the burials of the Nineteenth to Twenty-Sixth Dynasties, and in the older individual tombs, the coffins were made less expensively of gilded wood. One of the isolated tombs was found intact by Mariette; it contained the coffins of two bulls, both dating from the reign of Ramesses II. The south wall of the chamber bore a painted scene showing the king and the prince Khaemwase making offerings to the Apis. From the coffins came a variety of golden jewellery and amulets, some pieces being inscribed with the names of Ramesses or Khaemwase, together with a number of bull-headed statuettes. Prince Khaemwase took great interest in the Memphite necropolis, and seems to have been particularly devoted to the cult of the Apis bull. He organized the repair of the Fifth Dynasty pyramid of Unas, placing an inscription upon the monument to record the deed, and eventually had his own tomb prepared within the Serapeum itself. This burial was found by Mariette, who described the mummy as having a gilded mask and items of jewellery, but he failed to record the tomb in full detail.

From the Serapeum come many inscribed stelae of royal or private persons, varying from simple expressions of devotion to the Apis to more formal records of the date of death of the bull. A fine stela from the reign of Ramesses II begins:

Year 30, third month of summer, day 21 of the lord of the two lands Usermaatre-Setepenre, lord of diadems, Ramesses, may he be granted life like Re. It happened that the majesty of the Apis departed to heaven, to rest in the embalming-house under [the charge of] Anubis who is in the place of embalming, that he might mummify his body. The children of Horus raise him up while the lector-priest recites glorifications.[1]

At a later point in this text, reference is made to the Apis having completed seventy days in the place of embalming, showing that the length of time allowed for the process was the same as that for human mummification. Indeed, the rites of burial were the same for the bull as for any human interment, as is clear from the stelae, the example in question showing two officials performing the offices of lector-priest and *Sem*-priest. The former reads from a papyrus scroll the formula for the Opening of the Mouth ceremony to restore the living senses of the dead animal, while the latter presents the necessary ritual implements. A demotic papyrus in Vienna records the procedures which accompanied the mummification of the Apis bull, and confirms that the operation was highly ritualized. At an early stage in the proceedings, the bull was housed in a special booth, into which the priests entered to perform all the correct ceremonies. From this temporary shelter the body was transferred to the 'Place of Embalming' for the process of mummification. The instructions in the papyrus state that the corpse was to be laid out upon a bed of sand, to the accompaniment of the lamentations of the priests. The wrappings for the mummy were carefully prepared and were applied according to specific directions, which described the correct manner of wrapping the different areas of the body:

They must bring another *nebti*-bandage and divide it as they wish. They must make the feet and legs fast to their clamps on the board. They must lay a linen cloth over the god [and] they must make the *skr*-stuff go under the board. It must be two palms in width. They must three times wrap it to the upper side of the god before and behind the navel.[2]

The description of binding the mummy to a wooden board accords well with discoveries made in the excavation of the tombs of the sacred Buchis bulls at Armant, which lay in an underground cemetery similar to the Serapeum, but of more modest construction. This burial-place was termed the 'Bucheum' by the excavators. Amongst the remains of the mummies were found many bronze or iron clamps of the type shown in figure 80, which can only be the 'clamps on the board' mentioned in the papyrus. Other parts of this same text refer to making the various bandages fast to 'the clamps at the back', or 'the two front clamps'. From the evidence of the Bucheum tombs, it is clear that the body was fastened on to a board by passing the bandages through the loops of the clamps, which had been driven into the wood beforehand. The close agreement between the text concerning the mummification of the Apis and the actual remains in the burials of Buchis shows that the procedures must have been essentially similar for each kind of bull. The amount of actual embalming treatment performed on the animals, apart from the bandaging, seems to have been fairly limited. Evidence from the Vienna papyrus and from the excavation of the Bucheum shows that no incision was made in order to remove the internal organs, the process being restricted to the dissolution of the viscera by means of fluids introduced through the

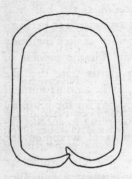

Fig.80.Clamp for the mummy of a bull

Fig.81.The Apis bull on a bier

anus. This is the same as the second technique of mummification described by Herodotus, in his comments on human embalming. The presence of Canopic jars in some of the early Apis burials at Saqqara might seem to imply that certain bulls had received more elaborate treatment, but on the other hand it is quite possible that the Canopics were purely ritual. Mariette does not state whether the jars had any contents.

On the site of the ancient city of Memphis are the remains of a structure which formed the mummification-place of the Apis bulls in the Twenty-Sixth Dynasty. The most striking features of this building are the massive alabaster tables, in the form of low couches, upon which the bodies of the sacred animals were laid during embalmment. Each of these tables is equipped with a sloping top, to drain the fluids used in the process into an outlet at one end. After completion of embalmment in this building, the wrapped corpse would have been placed upon a bier for transport to the desert plateau at Saqqara, to rest in the tomb which had been prepared for it in the Serapeum (fig. 81). On reaching the lower desert slopes, the burial cortege would have arrived at the religious and administrative centres which lay along the eastern edge of the plateau, from which the route to the Serapeum was marked by an imposing avenue of sphinxes, at least from the Thirtieth Dynasty. This was the avenue discovered by Mariette in 1851, in the course of excavations which were to lead him eventually to the Serapeum itself. Towards the western end of the route there was a temple built by Nectanebo II and dedicated to the Osiris-Apis, although this structure has been entirely destroyed. Some of the stones from the temple were re-used in the later construction of the Coptic monastery of Jeremias at Saqqara, among them a large sandstone stela belonging to the second year of the reign of Nectanebo II, upon which some details of the establishment and furnishing of the temple are recorded. The building was called, 'The Place of the Living Apis', and must have been richly decorated, its doors being overlaid with gold and silver. Most of the major cemeteries of sacred animals would originally have had temples nearby, in which the cult of the appropriate deity could be perpetuated, but these places of worship have generally not survived the passage of time so well as the burial installations they were intended to serve.

The burials of Buchis, sacred bull of Armant and the surrounding region, have already been mentioned in connection with the mummification and wrapping of the animals. Buchis was linked with various Egyptian divinities, being most closely associated with the solar-god Re and also with Montu, the god of Armant. The tombs of the Buchis bulls differed from those of Apis in that some were built structures covered by vaulting rather than rock-hewn sepulchres. The burials were all of a late age, ranging from the Thirtieth Dynasty to the Roman Period. The richness of the tombs varied greatly, some having a considerable amount of funerary equipment, while others were buried without even a sarcophagus. For some of the latest burials no attempt was made to prepare a new vault; instead, the mummies were simply left in the passages which linked the earlier tombs. As with the burials of Apis, stelae were inscribed giving the dates of birth, installation and death of the sacred bulls. An extract from the stela of Ptolemy IV reads:

... On this day the majesty of this noble god went up to heaven, the beneficent *Ba*, the living *Ba* of Re, the manifestation of Re, who was born of Ta-amen. The length of his life was 18 years, 10 months, 23 days. The day on which he was born was Year 13 Epep 20 in the life of the King of Upper and Lower Egypt, Ptolemy, living forever, beloved of Isis, in the district of Ombos. He was installed in Armant in Year 25, Thoth 15. [May he remain] on his throne for ever and ever. The majesty of this noble god went up to heaven in Year 8 Paoni 12...[3]

The upper parts of these stelae, above the text, usually bore a scene, in relief, of the king presenting offerings or incense to the bull, which is shown either standing upon a raised dais or couched upon a bier (plate 32). For burial, the bull was decked out in its regalia, a gilded wooden crown with inlays of glass being set between its horns. Artificial eyes of stone or glass in a bronze frame were applied to the face, and the whole head was plastered and gilded. Similar and even more lavish decoration would have been conferred on the Apis bulls at Memphis, but the archaeological record from the excavation of the Serapeum is not so complete as that for the Buchis burials.

Another important divine bull was Mnevis, worshipped and buried at Heliopolis in Lower Egypt. Only two Mnevis tombs have been found, belonging to the reigns of Ramesses II and Ramesses VII, but the excavation of these burials was carried out in such a manner as to yield little information. The tombs were individual structures, consisting of limestone chambers sunk into the ground, covered by horizontal roofing-slabs (fig. 82). Canopic jars were found with the burials, but, like the Canopics of the Apis bull, these may have been supplied for ritual purposes. There are close affinities between Mnevis and Buchis, since both were regarded as the embodiment of Re.

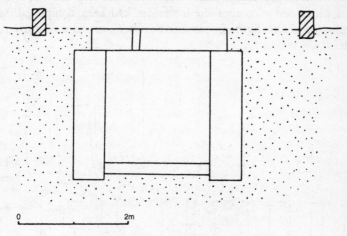

0   2m

Fig.82. Section of the tomb of a Mnevis bull

As a natural extension of the provision of burial-places for sacred bulls, cemeteries of similar character were developed in the Late Period for the mothers of these animals, since the cows were also regarded as divine. The mothers of Buchis were interred in a sep-arate series of tombs close to the Bucheum at Armant, the earliest cow-burial belonging to the reign of Nectanebo II. Some were equipped with stone sarcophagi like those of the bulls, but only one inscribed stela for a cow was discovered, dating from the time of the Emperor Commodus. Many of the tombs were covered by vaults of mud- or burnt-brick, as were the connecting passages of the complex. A more recent discovery is the finding of the cemetery of the Mothers of Apis at Saqqara, cut in a rock-hewn gallery under the western side of the plateau, some distance north of the Serapeum (fig. 83). The layout of the place is similar to the Late Period galleries of the Apis bulls, although on a much smaller scale and far more ruined. The axial passage is flanked on either side by sunk emplacements for sarcophagi, which had been deliberately smashed to fragments by Coptic intruders. From the burial-places came only scant remains of the mummies, amounting to loose cow-bones and pieces of linen. Each vault was originally lined with fine limestone and, after the interment had been completed, was sealed off from the main passage by a wall of the same material.

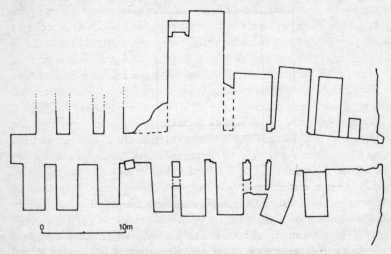

Fig.83.Plan of the burial place for the Mothers of Apis

The exterior of this blocking was then embellished with inscriptions of the priests, while the stonemasons who were responsible for the cutting of the vaults added their own small stelae in niches in the rock walls of the corridor. Both kinds of inscription were usually written with black ink in the demotic script, and were far less elaborate than the stelae of the Serapeum. From the evidence of the texts, the earliest burial took place in the first year of Psamouthes (393 B.C.) and the latest in Year 11 of Cleopatra (41 B.C.).

However, it is known that the cows were already given ceremonial burial in the Twenty-Sixth Dynasty, so it would appear that an earlier group of tombs still awaits discovery at Saqqara.

Outside the gallery of the sacred cows was a temple built by Nectanebo II, the king that was responsible for the construction of the temple at the Serapeum. The main sanctuary of the building seems to have been dedicated to Isis-mother-of-the-Apis, and to Apis himself, providing a centre in which the cult of the divine cows could be perpetuated. But the temple was not simple in plan, since it also contained separate chapels for two other underground cemeteries of sacred animals. This section of the Saqqara necropolis was honeycombed with such burial-places, and from the temple terrace there opened two galleries into the rock, one devoted to the burials of sacred baboons and the other to falcons. These cemeteries are of a somewhat different character to the tombs of the bulls or cows, because the baboons and falcons belonged to the type of animal cult in which all members of a species were regarded as divine representatives. In some cults of this type a particular animal was chosen periodically as the incarnation of the god, as at Edfu, where the sacred falcon had to be selected and displayed from the temple pylon. But the status of the chosen animal was not so high as that of the Apis bull, who reigned alone among bulls for his lifetime. The elevation of one bird to be the reigning sacred falcon did not cancel the sanctity of other falcons, which were kept in some numbers within the temple complex. The necessity of finding burial-places for large numbers of animals enforced a fairly modest style of interment, although the quantity of animals involved required a cemetery of some considerable size. At Saqqara, the baboon galleries contained over four hundred burials, but the falcons ran into hundreds of thousands, and consequently the individual treatment of the birds was less elaborate than that of the apes. The baboon gallery is on two levels, the lower having been cut after the upper level had been entirely filled with mummies. The animals were embalmed and placed in wooden boxes, which were set into recesses cut in the walls of the passages. The mummy was consolidated in its box by filling the interior spaces with gypsum plaster, thereby setting the corpse rigid in a plaster case, enclosed by the wooden boards of the box. Each container was sealed into its recess by a limestone slab, on which were written brief details of the baboon, including its name and date of burial. Unfortunately, only a single mummy remained in its original location, the remainder having been destroyed during the early Christian period.

The entrance to the falcon galleries lies in the southern part of the temple terrace of Nectanebo II and consists of a narrow, twisting staircase leading to a rough-hewn corridor. This passage winds on into the rock with side-galleries at intervals. The passages are about 2.5 m wide by 3 m high, and extend for a total distance of over 600 m, each lateral gallery being completely filled with pottery jars containing the mummies of the sacred falcons (fig. 84).

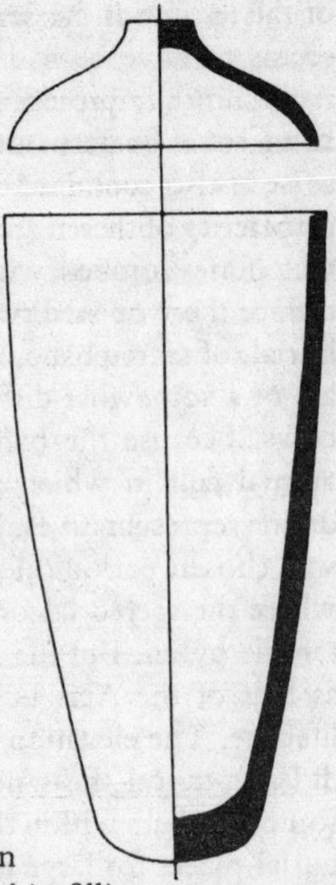

Fig.84.Pottery jar of the type used for falcon mummies

Many of the birds had been carefully wrapped in intricate linen bandaging, and some had painted plaster masks over the faces. After they had been sealed into their pottery containers, the jars were laid in regular layers inside the catacombs, with a thin filling of clean sand between each row. As a gallery became full it was closed off from the axial corridor by a stone or brick wall, or, in some cases, by mud–plaster applied directly over the ends of the stacked pots. Some birds received special treatment: at intervals along the passages there were niches cut in the rock walls, containing the remains of a falcon mummy within a coffin of wood or limestone. Appearances can be deceptive, however, as some of the finest mummies were found inside plain pottery jars, while more elaborate containers were often found to hold only a few bones wrapped in linen and consolidated into a solid mass with resin. Not all the mummies were those of falcons, for amongst the burials were found remains of ibises and a few very large pottery jars containing what were probably mummified vultures. Mixed in with the pots in the galleries were various objects, including bronze or glazed composition figures of divinities and sacred animals, bronze ritual equipment from the temple and relic boxes of metal or wood. Burying such items with the birds was a method of disposing of excess material which could not be re-used owing to its sacred connections. The relic boxes are an interesting feature of all major animal cemeteries. They consist of rectangular containers of bronze or wood, in which a few bones of the sacred animal could be placed, with a figure of the appropriate creature on top of the box (fig. 85). Most examples from the falcon galleries at Saqqara bore images of falcons, as one would expect, but relic boxes for ibises, ichneumons, snakes and even a scarab were also found.

Fig.85.Bronze relic box for a falcon

The cemeteries of the cows, falcons and baboons at Saqqara lie in an area which seems to have been designated a special animal necropolis in the Late and Ptolemaic Periods, for in the vicinity are yet more underground galleries, this time devoted to the burials of ibises. These are situated to the north and south of the temple of Nectanebo II, forming two separate complexes of great extent, similar in style to the falcon galleries, although with slightly larger corridors. It is estimated that something approaching half a million mummified birds lie in these burial-places, each one contained in the usual pottery vessel. The builders of the galleries had considerable problems with earlier tomb-pits, which honeycomb the rock in this area; every so often the tunnellers would cut into a shaft, and would be forced to divert the passage or provide support for the filling before they could proceed. Many of these pits have now spilled their rubble into the corridors, while in other cases the filling possesses sufficient cohesion to remain suspended over the void, presenting a cause of concern to those who excavate beneath. It is by no means uncommon at Saqqara for there to be sudden subsidence of patches of desert, as shafts collapse or the roofs of underground tunnels give way.

Saqqara is a good example of the way in which cemeteries of particular animals could develop away from the original cult-centre of the god with whom they were associated. The baboons and ibises were the sacred animals of Thoth, god of writing and wisdom, who had his main religious centre at Hermopolis in Middle Egypt; the falcons represent Re, worshipped at Heliopolis, and only the Apis bull, together with his mother, the Isis cow, originate from the Memphite district. These are not the only animals buried at the site: on the eastern side of the plateau lies the subterranean cemetery of the dogs or jackals sacred to the embalmer-god, Anubis, and further to the south are the burials of cats, here considered as the animal representatives of Bastet. Other animal burials are known only from texts and their location on the ground is still to be determined; these include a cemetery of rams and, most surprisingly of all, a possible burial-place for lions, mentioned in a Greek papyrus.

Subterranean galleries like those beneath the Saqqara plateau are known at Tuna el-Gebel, the necropolis of Hermopolis Magna. They date from the Late and Graeco-Roman Periods, and are devoted to the burials of ibises and baboons, both representatives of Thoth, chief divinity of the city (plate 34). The galleries at Tuna are somewhat larger than their Saqqara counterparts, and they possess many more niches in the walls for individual ibis burials. The latter were contained in small coffins of wood or stone, often with a figure of an ibis sculpted upon the cover. In certain of the passages, rows of such coffins in limestone were found beneath the masses of burials in pottery jars; they were set across the corridors with eight coffins in each row. This number is significant; it is a symbolic reference to the Egyptian name of the town of Hermopolis, which was simply the numeral 8. The reason for the city

being known as 'Eight-Town' was due to an early belief that it had
been the home of a group of eight divinities who were responsible
for the creation of the world. By placing the ibis-coffins in rows
of eight, the Egyptians were simply re-stating the connection of
Thoth with his city. He is normally referred to in ancient inscriptions as 'Thoth, the twice great, the Lord of Hermopolis', the name
of the city being written with eight strokes (fig. 86). Hermopolis
is the Greek name for the city, given because the Greeks associated
Thoth with Hermes.

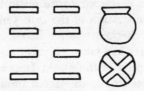

*Fig. 86. The writing of the name of the city
later called Hermopolis Magna*

Baboons were interred in the same complex as the ibises at Tuna,
the wrapped corpses being placed in coffins of stone or wood and
set in recesses in the walls. One mummy found intact was equipped
with amulets of gold and glazed composition, attached on the outside of the wrappings. On the desert close to the necropolis some
evidence was found of the sacred park in which the live ibises were
kept. We know from textual sources that both ibises and falcons
were kept at Saqqara, and the remains of birds' eggs found in
excavations at that site may indicate areas in which the creatures
were bred. The administration of any sacred animal cult-centre and
necropolis involved considerable organization and certainly provided employment for many individuals. In addition to the priests
of the temples and the embalmers, there must also have been people
involved in the provision of food for the animals, stonemasons for
work in the galleries, scribes, and persons engaged in pottery manufacture. The last-named must indeed have felt secure in their
employment, having been authorized to produce the hundreds of
thousands of pots required as containers for bird mummies. Much
of our information about the administration of the ibis cult at
Saqqara comes from demotic ostraca – memoranda written on

sherds of pottery – found on the site. One text refers to the bringing of food for the 60,000 ibises, which, if the figure is accurate, gives some idea of the number of birds involved. It has been estimated that the average rate of burial for ibises at Saqqara must have been in the order of 10,000 birds per annum. There was apparently a mass burial of mummified ibises once a year, the whole process being a rather formal occasion, including a funeral procession to the galleries accompanied by members of the priesthood. The affairs of animal burial, however, did not always run smoothly, and the Saqqara texts describe reforms instituted to stamp out corruption in the administration of the cult. One irregularity which seems to have been checked was the burial of empty pots by the embalmers, when they had taken payment for the complete mummification and wrapping of an ibis. At Tuna el-Gebel, one official, at least, was more devoted to the sacred animals. A certain Ankhhor, High-Priest of Thoth, prepared his own tomb in the ibis catacombs and his stone sarcophagus was found guarded by fifteen gilded wooden statues of the ibis. This unusual burial of a human being in an animal cemetery is paralleled by the interment of Prince Khaemwase in the Serapeum.

The vast numbers of ibises mummified and buried in the later stages of Egyptian civilization present a problem over the circumstances surrounding the death of the birds. It would seem impossible to have reached such a death-rate if each animal had been allowed to live its natural lifespan, and we are faced with the possibility that the birds may have been deliberately killed. This probability is not limited to ibises, but would apply equally to all those cults in which the mass burial of thousands of creatures was involved. Of course, the dispatch of the animals would have been accomplished in some ritual manner, as befitting divine representatives. It is quite probable that the animals were drowned, although we have no direct evidence, but we know that humans who died by drowning were accorded special reverence and elevated to divine status.

Not all the animal cemeteries in Egypt took the form of underground tunnels. At Abydos, ibises were found in large pots which had simply been buried in the ground at no great depth. These pots differed from the type employed at Saqqara in that they were of sufficient size to contain a number of mummies. The tops of the vessels were generally closed by two or three mud-bricks laid across the mouth. Abydos also possesses a subterranean cemetery for dogs, probably considered here as the divine representatives of Khentamentiu, an important necropolis-god of the district. Cats were interred at Bubastis and Speos Artemidos, in addition to the burials at Saqqara already mentioned. At the former site the cats were sacred to Bastet, while at Speos Artemidos they represent Pasht, a lioness-headed goddess. The Bubastis cemetery was explored by Edouard Naville, working for the Egypt Exploration Fund in 1888, and he found deep pits lined with brickwork, filled with the remains of the animals. On discovering evidence of burning, Naville assumed that the bodies had been cremated, but this seems very unlikely. Cremation was not a custom with any appeal to the Egyptians, since their entire mortuary belief revolved around the preservation of the body. Also, there would have been little point in going to the trouble of embalming the cats if they were to be burnt. Remains of burning are, in any case, not uncommon in animal cemeteries, as the result of accidental fires or the deliberate vandalism of plunderers. At Dendera in Upper Egypt, a mixed cemetery of various animals had burned so fiercely that the mud-bricks with which the passages were lined had become completely vitrified. This burial-place had been constructed by building tunnels of brickwork in trenches cut in the desert surface, and then re-covering them with sand. In this way an underground structure could be created without tunnelling, and it may be that the quality of the rock was too poor for direct undercutting. The cemetery was begun in the Eighteenth Dynasty and had been extended in several phases down to the Roman Period. Its various sections contained mummies of birds, gazelles, cats, ichneumons and snakes, although many of the tunnels were found to be empty or simply filled with clean sand when Petrie explored the complex in 1898.

It may seem strange that the vast majority of animal burials belong to the later stages of Egyptian civilization, when one might have expected these primitive cults to have been replaced by more intellectual religious concepts. This is not to say that advanced ideas did not exist, for they certainly did, but, owing to Egyptian conservatism, they had not replaced earlier beliefs. As explained earlier in this chapter, animal cults persisted right through the history of Egypt. However, the most remarkable feature is the excessive zeal displayed over the provision of temples and cemeteries for animals in the Late and Ptolemaic Periods, and it seems that the explanation of this phenomenon lies in political considerations. During this part of their history, the Egyptians were repeatedly dominated by foreigners – first the Persians and then the Greeks. The extension of animal worship at this time may well have been part of a nationalistic movement, probably inspired by the priesthood, intentionally exaggerating the most characteristic features of Egyptian culture. Another aspect of the same process is seen in the increasing complexity of the hieroglyphic script used for temple inscriptions. If this interpretation is correct, then the vast animal cemeteries of the Late Period are to be viewed as a final attempt by the Egyptians to assert the superiority of their traditional culture.

Animal burials, in addition to the examples discussed above, are plentiful throughout Egypt, and it would be pointless to describe each cemetery individually, as the general characteristics are much the same. However, a few cults deserve special note. The sacred rams of Elephantine belonged to the same type of cult as that of the bulls, with a single animal reigning at any one time. At the death of the ram the corpse was embalmed and wrapped, decorated with its regalia, including a miniature crown, and interred in a large stone sarcophagus. The ram of Elephantine was sacred to Khnum, god of the First Cataract region. Far to the north, at Mendes in the Nile Delta, another sacred ram was worshipped under the name Banebdjed, which means simply 'The Ram, Lord of Mendes'. Crocodiles were buried in the Fayum and at Kom Ombos, the animals at both places being the representatives of Sebek. The mummies were buried in very large numbers and included crocodiles of all sizes, together with a quantity of eggs. Many of the animals were preserved in rather summary fashion by the extensive use of black resin, transforming the mummy into a very heavy solid mass. Some examples proved to be of exceptional interest, however, owing to the use of discarded papyrus documents by the embalmers for the packing of the mummies or the manufacture of cartonnage wrappings. This remarkable re-use of the waste paper of the Ptolemaic Period has turned a number of crocodile mummies into valuable sources of information. Among the crocodile burials of the Fayum were a number of fake mummies, consisting of a bundle of reeds wrapped up with an odd bone or two, which may represent evidence of corrupt practices among the embalmers, such as is known from the sacred ibis necropolis at Saqqara.

Individual animal mummies were sometimes placed inside a hollow compartment within a wooden statue of an appropriate divinity, dog mummies occurring in figures of Anubis and cats in figures of Bastet or Wadjet. Some such figures may well have served as cult-statues in temples, additional sanctity having been gained by the inclusion of the sacred animal within the image. The practice may seem bizarre to us, but it is not far removed from the preservation of sacred 'relics' in churches. Probably the most unusual resting-place for an animal was that of the baboon interred with the God's Wife of Amun, Makare, of the Twenty-First Dynasty. It is difficult to see any connection with animal-worship in the placing of the baboon in the coffin of the priestess, and, since Makare died in childbirth, it has been suggested that the mummified baboon was supplied deliberately as a substitute child mummy. Other examples of animal remains wrapped up in the style of child mummies are known from the Graeco-Roman Period, but these are probably to be explained as cases of fraudulent embalming to disguise the accidental loss or destruction of the body.

FUNERARY ARCHITECTURE

During the examination of various aspects of Egyptian funerary archaeology in the foregoing chapters of this book, it has been possible to include details of tomb design only in so far as they were directly linked to the subject under discussion – the counter-measures to tomb-robbing and the effect of the offering cult on tomb development being obvious examples. It is, however, well worth while to study funerary buildings in more depth, to obtain some idea of the range of structures produced over the three-thousand-year span of Egyptian civilization, together with their chronological development and methods of construction. A number of general surveys of tomb development have been produced and all have tended to treat the subject from the chronological point of view, tracing the changes in tomb design from earliest times onwards. Another way of dealing with the material is to adopt the typological approach, to give a survey of the variety of Egyptian tomb-types and to list chronological and regional differences under each class. The latter method has been chosen here since it offers a better opportunity of presenting an overall view of the different funerary buildings in a comprehensible form for the non-specialist. One problem in classifying Egyptian tombs is deciding whether to distinguish the styles by variations in the form of the superstructure or substructure. In fact, the divisions have to be somewhat arbitrary, because many tombs have had their super-structures entirely destroyed, leaving only their underground parts for consideration. Basically, the following types of tomb can be distinguished:

1. Simple pit-graves
2. Mastaba-tombs
3. Rock-cut chapels
4. Pyramid-tombs
5. Built mortuary chapel-tombs.

Within each of these five groups there exist a number of subdivisions, which will be examined in turn. This survey is primarily concerned with the development of private tombs, since the royal monuments have already received a fair amount of description and require only brief comments to fill out the details.

Type 1: simple pit-graves

The simple grave, consisting of a pit in the ground just large enough to accommodate a body and a few grave-goods, is the earliest form to appear in Egypt, being characteristic of the Predynastic Period (plate 36). However, it must not be thought that this kind of burial disappeared in the more highly developed Dynastic age; in fact, the simple grave, or various adaptations of it, persisted right through to the last stages of the ancient civilization, although its longevity was more the result of poverty than of choice. Burial-places of this class vary considerably in quality of construction, a reflection of variations in wealth among the poorer section of the community. Already in the Predynastic Period we see the introduction of a lining of wood or brick to the pit and the provision of roofing; towards the end of the period the first multi-chambered substructures occur (fig. 87).

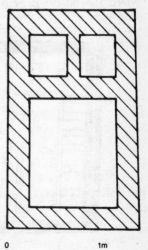

0   1m

Fig.87. Late Predynastic tomb with store-chambers in the substructure

Very simple pits are known from the Early Dynasties, a large proportion of them being satellite burials around the larger tombs of royalty or nobility. In fact, there is evidence from Saqqara to show that certain of these tombs possessed small brick mastaba superstructures of their own, and consequently they should properly be classed with other mastaba-tombs. However, the vast majority of small satellite graves have lost their superstructures entirely, and, rather than place the whole series with the mastaba-tombs on the basis of only a handful of better-preserved examples, it is safer to class these graves by the form of their substructures and to group them with the simple pits. In the same way, the Predynastic graves could probably be classed as 'tumulus-graves', since that is what they seem to have been before their superstructures were eroded away.

The Abydos royal tombs are a special group, which can be described as very much enlarged and elaborated versions of the simple pit, with internal subdivisions of the chamber in brick and wood (fig. 88). From the reign of Den onwards, they possess the added refinement of a stairway descent to the pit.

During the Third Dynasty, numerous shallow pits were prepared around the large tombs of the wealthy at sites like Saqqara.

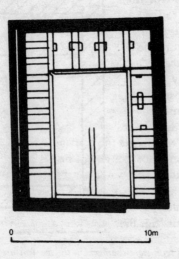

Fig.88.Plan of the tomb of Uadji at Abydos

0   10m

These graves differed from the satellite burials of the preceding dynasties in that they were not intended for servants buried at the same time as the owner of the larger tomb, but were later additions. Some of them were actually cut into the structure of the big mastabas, as burial in or around the superstructure of a large tomb seemed to have some attraction for lesser individuals. A similar situation obtained later in the Old Kingdom, when dozens of shallow pits were sunk in the streets alongside the stone-built mastabas of Giza and Saqqara (fig. 89). In Roman times, something of the same desire to insert small tombs into the fabric of larger and earlier monuments persisted, and rough pits to accommodate limestone coffins were cut into the structure of Old Kingdom pyramids and their temples.

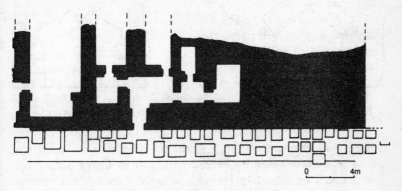

Fig. 89. The accumulation of small pits beside a large
mastaba of the Old Kingdom

From the late Old Kingdom right down to the latest times there are plentiful examples of simple pit-graves for poor burials, often with some kind of brickwork cover over the body (and coffin, if any container was provided). The disposition of the bricks can take the form of a true arch, a rough corbel-vault or different styles of gabled structure. The brick covering is often supported on low lining walls of the same material around the interior of the pit. All the different styles occur contemporaneously, because these graves were so simple that there was little scope for any development. In figure 90 a grave of the late Old Kingdom and another of the Eighteenth Dynasty are illustrated in cross-section to show how the gabled brickwork around the burials is virtually identical in construction, despite the long time-span between the two monuments. This kind of arrangement could almost be described as a brick coffin, built around and over the extended body. In the case of wealthier individuals, larger versions of these bricked substructures were constructed beneath mastabas, as will be described in the next section. Simple brick-lined pit-graves do not seem to be restricted geographically; they are known at sites from the Delta to Nubia.

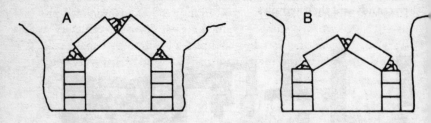

Fig. 90. Gabled brick tombs of the Old Kingdom (A) and New Kingdom (B)

One very characteristic style of the pit type of burial is the so-called 'pan-grave' used by Nubians resident in Egypt during the late Second Intermediate Period and early Eighteenth Dynasty. The name of these graves is derived from their simple form – a shallow pit in the desert surface – and they are not greatly different from some Predynastic graves.

The evolution of pit-graves, leaving the special case of the Abydos royal tombs aside, can be summarized as the transition from the unlined circular or oval early Predynastic grave to a brick-lined rectangular one by the Naqada II period, and the subsequent introduction of deeper pits in the Early Dynastic Period and Old Kingdom, followed by the addition of brickwork over the burial. After this stage, reached by the late Old Kingdom, there was little further progress, since the development was limited by the lack of wealth of the tomb-owners. In the Roman Period there are many brick-covered graves which show no improvement over those of the late Old Kingdom, apart from the occasional use of burnt bricks in place of the more common sun-dried variety. The lack of change is a good confirmation of the view expressed by Reisner many years ago, that the main advances took place in the wealthy tombs and were imitated by the less well-off according to their means.

Type 2: mastaba tombs

The origin of the name 'mastaba' and some description of the form of superstructure to which the term is applied have been given in Chapter 3, allowing us to proceed directly to a more detailed consideration of the evolution of this style of tomb. That simple brick mastabas with gravel filling stood above unlined pits as superstructures is known from the First Dynasty cemetery at Tarkhan, where the earliest examples of offering-chapels built against the side of the mastaba also occur (fig. 91). Prior to the

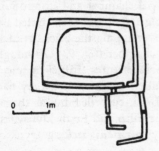

Fig.91.Early First Dynasty tomb at Tarkhan with a simple offering-chapel

reign of Den in the First Dynasty, mastabas were constructed above burials after the interment had been completed, but the introduction of the stairway entrance at this date allowed the superstructure to be built in advance. The characteristic feature of the large mud-brick mastaba of the First Dynasty is the palace-facade panelling on the exterior faces, revivals of which are found on certain tombs of the Third Dynasty (fig. 92). The main trends

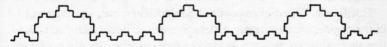

Fig.92.An example of palace-facade panelling

in the development of the mastaba during the First Dynasty are the gradual disappearance of the niched facade, together with the transference of the storerooms from the superstructure to the substructure, as noted in Chapter 3. By the Second Dynasty, the mastaba-tomb had been simplified to a plain rectangular structure with only two offering-niches in the east face, but the subterranean levels tended to become more extensive than before (figs. 9, 11). Access to the underground apartments was gained by means of a stairway, at first descending from the valley side, but later from the north. It is in the Second Dynasty that differences appear between the tombs of the Memphite region and those of Upper Egypt, where technological innovations were adopted more slowly. The deep rock-cut burial chambers do not appear in the south until some time after their introduction at Memphis; instead, the more shallow substructure cut in the desert gravel and entered by a short stairway remained in use. Good examples of this type occur at Naga ed-Deir, where the burial chamber and storerooms were built of brick in a pit cut in the ground, and then roofed by corbel-vaulting. This is a system of overlapping the bricks at each course until the roof closes over the chamber (fig. 93). Although most of the tombs had lost their superstructures, sufficient traces were found above some of the chambers to show that they had consisted of small brick mastabas. Brick-corbelled burial chambers under mastabas also occur in the Fifth and Sixth Dynasties, but in these later versions the stairway entrance is lacking.

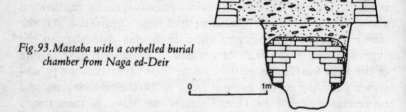

Fig.93.Mastaba with a corbelled burial
chamber from Naga ed-Deir

0   1m

During the Third Dynasty, the substructures of mastaba-tombs in the region of the capital at Memphis developed rapidly to adopt the vertical shaft descent to the burial chamber in place of the stairway. The transition was made in a number of stages, in which

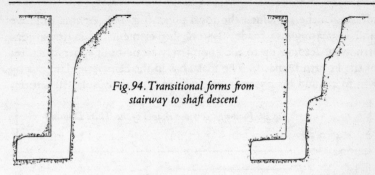

*Fig.94. Transitional forms from
stairway to shaft descent*

the stair was used in conjunction with the new shaft, or the shaft
itself descended in two or three large steps (fig. 94). Of course,
the change did not occur simultaneously at all levels of society,
because the new fashions were adopted most readily in the rich
tombs, among which we find examples of the true vertical shaft at
the very beginning of the Third Dynasty. Smaller mastabas, on the
other hand, retained the old stairway descent considerably longer.
The number of rooms in the substructure, very large during the
Second Dynasty, was steadily reduced in the following dynasty,
and by the Fourth Dynasty it was usual practice to have only a
single large chamber at the foot of the vertical pit in the rock. At
this date the location of the chamber was shifted from the south
side of the pit to the west. Gradually, the new style of rock-cut
substructure was adopted throughout the country, although the
stairway approach took some time to disappear finally from
Upper Egyptian tombs.

Concurrently with the development of
the underground section of the tomb, the
mastaba superstructure underwent steady
change as the southern offering-niche
grew in complexity to form a truly
enclosed chapel, often of cruciform shape
(fig. 95). Certain tombs, particularly
the brick mastabas of the early Old
Kingdom, made use of the so-called
'corridor chapel', which enclosed the
full extent of the valley side of
the superstructure, but the southern

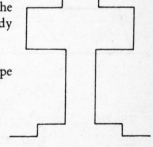

*Fig.95. Plan of a cruciform
chapel of the Second Dynasty*

offering-niche remained the focal point (fig. 96). At this time we find increasing use made of stone for elements of mastaba construction, leading up to the completely stone-built superstructures of the Fourth Dynasty. The mastabas in the cemeteries laid out by Khufu around his pyramid at Giza are essentially solid structures,

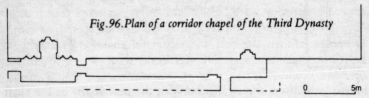

Fig.96.Plan of a corridor chapel of the Third Dynasty

the outer faces of which were cased with fine limestone and smoothly dressed. Through the body of the mastaba descend one or two square shafts, cut vertically into the bedrock to open into the burial chamber on the west side at the base (fig. 97). The chapels of these tombs were often built as separate constructions of brick against the southern end of the east face, so as to enclose and protect the false-door stela which now took the place of the earlier offering-niche at this point (fig. 98). Much greater use of inscriptions and reliefs was now possible, as the stone parts of the tomb provided a suitable medium for carving. The wholly exterior chapels gradually gave rise to a type in which the rooms of the chapel were partly built within the superstructure and partly added to the outside, the beginning of the process which was to lead to the cult-rooms being included completely inside the mastabas of the later Old Kingdom (plate 37). The use of stone for

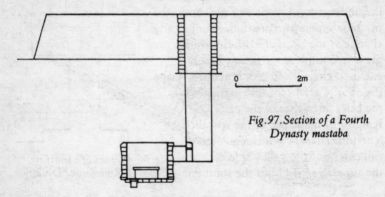

Fig.97.Section of a Fourth Dynasty mastaba

tomb-building soon became standard in the monuments of the rich, especially at Giza, but mud-brick mastabas remained in common use throughout the Old Kingdom for poorer burials. In the early Fourth Dynasty cemetery at Meydum an interesting variant type of tomb occurs, in which both the burial chamber and the sloping approach corridor were built of masonry in a large trench cut in the ground (fig. 99). This style involved considerably more labour to construct than the rock-cut shaft and chamber, and did not remain popular for long, although some examples of the sloping corridor as an alternative to the vertical pit are found in later tombs.

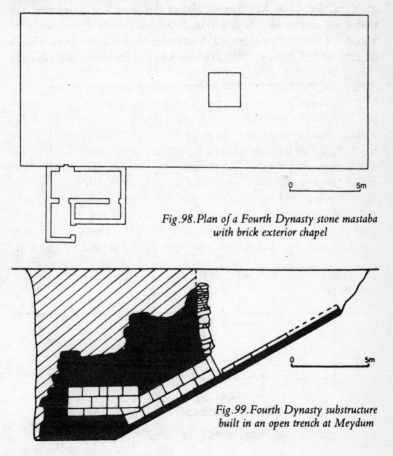

Fig.98. Plan of a Fourth Dynasty stone mastaba
with brick exterior chapel

Fig.99. Fourth Dynasty substructure
built in an open trench at Meydum

The history of the mastaba throughout the remainder of the Old Kingdom is largely concerned with the growth of the interior mortuary chapel, as described in Chapter 3. The stone mastabas of the Fifth and Sixth Dynasties show a fair amount of variation in plan as a number of different styles emerged. The trend towards increasing the number of rooms within the superstructure was not carried through in all tombs, so that even in the Sixth Dynasty there are still examples of large stone mastabas of virtually solid construction. A good example of this is the huge tomb of Neferseshemre at Saqqara, which possesses a chapel on its eastern side of small proportions in relation to the area of the whole mastaba (fig. 100). In other tombs of the same age, however, the entire superstructure is filled with internal rooms, the walls of which are normally decorated. Smaller mastabas of the period were constructed of stone or brick, or a mixture of the two materials, and

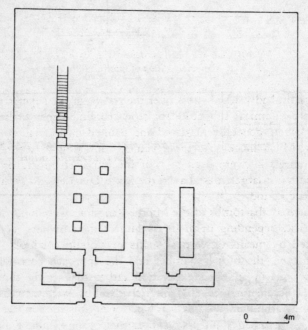

Fig.100.Plan of the mastaba of Neferseshemre at Saqqara

contained two or three rooms in the superstructure. The shafts of these tombs descend vertically to the burial chambers, which open from the west side and extend to the south in the majority of cases, in order to place the burial directly below the offering-chapel (fig. 101). Many small mud-brick mastabas of the late Old

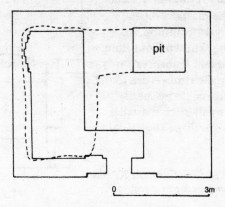

Fig. 101. Plan of a small mastaba of the Sixth Dynasty, showing position of substructure

Kingdom had vaulted roofs over the rooms in the superstructure, as an economical substitute for stone roofing-slabs. These brick vaults were generally plastered and painted on their interior surfaces. Much more substantial vaults, consisting of several rings of brickwork, were used to roof the burial chambers or access corridors of larger mastabas in the Sixth Dynasty and First Intermediate Period.

The mastaba-tombs of the Middle Kingdom were built of stone or brick, depending upon the wealth of their owners, and were entered by means of vertical shafts or sloping corridors. In the latter type, the burial chamber and the approach corridor were often built in an open excavation rather than being tunnelled. The elaborate corridors of some richer tombs, with their complex blocking arrangements and heavy masonry construction, are imitative of the passages in the royal pyramids of the Middle Kingdom. Similar imitation led to the use of gabled roofing-slabs over the burial chambers, with brick relieving arches above (fig. 102). The poorer tombs were usually brick-built, with vaulted burial chambers entered from shallow pits. Brick-vaulted chambers situated just below the ground surface and covered by the mastaba superstructure are very common, examples being known from Edfu, Qatta, Abusir and Kubaniya. Rock-cut burial chambers are found at Abydos, accessible by means of pits from small brick mastabas of almost square shape (fig. 103).

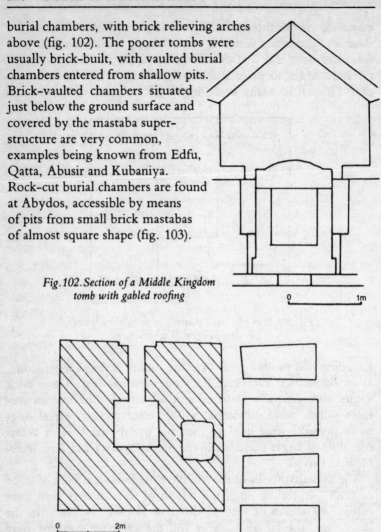

Fig.102.Section of a Middle Kingdom tomb with gabled roofing

Fig.103.Plan of a brick mastaba of the Middle Kingdom at Abydos

The greatest age of the mastaba-tomb, without doubt, was the period between the beginning of the First Dynasty and the fall of the Old Kingdom. The Middle Kingdom mastabas continue the older tradition to some extent, but the major emphasis of Middle Kingdom tomb development was centred on the rock-hewn cliff-tomb. By the New Kingdom the mastaba had evolved into a new form, so different from the original design of the monument that it can no longer be described as a mastaba at all, but rather as a chapel-tomb. These buildings, which imitate the layout of small temples in their plan, are described below under Type 5.

Type 3: rock-cut chapels

The form of Egyptian burial-place usually described as a rock-tomb should really be termed a rock-cut chapel. Nearly all tombs of the Dynastic Period had *substructures* in the bedrock; the deciding factor is whether the cult-rooms of the monument, in which the offering ritual was performed, were hollowed from the rock. In this case the two parts of the tomb – both chapel and sepulchre – had been taken below ground, instead of building a chapel on the surface above the burial chamber. Rock-cut chapels were best suited to those regions of the Nile Valley in which substantial desert cliffs are found, since these provided excellent locations for the cutting of the tombs directly into the hillside.

Rock-hewn chapels originate in the Old Kingdom and are not uncommon, although most examples of the period are of no great size. They occur not only in the cliffs of Middle and Upper Egypt, but also in parts of the Memphite necropolis, inserted into the edges of slight escarpments or even in the sides of old quarries. Inside the rock-cut chapel there is normally a false-door stela at which the offering formula could be recited, and the walls might be decorated with paintings or reliefs from the repertoire of Old Kingdom tomb art. Sometimes the chapels served for the cult of several individuals buried in separate chambers below floor-level, in which case there are multiple false doors. Communication between the chapel and the burial chamber was by means of a vertical pit in the floor, or a sloping corridor descending from the rear of the chapel (fig. 104). Rock-tombs gained in popularity during the First Intermediate Period, a time which saw the development of considerable provincial cemeteries containing this kind of monument. As the chapels grew larger, pillars were included in the architectural design by leaving sections of the rock standing.

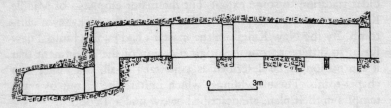

Fig.104. Section of a rock-cut tomb of the Old Kingdom

Gradually rock-tombs became more elaborate and assumed a longer, narrow form as they were carried deeper into the cliffs. From the Middle Kingdom there are many fine examples of decorated rock-cut chapels at various sites throughout Middle and Upper Egypt, belonging to the powerful governors of individual districts. Each necropolis has its own distinctive features, but the general scheme of such tombs includes an impressive facade, often with a columned portico, a spacious, pillared hall within the cliff and a shrine at the end of the tomb for a statue of the deceased (plate 38). The placing of the shrine at the end heightened the axial nature of the plan and led to the development of a chapel resembling the form of a small temple. At Beni Hasan, the tombs of the Twelfth Dynasty nomarchs contained very large chapels with fluted or polygonal columns arranged symmetrically around the middle axis (fig. 105), while the rock-cut tombs of Thebes and Aswan consisted of narrower corridors, driven into the cliffs for considerable distances (fig. 106). Rock-cut chapels were often embellished by the provision of some kind of exterior courtyard and approach, with either a row of columns along the back of the court, or brick pylons built against the cliff at the tomb entrance. The most impressive approaches were constructed for the local princes of Qau, whose tombs possessed grand porticoes and covered causeways leading up to the rock-cut chapel, in an imitation of the royal pyramid complex (fig. 107).

Although the rock-tombs of the Middle Kingdom are imposing and numerous, the greatest use of this type of tomb is found in the New Kingdom necropolis of Thebes. The typical chapel in this cemetery consisted of a doorway into a transverse hall, behind which was a corridor running straight into the cliff. At the end of

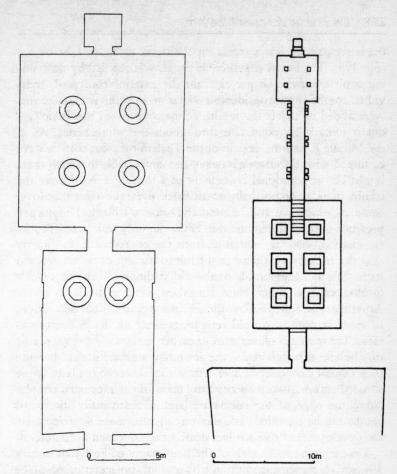

Fig.105.Plan of the tomb of
Amenemhat at Beni Hasan

Fig.106.Plan of the tomb of
Sirenput II at Aswan

Fig.107.Plan of the tomb of Wahka I at Qau

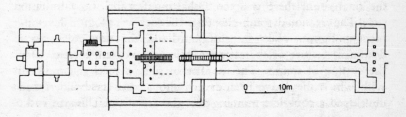

the latter passage was a recess for the statue or stela of the owner (fig. 108). The burial chamber, as usual, was reached by descending a pit from the chapel or from the exterior courtyard. Individual tombs show considerable variation in plan, as extra rooms were added to reflect the wealth of the owner, but this basic layout is remarkably consistent throughout the whole series. As in the Middle Kingdom, certain of the Theban rock-cut chapels were equipped with elaborate gateways and courtyards, in which there might be the additional refinement of a tomb garden. Above the tombs there were normally small brick pyramid superstructures, some of which can still be seen at Dira abu'l Naga. Despite the presence of these pyramids, the tombs can only be classed as rock-cut chapels, since the entrance from the courtyard leads directly into the rock-hewn chambers of the tomb and does not descend from below the pyramids in the old tradition. Rock-cut chapel-tombs occur at other New Kingdom sites, particularly at El-Amarna, where they follow the Theban style in all but decoration. In more remote provincial cemeteries the New Kingdom tombs retain the more obsolete forms of earlier periods. The royal tombs of Thebes, although rock-cut, are really a separate class because they consist of the sepulchres without the chapels; the latter were situated some distance away in the form of the mortuary temples along the edge of the cultivated land. Consequently, the royal tombs can be regarded as highly complex rock-cut substructures, the development of which has already been outlined in Chapter 4.

True rock-hewn chapels of the later stages of Egyptian history are not so numerous, although this tomb-type continued to be used. The Twenty-Sixth Dynasty tomb of the vizier Bakenranef is a good example, and consists of a series of rooms cut into the escarpment at Saqqara (fig. 109). The axial plan, descended from the earlier history of the rock-tomb, is here perpetuated, and in the final room there was the archaizing feature of a false-door stela. The creation of tomb-chapels in the rock was a logical development in Egypt, where the cliffs bordering the Nile Valley are a dominant feature of the country, offering excellent locations for the cutting of tombs. The number of such chapels and the skill with which they have been carved shows that the builders had developed a complete mastery over the art of tunnelling in rock.

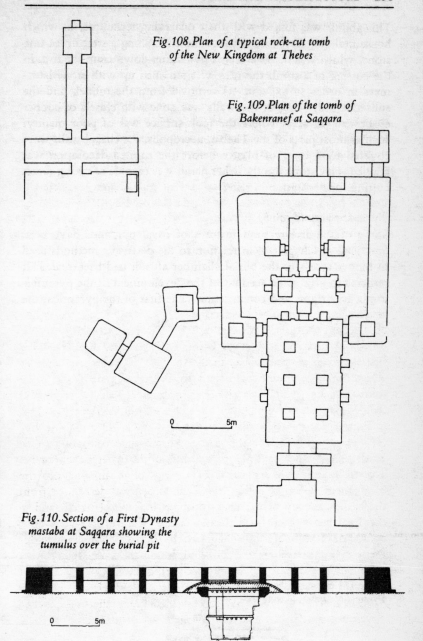

Fig.108. Plan of a typical rock-cut tomb
of the New Kingdom at Thebes

Fig.109. Plan of the tomb of
Bakenranef at Saqqara

0   5m

Fig.110. Section of a First Dynasty
mastaba at Saqqara showing the
tumulus over the burial pit

0   5m

This ability was linked with their quarrying technique, in which horizontal galleries were cut into the cliffs along a stratum of fine stone, which was then extracted by cutting down from the top. In the cutting of a tomb the rock was smashed up with stone hammers in order to expedite its removal from the tunnel, and the subsequent dressing of the walls was done with chisels of copper or bronze. In areas where the rock surface was of poor quality, such as most parts of the Theban necropolis, the chapel walls were covered by a layer of plaster before the painted decoration was applied. Fine stone, on the other hand, was capable of taking direct cutting for decoration in relief.

Type 4: pyramid-tombs

Some of the architectural features of royal pyramids have been described in Chapter 4, in relation to the defensive methods used to hinder access to the burial chamber after it had been sealed. It remains to give some account of the development of the pyramid-tomb, its origins and construction. The first of the pyramids, the

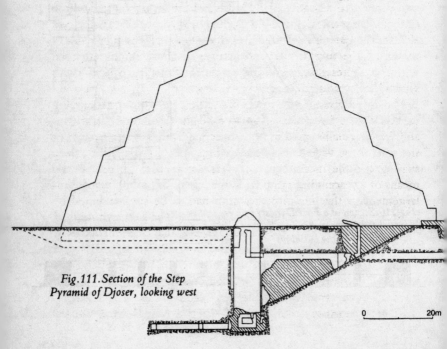

Fig.111.Section of the Step
Pyramid of Djoser, looking west

0   20m

stepped monument of Djoser at Saqqara, represents a dramatic achievement in early building technique for which Imhotep, the architect and chief minister of Djoser, must have been largely responsible. Although the structure was built first as a mastaba and subsequently enlarged by stages into the six-stepped pyramid we see today, it was planned from the outset as a pyramid-tomb. It has been suggested that the origin of the step-pyramid form may have been the stepped tumulus of brick which was discovered within the superstructure of the First Dynasty mastaba 3038 at Saqqara. This tumulus is itself paralleled by earlier examples at the same site, consisting of plain tumuli of rubble, cased with a layer of brick, incorporated into the mastaba superstructures of several large tombs (fig. 110). The location of the tumulus inside the palace-facade mastaba has been compared with the Step Pyramid within its enclosure wall of the same design. This link may well be correct, but the origin of the tumulus itself is not so clear. Its presence seems to be an attempt to fuse two kinds of superstructure in a single unit, although suggestions that the tumulus represents the burial customs of the south and the niched mastaba those of the north seem highly dubious. It is more probable that the two elements imitate different features of the royal tombs at Abydos, a model of the tumulus superstructures of those tombs enclosed within a representation of the so-called 'funerary palaces' with which they were associated.

The Step Pyramid of Djoser, the earliest large stone monument erected by the Egyptians, rises to a height of about sixty metres and was originally cased in fine limestone from Tura on the opposite side of the valley. Its burial chamber lies at the foot of a deep shaft under the monument and was designed to be reached by means of a descending ramp from the north, but following the enlargement of the pyramid the ramp had to be supplemented by tunnelling (fig. 111). The later pyramids of the Third Dynasty, that of Sekhemkhet at Saqqara and the 'Layer Pyramid' of Zawiyet el-Aryan, were each left incomplete, but they possessed tunnelled entrances to the burial chambers, in the former case cut from an open ramp and in the latter from the side of a vertical shaft. The mortuary temples of the step pyramids were situated on the northern side for the reasons given in Chapter 6. At the close of the Third Dynasty or commencement of the Fourth, the Meydum pyramid exhibits a transitional phase from stepped monument to true pyramid. Built originally as a monument of seven steps and later enlarged to eight, the final design added yet more masonry to fill in the steps and create the first straight-sided pyramid. At Meydum we also find the earliest example of the standard Old Kingdom pyramid complex, including a mortuary temple on the eastern side, a causeway and a valley temple. The entrance passage to the pyramid of Meydum descends from an opening in the north face until it terminates in a vertical shaft, which leads upwards into the burial chamber (fig. 112). Similarities to this pattern are evident in the two pyramids of Sneferu at Dashur, in both of which we also find corbelled ceilings like that in the pyramid at Meydum. The Dashur stone pyramids are considerable monuments, the northernmost being only slightly inferior in size to the Great Pyramid of Khufu at Giza.

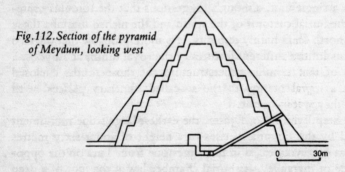

Fig.112.Section of the pyramid of Meydum, looking west

0   30m

The Giza pyramids have been discussed in such detail in other publications that there is no need to comment upon them at length. Their interior corridors exhibit some variation in arrangement, owing to several changes in plan during the construction of each monument. At Giza we see the continued development of the pyramid superstructure to attain even greater size and accuracy of construction in the pyramid of Khufu, which reached a height of 146 m and measured 230 m along its base. This achievement marks the zenith of pyramid-building in the Old Kingdom, and although the pyramid of Khafre was only about three metres lower than the Great Pyramid, subsequent royal pyramids were all much smaller. That of Menkaure rose to only 66 m, but had the distinction of granite casing-blocks for a substantial number of courses. King Djedefre, who ruled between Khufu and Khafre, built his pyramid at Abu Roash, further north, and, rather surprisingly, utilized the obsolete open trench descent to a deep pit substructure in place of tunnelling directly in the bedrock. The same kind of descent is found in the Unfinished Pyramid of Zawiyet el-Aryan, thought also to be of Fourth Dynasty date.

The rather diverse styles observed in the pyramid-tombs of the Fourth Dynasty coalesce into a more standard type in the later part of the Old Kingdom, in which simple corridor entrances from pavement level on the north side are the rule. The construction of the monuments is much inferior to the work of the Fourth Dynasty, and consists of very rough masonry and rubble contained within the outer casing of the pyramid. Each completed pyramid originally had its own mortuary temple, causeway and valley temple on the east side, except in the case of Userkaf, where the location presented technical problems and the mortuary temple was shifted to the south. From the reign of Unas, the chambers of the pyramids were inscribed with the Pyramid Texts.

Throughout the Old Kingdom, the pyramid-tomb had remained a royal prerogative, a tradition which continued in the Middle Kingdom, when the pyramid superstructure reappears. The tombs of the kings of the Eleventh Dynasty at Thebes possessed small brick pyramids built over the rock-cut substructures, but hardly any traces of these pyramids have survived. A larger stone-built pyramid was long thought to have stood in the mortuary temple of King Mentuhotpe II at Deir el-Bahari, but it has recently been suggested that this monument was not a pyramid at all, but an unusual kind of square mastaba. The problem is not yet entirely resolved; the fact that the pyramidal form was current for royal tombs in both the Eleventh and Twelfth Dynasties would make the construction of a different kind of tomb by Mentuhotpe II a distinct break with tradition, but such events are not unknown in Egyptian tomb development, an example being the adoption by Shepseskaf of a mastaba-tomb instead of a pyramid in the Fourth Dynasty.

Pyramids of the early Twelfth Dynasty were constructed of stone and are imitative of the Old Kingdom pattern with the entrance on the north. From the reign of Sesostris II the pyramids were built more economically in mud-brick with the addition of stone casing, and the entrance was moved away from the north face in an attempt at concealment. This change was combined with the introduction of complex interior passages and blocking arrangements, as described in Chapter 4. Other significant new features in pyramid construction at this period are the attempts to relieve the weight on the roof of the burial chamber by the use of huge gabled roof-beams and brick arches (fig. 113), and the lowering of heavy slabs by drawing away the sand which supported them.

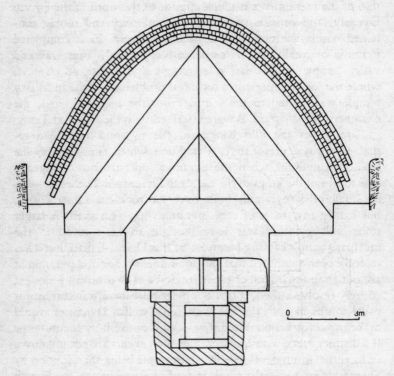

Fig.113.Section of the burial chamber in the pyramid of Hawara

Brick pyramids were still employed as the superstructures of royal tombs in the Seventeenth Dynasty at Thebes but they were of very small size and have not been preserved. In the New Kingdom, the pyramid was taken over by private individuals and used widely in the Theban necropolis, and also at Aniba in Nubia. These pyramids were small structures of white-plastered brickwork with an inscribed capstone at the apex. Small brick pyramids in private tombs are found also in later times, particularly at Abydos in the Thirtieth Dynasty. The latter pyramids are more worthy to be classed as pyramid-tombs than the New Kingdom examples at Thebes, since the burial chambers at Abydos were made within the pyramid itself, with a chapel attached on the exterior, instead of having both chapel and burial cut in the rock deep below the superstructure (fig. 114). Many of these private pyramids had a much steeper slope than the old royal monuments, which normally rose at an angle of about 52°. A steep slope is found also in the royal pyramids of Napata and Meroe, far to the

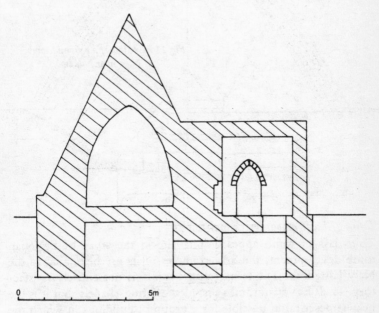

0   5m

Fig. 114. Section of a Late Period brick pyramid-tomb at Abydos

south of Egypt in what is now the Sudan. The perpetuation of the pyramidal form in Nubia was just one of the many influences which the Nubian civilization received from Egypt, although these pyramids differ greatly from the earlier royal pyramids of Egypt and have their own pattern of development. Essentially, they consist of a rock-cut burial chamber under the pyramid, entered by a stairway and tunnel, above which the mortuary chapel was constructed (fig. 115). In the earlier tombs the Egyptian influences are very marked, and include hieroglyphic inscriptions from the Book of the Dead on the walls and stone sarcophagi of Egyptian type, but the later pyramids at Meroe exhibit increasingly the characteristic local interpretation of Egyptian themes. Although the Meroitic pyramids are so different from their Egyptian antecedents, they are the last stage in a long tradition of royal tombs in this form, which they retained down to the middle of the fourth century A.D.

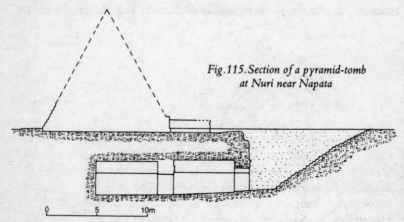

Fig.115. Section of a pyramid-tomb
at Nuri near Napata

0   5   10m

Type 5: built mortuary chapel-tombs

This class of tomb appears quite late in the story of Egyptian tomb development, the first examples of its use belonging to the New Kingdom. The term, 'chapel-tomb' is not entirely satisfactory, as all Egyptian tombs included offering-chapels, but it is the nearest description possible for a group of buildings in which the superstructure assumes the form of a small temple or shrine, built on the ground surface. As mentioned under Type 2, this tomb style may well be the latest development of the mastaba, in which the solid part of the superstructure has given way completely to the rooms of the offering-chapel and these rooms have been rearranged along an axial plan. This design is similar to that evolved for rock-cut chapels, as one would expect, since both types served the same function. The basic layout of a chapel-tomb superstructure is illustrated in figure 116 by the plan of a typical tomb of this class from El-Amra. The approach to the offering-place through

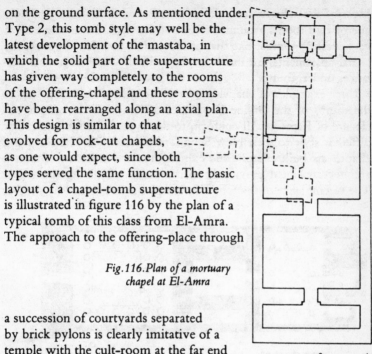

Fig.116.Plan of a mortuary
chapel at El-Amra

a succession of courtyards separated by brick pylons is clearly imitative of a temple with the cult-room at the far end of the building. This kind of tomb remained in use at El-Amra and the nearby cemetery of Abydos from the Eighteenth Dynasty to the Late Period, with variations of the basic plan between individual structures. It seems that the roofing of the inner rooms was vaulted in brick as in certain tombs of the same class at Aniba. Vaulted roofing was certainly employed in the chapel-tomb of General Horemheb at Saqqara, because the remains of the vaults still show. This tomb is a very large and grand example of the mortuary-chapel type, with decorated stone-lined walls and limestone columns around the courtyards (fig. 117). It stands in an area of the Saqqara necropolis where many more tombs of the same type probably exist, in an extensive but unexcavated cemetery of the New Kingdom.

The substructures of chapel-tombs were reached by shafts from the courtyards, descending to the burial chambers in the bedrock.

Most of the substructures are of small extent, consisting of only one or two rooms around the foot of the shaft, but in the case of very wealthy tombs, like that of Horemheb mentioned above, the burial apartments are much larger and run for considerable distances underground.

Later examples of chapel-tombs occur at Medinet Habu, where the tombs of the Divine Votaresses of Amun in the temple enclosure of Ramesses III conform to this type, although in a rather different style to their New Kingdom antecedents. The surviving chapels are built of stone and exhibit the same imitation of temple architecture noted previously in this class of building (plate 39). The resemblance of the tombs to temples is heightened by the fact

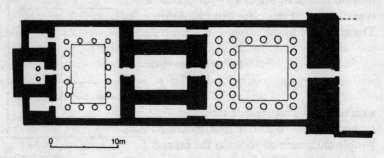

Fig.117.Plan of the tomb of General Horemheb at Saqqara

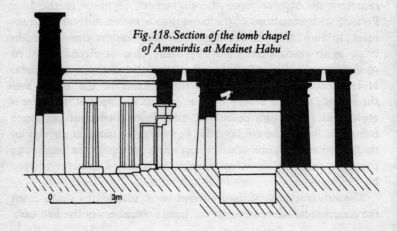

Fig.118.Section of the tomb chapel
of Amenirdis at Medinet Habu

that the stone walls of the chapels are decorated with reliefs showing the owners in religious scenes. The chapels had a pylon entrance, open forecourt and a vaulted sanctuary, below which lay the burial chamber at a shallow depth (fig. 118). Superstructures of a similar kind must have covered the burial chambers of the Twenty-First and Twenty-Second Dynasty kings at Tanis, but only the underground parts of these tombs have survived. No doubt the unrecovered tombs of the kings of the Twenty-Sixth Dynasty at Sais would have been of comparable pattern.

From the late Twenty-Fifth and Twenty-Sixth Dynasties there are very large examples of chapel-tombs in the region of the Theban necropolis known as the Asasif. These buildings have pylons and courtyards of monumental proportions above a rock-hewn substructure. They belonged to officials of extremely high rank at Thebes in the Late Period, including the well-known mayor of the city and Fourth Prophet of Amun, Montuemhat. The perimeter walls of the tomb-chapels were decorated on their exterior faces with a simplified version of the old palace-facade motif, revived for archaistic reasons. The underground passages in certain of these tombs resemble a royal burial-place in their extent and complexity, with a succession of corridors and halls separated by doors and stairways. In the Memphite necropolis at the same period the superstructures of the deep shaft-tombs described on p. 106 seem also to have consisted of brick-built chapels, to judge from the scanty evidence available.

In the latest examples of chapel-tombs it is interesting to note how the style of tomb changed to match the development of the temples upon which they were modelled. An excellent illustration of this process is afforded by the tomb of the High-Priest Petosiris at Tuna el-Gebel. The tomb chapel dates to the end of the Dynastic Period, around 340 B.C., and carefully imitates the temple buildings of that age. It is built entirely of limestone and has a front hall of columns in the style of a pronaos, an element not introduced into temple architecture until very late times. Behind the pillared hall is an inner room for the offering ritual, from the floor of which a shaft descends to the subterranean burial chamber.

In some respects the built chapel-tomb can be regarded as the most advanced development of Egyptian funerary architecture, because it dispenses with any traditional superstructure such as mastaba or pyramid and retains only the two essential elements of the tomb: the burial chamber and the offering-place. The necessity of providing these features in a single building, which could also offer reasonable security, taxed the ingenuity of the architects over the centuries and led to the creation of the various tomb styles outlined above. It is a measure of the achievement of the ancient tomb-builders that their designs not only served their purpose but also led to the production of many structures which can be admired as true masterpieces of architecture.

NOTES

Abbreviations

BM   British Museum (followed by collection number of
                    object in Egyptian Antiquities Department)

Lebensmüde   A. Erman, *Gespräch eines Lebensmüden mit seiner
                    Seele*, in *Abhandlungen der königl. Preuss. Akademie
                    der Wissenschaften*, Berlin, 1896.

Pyr.   K. Sethe, *Die altaegyptischen Pyramidentexte*, 3 vols.,
                    Leipzig, J. C. Hinrichs, 1908–22.

Urkunden   K. Sethe and W. Helck, *Urkunden des Aegyptischen
                    Altertums*, Leipzig, J. C. Hinrichs and Akademie-
                    Verlag, 1906–59.

2. Beginnings of Mummification

1 W. M. F. Petrie, *Seventy Years in Archaeology*, London, Sampson Low,
  1931, 175.
2 Petrie, *Naqada and Ballas*, 32.
3 Petrie and Wainwright, *The Labyrinth and Gerzeh*, 14, 15.
4 *Pyr.*, 735–6.
5 ibid., 1683–5.
6 ibid., 722.
7 ibid., 1500–1501.

3. Providing for the Dead

1 Gardiner, *The Tomb of Amenemhat*, 56.
2 *Lebensmüde*, 52–3.
3 Sethe, *Aegyptische Lesestücke*, Leipzig, J. C. Hinrichs, 1924, 93.
4 BM 10800. See Edwards, *Journal of Egyptian Archaeology* 57 (London
  1971), 120–24.
5 *Pyr.*, 134a–b.
6 ibid., 1610a–b.

7 A. H. Gardiner, *Hieratic Papyri in the British Museum*, 3rd series, London, 1935, II, pl. 18.

8 P. E. Newberry, *Beni Hasan*, I, pl. XXVI.

9 Sethe, op. cit., 98.

10 ibid., 88.

11 Peet, *Cemeteries of Abydos*, II, pl. XXIII, 5.

4. *Security of the Tomb*

1 A. H. Gardiner, *The Admonitions of an Egyptian Sage*, Leipzig, J. C. Hinrichs, 1909,2,8–2,9.

2 Papyrus BM 10052, 11,7–8.

3 *Pyr.*, 878.

4 J. de Morgan, *Fouilles à Dachour 1894–5*, Vienna, Adolphe Holzhausen, 1903, 97.

5 Papyrus BM 10221, 4,1–4,4.

6 Papyrus Leopold-Amherst, 2,4–3,2.

7 Papyrus BM 10054, recto 1, 3–7.

8 ibid., recto 2, 11.

9 Papyrus BM 10052, 13, 15–21.

10 ibid., 14, 23–4.

11 *Urkunden*, IV, 57, 3–5.

12 Herodotus, Book II, 169 (Heinemann 1920 edition).

13 *Pyr.*, 775.

5. *Preserved for Eternity*

1 Quoted in E. Amélineau, *Étude sur le Christianisme en Égypte*, Paris, E. Leroux, 1887, 141–3.

6. *The Egyptian Afterlife*

1 *Pyr.*, 1171–2.

2 Papyrus BM 9900.

3 Book of the Dead, 125a, Introduction.

4 W. Budge, *Book of the Dead, Text, II*, London, Kegan Paul, 1910, 144, 27–30.

5 ibid., 145, 33–6.

6 Hornung, *Das Amduat*, I, 126.

7 R. Lepsius, *Totenbuch*, Leipzig, G. Wigand, 1842, pl. 76.

8 J. de Morgan, op. cit., *mars-juin 1894*, 106, fig. 247.

9 BM 36627.

7. *Coffins and Sarcophagi*

  1 *Pyr.*, 616.
  2 *Urkunden*, I, 99, 10–16.
  3 BM 30842.
  4 BM 1001.

8. *Sacred Animal Cemeteries*

  1 M. Malanine and others, *Catalogue des stèles du Serapeum de Memphis*, Paris, Imprimerie Nationale, 1968, no. 5, 1–3.
  2 Spiegelberg, *Zeitschrift fur Ägyptische Sprache und Altertumskunde*, 56 (Leipzig 1920), 16–17.
  3 Mond and Myers, *The Bucheum*, III, pl. XXXIX, no. 6.

FURTHER READING

Source material for the study of Egyptian tombs and burial customs is plentiful, but tends to be scattered throughout scholarly articles or reports of excavation. This list gives the more important general and scholarly works, but preference has been given to those in English. For certain topics attention is drawn to bibliographies already published elsewhere.

C. Aldred, *Egypt to the End of the Old Kingdom*, London, Thames & Hudson, 1965.

T. G. Allen, *The Book of the Dead*, Chicago, University of Chicago Press, 1974.

C. A. R. Andrews and J. Hamilton-Patison, *Mummies*, London, British Museum Publications and Collins, 1978.

A. Badawy, *A History of Egyptian Architecture*, I–III, Cairo, Urwand Fils, 1954, and Los Angeles, California University Press, 1966–8.

G. Brunton, *Matmar*, London, Quaritch, 1948; *Mostagedda*, London, Quaritch, 1937; *Qau and Badari*, I–III, British School of Archaeology in Egypt, 1927–30.

Cambridge Ancient History, I–II, rev. ed., Cambridge, Cambridge University Press, 1970–75.

H. Carter, *The Tomb of Tutankhamen*, 3 vols., London, Cassell, 1923–33: new single volume edition, London, Sphere Books, 1972.

G. Caton-Thompson, *Badarian Civilisation*, London, British School of Archaeology in Egypt, 1928.

J. Černy, *Ancient Egyptian Religion*, London, Hutchinson, 1952.

W. R. Dawson, *A Bibliography of Works Relating to Mummification in Egypt*, Cairo, Institut Français d'Archéologie Orientale du Caire, 1929; 'Making a mummy', in *Journal of Egyptian Archaeology* 13 (London 1927).

W. R. Dawson and P. H. K. Gray, *Catalogue of Egyptian Antiquities in the British Museum: I, Mummies and Human Remains*, London, British Museum Publications, 1968.

D. E. Derry and R. Engelbach, 'Mummification', in *Annales du Service des Antiquités de l'Égypte* 41 (Cairo 1942).

D. Dunham, *Naga ed-Dêr: IV, The Predynastic Cemetery N. 7000*, Los Angeles, University of California Press, 1965.

I. E. S. Edwards, *The Pyramids of Egypt*, rev. ed., London, Michael Joseph and Penguin Books, 1972. See the detailed bibliography on pages 227–34.

W. B. Emery, *Archaic Egypt*, Penguin Books, 1978; *A Funerary Repast in an Egyptian Tomb of the Archaic Period*, London, Nederlands Instituut voor het Nabije Oosten, 1962; *Great Tombs of the First Dynasty*, I–III, Cairo, Service des Antiquités de l'Égypte, 1940, and London, Egypt Exploration Society, 1949–58.

R. E. Engelbach, *Introduction to Egyptian Archaeology*, Cairo, Service des Antiquités de l'Égypte, 1946.

R. O. Faulkner, *The Egyptian Coffin Texts*, I–III, Warminster, Aris & Phillips, 1973–7; *The Egyptian Pyramid Texts*, Oxford, Oxford University Press, 1969.

A. H. Gardiner, *Egypt of the Pharaohs*, Oxford, Oxford University Press, 1961; *The Attitude of the Ancient Egyptians to Death and the Dead*, Cambridge, Cambridge University Press, 1935; *The Tomb of Amenemhat*, London, Egypt Exploration Society, 1915.

J. Garstang, *Burial Customs of Ancient Egypt*, London, Constable, 1907.

H. Gauthier, *Cercueils anthropoides des prêtres de Montou*, Cairo, Service des Antiquités de l'Égypte, 1913.

J. E. Harris and K. Weeks, *X-Raying the Pharaohs*, London, Macdonald, 1973.

J. E. Harris and K. Wente, *An X-Ray Atlas of the Royal Mummies*, Chicago, University of Chicago Press, 1980. See the bibliography on pages 26–8.

W. C. Hayes, *Royal Sarcophagi of the Eighteenth Dynasty*, Princeton, Princeton University Press, 1935; *The Scepter of Egypt*, I–II, Cambridge, Mass., Harvard University Press, 1953–9.

E. Hornung, *Das Amduat*, I–III, Wiesbaden, Otto Harrassowitz, 1963–7.

T. G. H. James, *An Introduction to Ancient Egypt*, London, British Museum Publications, 1979.

K. A. Kitchen, *The Third Intermediate Period in Egypt*, Warminster, Aris & Phillips, 1973.

P. Lacau, *Sarcophages antérieurs au Nouvel Empire*, I–II, Cairo, Service des Antiquités de l'Égypte, 1904–6.

J. P. Lauer, *Saqqara: The Royal Cemetery of Memphis*, London, Thames & Hudson, 1976.

A. B. Lloyd, *Herodotus, Book II, Commentary 1–98*, Leiden, Brill, 1976. Especially pp. 351–66 with the bibliography there quoted.

A. Lucas, *Ancient Egyptian Materials and Industries*, 4th ed. revised by J. R. Harris, London, Edward Arnold, 1962.

A. C. Mace, *Early Dynastic Cemeteries of Naga ed-Dêr*, II, Leipzig, J. C. Hinrichs, 1909.

G. Maspero, *Sarcophages des époques persane et ptolémaiques*, I–II, Cairo, Service des Antiquités de l'Égypte, 1914–39.

R. Mond and O. H. Myers, *The Bucheum*, I–III, London, Egypt Exploration Society, 1934.

P. Montet, *Eternal Egypt*, London, Mentor Books 1964; *La Nécropole royale de Tanis*, I–III, Paris, Centre National de la Recherche Scientifique, 1947–60.

S. Morenz, *Egyptian Religion*, London, Methüen, 1973.

A. Moret, *Sarcophages de l'époque Bubastite à l'époque Saite*, Cairo, Service des Antiquités de l'Égypte, 1913.

E. Naville, *Cemeteries of Abydos*, I, London, Egypt Exploration Society, 1914.

E. Otto, *Egyptian Art and the Cults of Osiris and Amon*, London, Thames & Hudson, 1968.

T. E. Peet, *Cemeteries of Abydes*, II–III, London, Egypt Exploration Society, 1913–4; *The Great Tomb-Robberies of the Twentieth Egyptian Dynasty*, Oxford, Oxford University Press, 1930.

W. M. F. Petrie, *Amulets*, London, Constable, 1914, reprinted Warminster, Aris & Phillips, 1972; *Deshasheh*, London, Egypt Exploration Society, 1898; *Diospolis Parva*, London, Egypt Exploration Society 1901; *Medum*, London, D. Nutt, 1892; *Naqada and Ballas*, London, Quaritch, 1896; *Royal Tombs of the Earliest Dynasties*, I–II, London, Egypt Exploration Society, 1900–1901; *Shabtis*, originally published 1935, reprinted Warminster, Aris & Phillips, 1974.

W. M. F. Petrie and G. A. Wainwright, *The Labyrinth and Gerzeh*, London, British School of Archaeology in Egypt, 1912; *Meydum and Memphis*, III, London, British School of Archaeology in Egypt, 1910.

A. Piankoff, *Le Livre des Portes*, I–III, Cairo, Institut Français d'Archéologie Orientale du Caire, 1946, 1962; *Le Livre des Qererets*, Cairo, Institut Français d'Archéologie Orientale du Caire, 1946; *The Pyramid of Unas*, Princeton, Princeton University Press, 1968; *The Tomb of Ramesses VI*, New York, Pantheon Books, 1964.

G. A. Reisner, *Amulets*, Cairo, Service des Antiquités de l'Égypte, 1907; *Canopics*, Cairo, Service des Antiquités de l'Égypte, 1967; *The Development of the Egyptian Tomb down to the Accession of Cheops*, Cambridge,

Mass., Harvard University Press, 1936; *Early Dynastic Cemeteries of Naga ed-Dêr*, I, Leipzig, J. C. Hinrichs, 1908; *History of the Giza Necropolis*, I, Cambridge, Mass., Harvard University Press, 1942; *A Provincial Cemetery of the Pyramid Age, Naga ed-Dêr*, III, Oxford, Oxford University Press, 1932.

H. Schneider, *Shabtis*, I–III, Leiden, Rijksmuseum van Oudheden, 1977.

G. E. Smith, *Egyptian Mummies*, London, Allen & Unwin, 1924; *The Royal Mummies*, Cairo, Service des Antiquités de l'Égypte, 1912.

H. S. Smith, *A Visit to Ancient Egypt*, Warminster, Aris & Phillips, 1974.

E. Thomas, *The Royal Necropoleis of Thebes*, privately printed, Princeton, 1966.

J. Vandier, *Manuel d'archéologie égyptienne*, 6 vols., Paris, A. and J. Picard, 1952–78.

H. E. Winlock, *Excavations at Deir el-Bahari 1911–31*, New York, Macmillan, 1942; *Materials used in the Embalming of Tutankhamun*, New York, Metropolitan Museum of Art, 1941; *Models of Daily Life in Ancient Egypt*, Cambridge, Mass., Harvard University Press, 1955; *The Slain Soldiers of Neb-hepet-re Mentuhetep*, New York, Metropolitan Museum of Art, 1945; *The Tomb of Queen Meryetamun at Thebes*, New York, Metropolitan Museum of Art, 1932; *The Tomb of Senebtisi at Lisht*, New York, Metropolitan Museum of Art, 1916.

INDEX

Abbott Papyrus, 95, 97
Abu Roash, 235
Abusir, 226
Abydos, 19, 34, 50, 53, 56, 73, 160, 162, 191, 210, 211, 218, 226, 233, 237, 239
afterlife, beliefs about, 139–54
Ahhotpe (queen), coffin of, 175
Ahmose-Nefertari (queen): coffin of, 175; mummy of, 118, 136
Akhenaten (king), 23
Akhetaten, 23
Akhmim, 191
Alexander, 25
Alexandria, 16, 192
Amarna, El-, 23, 182, 230
Amenemhat, tomb of, 229
Amenemhat III (king), pyramid of, 84–7, 88
Amenemhat IV (king), pyramid of, 87
Amenemope (king), tomb of, 105
Amenemope, tomb of, 134
Amenhotpe, sarcophagus of, 183
Amenirdis, tomb of, 240
Amenophis I (king): mummy of, 101, 118; as a god, 157, 180
Amenophis II (king): mummy of, 119, 136; sarcophagus of, 182; tomb of, 99, 100, 101, 122, 137
Amenophis III (king), 23, 99; mummy of, 121; sarcophagus of, 181
Amenpnufer, 96–7
Ameny, sarcophagus of, 183
Ammit, 144–5
Amosis I (king), 22; mummy of, 101, 118
Amra, El-, 19, 239
amulets, 30, 52, 87, 96, 103, 108, 109–10, 115, 128, 136, 155–6, 172, 209

Amun (god), 23, 63, 97, 98, 99, 101, 102, 104, 106, 118, 123, 178, 179, 188, 195, 196, 240
Amun-Tefnakhte, tomb of, 108
Amyrtaeus (king), 25
Ani, papyrus of, 144–5
Aniba, 237, 239
animal cemeteries, 195–213
Ankhhor, priest of Thoth, 210
Ankhnesneferibre, sarcophagus of, 188
Anlamani (king), 186
Anubis, 52, 129, 145, 157, 180, 182, 192, 193, 199, 208, 213
Apis bull, 113, 196. 197–205, 208
Apopis, 153
Armant, 133, 192, 200, 202, 203
artificial eyes in mummies, 123, 124, 136, 202
Asasif, 241
Ashayt (princess), 114
Aspelta (king), 186
Assyrian invasion, 24
Aswan, 228, 229
Asyut, 55
Aten (god), 23
Atum (god), 153
Avaris, 22
Aw-ib-re (king), 158
Ay (king), 54; sarcophagus of, 182

Ba, 58, 59, 184, 190, 192
baboon burials, 205, 207, 208, 209, 213
Bakenranef (vizier), 230, 231
Banebdjed (god), 212
banquet: eaten at funeral, 131–2; left in tomb, 49; offered at tomb, 53
Bastet (goddess), 208, 211, 213
Behbeit el-Hagar, 160